LIVES
IN SCIENCE

a
SCIENTIFIC
AMERICAN
book

SIMON AND SCHUSTER · NEW YORK

TABLE OF CONTENTS

1. THE GREAT WORLD SYSTEM

With a rare talent for polemics, Galileo launched the idea of universal physical law in a public controversy; a Galilean law in another sphere declares: "Philosophy must be free." Newton did his work in one 18-month period and devoted most of the rest of his life to metaphysics and magic. Hooke, a man of many gifts and interests, independently proposed a force called gravity. A functionary of the First Republic, a Napoleonic count and a Restoration marquis, a plagiarist and an original, Laplace tried to keep the solar system from running down.

2. THE NEW WORLD SYSTEM

One 15-year-old Dublin boy was not persuaded by Laplace; he abandoned the classics for mathematics and went on to invent a strange new algebra which is only now finding application in the new world of modern physics. The revolution that heralded the new physics was advanced by the suggestion of another Dublin mathematician: if a yardstick does not give readings that fit the predictions of theory, then the length of the yardstick should be changed.

3. WHAT IS FIRE?

The enthusiasm of his friend Franklin led Priestley into science; the odors of a brewhouse attracted him to chemistry. A radical in politics but a conservative in science, he thought he had isolated "phlogiston." Lavoisier did the same experiments and gave them the right explanation, therewith securing the foundations of chemistry. In contrast to Laplace, Lavoisier took the French Revolution seriously and became its victim when hope and promise gave way to terror.

4. MAGNETISM AND ELECTRICITY

Franklin not only played with lightning but propounded much of the theory of electricity that is in force today. With a laboratory financed by the Crown, Faraday had ample facilities to make the discovery that electric current can be induced from a magnetic field—and to publish promptly. In Albany, New York, a high school teacher named Joseph Henry independently discovered electrical induction on his own funds and his own time; he published his results too late. One important consequence of their discovery was the electrification of civilization; of equal importance were the equations of Clerk Maxwell. These equations predicted the discovery of the radio spectrum, on the long side of the wave lengths of light, and of the X and gamma rays, on the short side, that opened the way to the breakdown of the atom.

5. THE STUDY OF LIFE

Harvey's demonstration of the circulation of the blood was a demonstration also of the power of the method of physics applied to questions of life. The *Origin of Species,* like Galileo's dialogues, raised a storm of public controversy; the anthropocentrists died hard in biology as they had in astronomy. By looking through surgical windows into the stomachs of his laboratory dogs, Pavlov found a way to investigate their nervous systems.

6. THREE MATHEMATICIANS

Because contemporary machine tools could not work to the tolerances he required, Charles Babbage was defeated in his lifelong effort to mechanize the computations of mathematics. Lewis Carroll accomplished little when he attacked logic seriously, but succeeded admirably in having fun with it. Before he was thirteen and was discovered by more senior mathematicians, Ramanujan had independently reconstructed most of modern number theory.

Portraits by Bernarda Bryson

INTRODUCTION

Among the 18 men whose biographies are recounted in this book, the reader will find two or three authentic giants, a hero or two, a saint and a rascal, sunny men of action and sour recluses and a selection of eccentrics, prodigies and sages. What brings them together here is that they lived their lives in science. They must be reckoned as still very much alive and vitally in our midst today. Their existence is massively bodied forth in the industrial system that dominates our landscape. Inside our heads their ideas shape the picture each of us makes of the universe and himself in it. The lives of these men go on changing the world as surely as they transformed the condition and the outlook of man in the four centuries spanned by their life stories.

Of course this book presents only a sampling of all of the many lifetimes that went into the history of science in this period. It is admittedly, also, a somewhat random sampling. The chapters in this book were originally designed as articles in the monthly issues of SCIENTIFIC AMERICAN. Assembled here, however, they gain in relevance from one another and present a rounded coverage of a number of pivotal developments in science.

The history of science is an unfortunately neglected aspect of history. The situation is explained, no doubt, by the impenetrability of that ivy-clad academic wall which sets the humanities apart from the sciences. There is no need to argue the instant relevance of science to current affairs. It is equally clear that a better understanding of the history of science can illuminate the political, military, economic and intellectual affairs of the past. This book demonstrates another usefulness of the history of science: the illumination of our understanding of science itself.

The historical approach shows, first of all, that science is only incidentally an accumulated body of knowledge. The making of observations, the collecting of data—the fact-finding process that is so plainly identified as "scientific"—appears as an adjunct to a more significant enterprise. The scientist wants to make sense out of what he knows. He asks questions with the aim of achieving a picture of experience that is more clearly connected and logically consistent. Such questions lead not only to new knowledge but to new questions and so push forward the boundaries of human experience.

This is a far cry from the popular image of the scientist as a digger of hard facts from some rich mine of certainty. The work of the scientist is seen to be more like that of the artist. In the words of George Bernard Shaw: ". . . the artist's work is to show us ourselves as we really are. Our minds are nothing but this knowledge of ourselves; and he who adds a jot to such knowledge creates new mind as surely as any woman creates new men."

In science, each addition to the mind of man must come as an extension of the edge of the known, not by a flash in the dark beyond. The giants of science always stand on the shoulders of giants. The first chapter tells the story of the giant Galileo. He proposed the idea of inertia as a way to tie the celestial mechanics of Kepler to terrestrial experience with falling bodies. Kepler had built his system on the hypothesis of Copernicus. Galileo's work in turn laid the foundation for Newton's classical synthesis of mechanics.

The continuity of progress in science is further underscored in this book by the frequent occurrence of simultaneity of discovery. We see Newton embarrassed by Hooke's independent intuition of the notion of gravity and are reminded of Newton's clash with Leibnitz for prior claim to the calculus. Lavoisier and Priestley both must be credited with the isolation of oxygen. Henry and Faraday simultaneously demonstrated the magnetic induction of electric current. Darwin was almost anticipated by Wallace in the publication of the theory of natural selection. Simultaneity of discovery happens too often in science to be described as coincidence. Its explanation lies in the unity of science that overrides the tendency to divide it up into special fields of knowledge. Scientists approaching the unknown from a common background of understanding and with the same motivations may be expected to ask similar questions.

Part 1 of this book is concerned with what we really mean when we say "the sun comes up" and "the apple falls from the tree." As commonplace, securely familiar notions, the rotation of the earth on its axis and the force of gravity may seem to fall in the category of incidental information, not relevant to the larger concerns of life. It is instructive to recall, therefore, that the idea of universal physical laws, operating in both the terrestrial and celestial realms, was once heresy. Galileo's crime might have been overlooked had he not written his great Dialogue "chiefly for gentlemen," in order· to enlist public opinion on the side of physics. Only two centuries after Galileo's trial and abjuration Napoleon was to ask Laplace where the Deity was to be found in his equations. He received the arrogant reply: "Sire, I have no need of that hypothesis." The success of physics had profoundly altered the world view of European civilization.

In the triumph of the Enlightenment, there was scarcely any doubt that calculus would encompass all that could be known. Yet before the last volume of Mécanique céleste came from the printer, Laplace had found a discerning and critical young reader. William Rowan Hamilton, at the age of 16, was enthralled by the vision, but he was challenged also by the difficulties which Laplace was content to gloss over and conceal. Hamilton did not succeed in constructing a new celestial mechanics. He did, however, discover a strange new algebra, in which ab may not at all times be equal to ba. Noncommutative algebra is used today to describe events in physics not dreamed of in the calculus.

George Francis FitzGerald is another radically original figure whose true stature could not be measured until the twentieth century. He suggested the insouciant notion that the yardstick might be contracted and the clock slowed down in order to make the equations of motion come out right. Today everybody appreciates the common sense of this suggestion in a world where we know that $E = Mc^2$ and where it has been shown that short-lived particles actually live longer when they are accelerated close to the speed of light.

The more than coincidental discovery of oxygen by Priestley and Lavoisier presents a clear demonstration of the importance of theory in the understanding of what is observed. Both men did ingenious experiments which isolated the principal agents and products of combustion. Priestley, a political heretic, was a resolute conservative in science. He was satisfied with the ancient phlogiston hypothesis and succeeded in "saving" it when he explained his results. Lavoisier started with a different hypothesis about the nature of combustion. As a result, he correctly identified oxygen as an element and carbon dioxide as a compound. His explanation of fire opened up the realm of chemistry to exploration by the methods of physics.

Strangely enough, history shows that man began to understand electricity even before he cleared up his misunderstanding of fire. But Benjamin Franklin was an elegant theorist as well as a daring experimenter. The man "who snatched the lightning from the sky and the scepter from the hand of the tyrant" did more than show that lightning was the same as the spark at the knuckle. His concepts of a single electric "fluid," of direction of flow and of conservation of charge remain embedded in electrical theory today.

In his role as statesman, Dr. Franklin tried to accelerate the acclimatizing of science at the edge of the American wilderness. Two generations later, however, de Tocqueville observed that the new nation "required nothing of science but its special application to the useful arts and the means of rendering life more comfortable." The story of Joseph Henry bears cruel witness to the acuity of this observation. No one among Henry's countrymen could see any immediate utility in his magnets and coils of wire.

His discovery of electrical induction in the year 1831 went un-published until 1833, after Faraday had won world fame with the announcement of his discovery of the same effect.

As an immediate consequence of the Faraday–Henry work, the first primitive dynamos were soon spinning on both sides of the Atlantic. But, in accord with the contrast between Faraday's Royal Institution and Henry's schoolroom workshop, it was in England that the really deep significance of their experiments was recognized. Clerk Maxwell sought a comprehensive mathematical expression for the experimental picture of electricity and magnetism. His equations tied electromagnetic phenomena unexpectedly to light. They showed, moreover, that the spectrum of light is but a narrow band in the total spectrum of radiant energy. Experiments suggested by the equations soon thereafter demonstrated the existence of the invisible radio waves. The equations alerted experimenters equally to the possibility of radiation in wave lengths shorter than light. With the discovery of X rays and gamma rays, the way was opened to atomic and nuclear physics.

This narrative shows, incidentally, why Maxwell is ranked with Newton in the history of science. He was a system-builder who gave meaning and direction to the work of preceding and succeeding generations of scientists.

Harvey, Darwin and Pavlov are scientists of a different sort. The processes of life do not yield to exact measurement or to expression in the mathematical terms that work so well for the less complex situations of physics. A discovery in biology might, in some ways, appear a lesser feat of the intellect than, say, the Maxwell equations. But what scale will fairly weigh the sensitivity of perception that discerned the valves in the veins, the reach of the imagination that reconstructed the transformation of the Galápagos finches, or the sheer originality of the experimenter who measured the secretion of gastric juices as an indicator for unseen processes in the nervous system? The spectacular success of the scientific method in the realm of physics has engaged public attention in recent years. But the life sciences have even more direct relevance to the welfare of man and to his inner life. Harvey showed that the laws of mechanics obtain in the chambers of the heart. Darwin, no less than Galileo, displaced man from the center of creation. Pavlov opened the way to rational investigation of behavior and personality.

Three apparently lesser figures are the heroes of the last section of the book. But fame might shine more brightly upon Babbage had he been born a half century later, and upon Ramanujan had he lived to do his work. As for Lewis Carroll, the author of the third most quoted writings in the English language (after the Bible and Shakespeare) is certainly the most-quoted scientist in history.

THE EDITORS *

* Board of Editors: Gerard Piel (Publisher), Dennis Flanagan (Editor), Leon Svirsky (Managing Editor), James R. Newman, E. P. Rosenbaum, James Grunbaum (Art Director).

PART 1 THE GREAT WORLD SYSTEM

I. GALILEO *by I. Bernard Cohen*

II. ISAAC NEWTON *by I. Bernard Cohen*

I. Bernard Cohen is associate professor of the history of science and of general education at Harvard University. He graduated from Harvard College in 1937 and stayed on as an instructor in physics while he undertook his graduate studies in the history of science under the late George Sarton. The war and the instructing of platoons of Naval V-12 and Army ASTP students delayed the conferring of his Ph.D. until 1947. Cohen is the editor of *Isis,* the history-of-science journal, and author of "Science: Servant of Man," a book that argues persuasively the case for more generous public support of fundamental research.

III. ROBERT HOOKE
   by E. N. da C. Andrade

For many years professor of physics at London University, E. N. da C. Andrade has more recently been known for his studies in the history of science. He was born in London in 1887 of a family of Portuguese descent. He went to University College in London, began to study the structure of metals and discovered what is now known as Andrade's law for the creep of metals. He then obtained a Ph.D. *summa cum laude* at the University of Heidelberg and joined Ernest Rutherford's laboratory at Manchester. In 1913 he obtained the first measurement of the wave lengths of gamma rays. He saw active service in France in World War I and afterwards taught physics at the Artillery College until 1928, when he was appointed to the London University faculty. Andrade has received many honors and has been a Fellow of the Royal Society since 1935. He has a notable collection of seventeenth-century scientific books, though much of it was destroyed in German bombings.

IV. LAPLACE *by James R. Newman*

Born in New York City in 1907, James R. Newman hastened through his undergraduate training in mathematics at the City College of New York and through Columbia Law School and was admitted to the bar at the early age of 22. That portion of his talents not engaged in the practice of law found a pleasant preoccupation in collaboration with the late Edward Kasner in the writing of *Mathematics and the Imagination*. Published by Simon and Schuster in 1940, it is still selling 82 copies per month and has aggregated the impressive total of 14 printings and 42,000 copies. During the war Newman served in a variety of responsible civilian capacities in the War Department, the War Production Board and at the U. S. Embassy in London. As one of the few nonscientists in government not taken unawares by the success of the Manhattan Project, he was able to play a uniquely effective role as adviser to the Senate Committee on Atomic Energy, in support of a civilian Atomic Energy Commission against the powerful proponents of military control. Upon the organization of the "new" SCIENTIFIC AMERICAN early in 1948, he joined its board of editors and has conducted its book review department.

GALILEO

by I. Bernard Cohen

PROBABLY no single name in the annals of science is as well known as that of Galileo. Yet so conflicting are the opinions in the literature on his work that it is difficult for the average scientist to find out exactly what Galileo did. Some writers tell us that Galileo was an empiricist who inaugurated the "scientific method" of learning "general truths of nature," and they illustrate by citing his supposed discovery of the laws of falling bodies by patient observation of what happened when balls of unequal weight were dropped from the Leaning Tower of Pisa. Others say that, on the contrary, Galileo never learned anything by making experiments; he used them only to check results which he had already obtained by mathematical reasoning and deductions from a priori assumptions. Many writers hail Galileo as the father of modern science. Others argue that almost everything Galileo did in science had been begun in the late Middle Ages. Many commentators agree with Sir David Brewster, who wrote of Galileo as one of the "martyrs of science." Others accept A. N. Whitehead's remark that Galileo's punishment by the Roman Inquisition was only "an honorable detention and a mild reproof before dying peaceably in bed."

What shall a scientist do when he is faced with making a choice between diametrically opposed points of view held by such respected writers? The example of Galileo provides one of the best possible arguments for the need of a continuing and increasing scholarship in the history of science. For if we are to understand the true significance of what Galileo did in physics and astronomy, obviously we must first have a clear picture of the scope and nature of the science that existed at the time he did his work, and next a knowledge of the history of physical science since his time, so that we may evaluate those elements which have proved most fruitful for the development of science.

The difficulty in interpreting Galileo stems in large part from the nature of his own thought and writings. He lived in that fertile period which marks the end of the Middle Ages and Renaissance and the beginning of the era of modern science. Thus he was a transitional figure with one foot in the past and the other striding into the future. Considering this state of affairs, one would need an unwarranted vanity to attempt to patch up all the contradictions in the various interpretations that have been made during the last hundred years. Yet certain clearly marked aspects of Galileo's achievement do emerge.

Galileo was a physicist, an astronomer and a mathematician. The first significant contribution to astronomy by Galileo occurred in 1604 while he was a professor in Padua, a post he had received in 1592 at the age of 28. The occasion was a new star seen in the heavens, a nova, which had aroused great interest among scientists, students and laymen everywhere. In a public lecture Galileo demonstrated, on the basis of careful observation, that the new star was truly a star. It could not be a mere meteor in the earth's atmosphere, for it had no parallax and must be very distant, among the fixed stars well beyond our solar system. Galileo predicted that the nova would be visible for a short while and then would vanish into obscurity.

The boldness of this assertion is difficult to realize today. The outlook on the external world then was largely Aristotelian; it was generally believed that the heavens were perfect and unchangeable and subject neither to growth nor to decay. Only the earth, the center of the universe, could change. The laws of physics on earth were essentially different from those in the celestial beyond.

Galileo's assertion that the perfect and unchangeable heavens might witness growth and decay brought him into immediate conflict with the Aristotelians. The latter, as one of Galileo's biographers, J. J. Fahie, puts it, were probably as much "annoyed

BERNARDA
BRYSON

at the appearance of the star" as at Galileo's "calling attention to it so publicly and forcibly." In any event, Galileo was a better target than the star. Galileo was never one to shrink from controversy, and he seized the opportunity to repudiate the old physics of Aristotle, which he held to be inadequate, and with it the Ptolemaic, or geocentric, system of the universe.

Galileo had already been a confirmed Copernican for some time, although he had not dared to publish his arguments, "fearing," as he said in a letter to Johann Kepler, "the fate of our master, Copernicus." Soon after his studies of the new star, however, Galileo was provided with an extraordinary opportunity to vindicate the Copernican idea. This occasion was the most important event in Galileo's career as an astronomer. He wrote:

"About ten months ago a rumor came to our ears that an optical instrument had been elaborated by a Dutchman, by the aid of which visible objects, even though far distant from the eye of the observer, were distinctly seen as if near at hand; and some stories of this marvelous effect were bandied about, to which some gave credence and which others denied. The same was confirmed to me a few days after by a letter sent from Paris by the noble Frenchman Jacob Badovere, which at length was the reason that I applied myself entirely to seeking out the theory and discovering the means by which I might arrive at the invention of a similar instrument, an end which I attained a little later, from considerations of the theory of refraction; and I first prepared a tube of lead, in the ends of which I fitted two glass lenses, both plane on one side, one being spherically convex, the other concave, on the other side."

Thus in his great book *The Sidereal Messenger*, which he published in Venice in 1610, did Galileo describe his introduction to the telescope. There are several independent claimants to the invention, but there is no doubt that Galileo was the first to turn the telescope to observation of the heavenly bodies. It was an experience unique in the history of man. For millennia the heavens had been viewed only by the naked eye, and no one knew what glories might exist beyond the range of man's unaided vision. Wherever Galileo pointed his telescope he found extraordinary and astonishing new facts.

Galileo first examined the moon. His conclusion was "that the surface of the Moon is not perfectly smooth, free from inequalities and exactly spherical, as a large school of philosophers considers with regard to the Moon and the other heavenly bodies, but . . . on the contrary, it is full of inequalities, uneven, full of hollows and protuberances, just like the surface of the Earth itself, which is varied everywhere by lofty mountains and deep valleys." Galileo even determined the height of the mountains on the moon, and his results agree with modern determinations in order of magnitude. He believed at first that the dark and light areas on the moon's surface represented land and water, but we must remember that even today beginning students of astronomy, on first looking at the moon or at a photograph of it, have the same impression.

Next Galileo turned to the stars, and at once discovered a difference between the fixed stars and the planets, or wanderers. "The planets present their discs perfectly round, just as if described with a pair of compasses, and appear as so many little moons, completely illuminated and of a globular shape; but the fixed stars do not look to the naked eye [as if they were] bounded by a circular circumference, but rather like blazes of light shooting out beams on all sides and very sparkling, and with the telescope they appear of the same shape as when they were viewed by simply looking at them. . . ." Galileo also noted that the telescope brought within the range of vision "a host of other stars, which escape the unassisted sight, so numerous as to be almost beyond belief. . . ."

The next subject of his observation was the Milky Way, which, to his astonishment, he found to be "nothing else but a mass of innumerable stars planted together in clusters." Furthermore, all of the "nebulosities," whose nature had long been a topic of dispute, also proved to be masses of stars.

Galileo reserved for last in his account "the matter, which seems to me to deserve to be considered the most important in this work, namely, that I should disclose and publish to the world the occasion of discovering and observing four PLANETS, never seen from the very beginning of the world up to our own times. . . ."

He had been examining the planet Jupiter on the seventh day of January in 1610 when he noticed "that three little stars, small but very bright, were near the planet; and although I believed them to belong to the number of the fixed stars, yet they made me somewhat wonder, because they seemed to be arranged exactly in a straight line, parallel to the ecliptic, and to be brighter than the rest of the stars, equal to them in magnitude. . . . On the east side [of Jupiter] there were two stars, and a single one towards the west. . . . But when on January 8th, led by some fatality, I turned again to look at the same part of the heavens, I found a very different state of things, for there were three little stars all west of Jupiter, and nearer together than on the previous night, and they were separated from one another by equal intervals, as the accompanying illustration shows."

Night after night Galileo continued to observe this group of "stars," and finally he "decided unhesitatingly, that there are three stars in the heavens moving about Jupiter, as Venus and Mercury round the Sun; which at length was established as clear as daylight by numerous other subsequent observations. These observations also established that there are not only three, but four erratic sidereal bodies performing their revolutions round Jupiter. . . ."

Galileo wrote that the discovery of Jupiter's four moons, which he called "planets," provided "a notable and splendid argument to remove the scruples of those who can tolerate the revolution of the planets round the Sun in the Copernican system, yet are so disturbed by the motion of one Moon about the Earth . . .

for now we have not one planet only revolving about another
. . . but four satellites circling about Jupiter, like the Moon about
the Earth, while the whole system travels over a mighty orbit
about the Sun in the space of twelve years." Galileo discovered
another important fact: that the planet Venus has phases like
those of the Moon; it waxes and wanes from a full orb to a thin
crescent. "From the observation of these wonderful phenomena,"
wrote Galileo, "we are supplied with a determination most con-
clusive, and appealing to the evidence of our senses, of two very
important problems, which up to this day were discussed by the
greatest intellects with different conclusions. One is that the
planets are bodies not self-luminous (if we may entertain the
same views about Mercury as we do about Venus). . . . The
second [is] that we are absolutely compelled to say that Venus
(and Mercury also) revolves round the Sun, as do also all the
rest of the planets. A truth believed indeed by the Pythagorean
school, by Copernicus, and by Kepler, but never proved by the
evidence of our senses, as it is now proved in the case of Venus
and Mercury."

The discovery of the phases of Venus directly challenged the
accepted Ptolemaic system. According to this system, Venus
moved in an epicycle, a circular orbit whose center always lay
between the earth and the sun. If this were true, then Venus,
shining, as Galileo showed, by reflected light from the sun, might
be seen in some of its crescent phases, but we would never expect
to see Venus as a half circle, a full circle, or any phases between.
Yet Galileo observed all these phases.

Galileo's discoveries made the Copernican system "philosophi-
cally reasonable" by showing that the earth was like the other
planets and the moon. By observing the dark half of the quarter-
moon, faintly illuminated by earthshine, he demonstrated that the
earth shone just like the planets. If observed through a telescope
located on the moon or on Venus, the earth would exhibit phases
like theirs. As Galileo put it, "The Earth, with fair and grateful

exchange, pays back to the Moon an illumination like that which it receives from the Moon nearly the whole time during the darkest gloom of night."

The sun, by contrast, was self-luminous and thus set apart from the earth, the moon and the planets. If any single body was especially constituted to be at the center of the universe, surely it was the sun and not the earth! And as a model for this picture of the solar system, with the sun at the center and its attendant planets circling it, there was Jupiter with its four satellites revolving about it in the same way.

Galileo's lifework shows a unity of purpose and achievement that is rare among men of science. His work in mechanics fitted in with his work in astronomy like an adjacent piece of a jigsaw puzzle. It is clear from his writings that Galileo was at heart a gadgeteer with true mechanical feeling and inventive genius. One of his earliest discoveries was that a pendulum always makes a complete swing in the same period of time, no matter what the length of the swing. He speedily applied this discovery to the invention of the "pulsilogium," a device for mechanically recording and comparing pulse rates. Aside from his natural bent for mechanics, however, Galileo was strongly attracted to this subject because, in part at least, he thought of it as a cosmological science, the link between earthly and celestial phenomena. If he could find the laws of motion on earth, he could apply them to the motions of the planets and the stars. It was thus his ambition to show that if one adopted the Copernican system, the planets followed their patterns in the heavens by regular and simple laws, and not, as in the older theory, because each was guided by a "special intelligence."

In seeking a universal science of mechanics that would apply equally to the heavens and the earth, Galileo was, of course, flying directly in the face of the contemporary point of view. The Aristotelian conception made a sharp distinction between motion on the earth and moon and motion in the translunar, "celestial" universe. In the sublunar world, "natural motion" occurred in a straight line. An apple fell downward from the tree because it was "heavy" and its natural place was "down"; to make it go in any other direction contrary to its nature required a "violent motion." In the translunar world, by contrast, the natural motion was circular, as befitted the perfect material out of which the celestial bodies were made.

By showing the similarity between the earth, moon and planets, which indicated that they must obey the same laws, Galileo brought terrestrial and celestial phenomena within one universal physics. The revolution in physical thinking effected by Galileo may be thought of as concentrating men's attention on change and on motion. He proved that even the sun, that most "perfect" of all heavenly bodies, was subject to change, for when viewed by Galileo's telescope it showed changing spots! Anyhow, as Galileo put the matter, it was no "great honor" for bodies to be immutable and unalterable, nor was the earth "corrupt" because it changed.

"It is my opinion," he asserted, "that the earth is very noble, and admirable, by reason of so many and so different alterations, mutations, generations, etc., which are incessantly made therein; and if without being subject to any alteration, it had been all one vast heap of sand, or a masse of jasper, or that . . . it had continued an immense globe of christal, wherein nothing had ever grown, altered, or changed, I should have esteemed it a lump of no benefit to the world, full of idleneses, and in a word superfluous. . . . What greater folly can there be imagined, than to call jems, silver and gold pretious; and earth and dirt vile? For do not these persons consider, that if there should be as great a scarcity of earth, as there is of jewels and pretious metals, there would be no prince, but would gladly give a heap of diamonds and rubies, and many wedges of gold, to purchase onely so much earth as should suffice to plant a Gessemine in a little pot, or to set therein a China Orange [tangerine], that he might see it sprout, grow up, and bring forth so goodly leaves, so odoriferous flowers, and so delicate fruit? It is therefore scarcity and plenty that makes things esteemed and contemned by the vulgar."

We shall consider here only three aspects of Galileo's mechanics: the law of falling bodies, the principle of inertia, and the resolution and composition of independent motions. The law of falling bodies is the most celebrated of Galileo's discoveries. Modern scholarship has shown that Galileo's work on falling bodies was original not so much in his own statement of the law as in the particular use he made of it. Aristotle had said that the speed of a given falling body depended on the resistance of the medium in which it fell, e.g., a stone obviously will fall faster in air than in water. He had also said that if two bodies were to fall in a resistant medium like air, their speed would depend on their weight. Even before Galileo, many writers had expressed their doubts concerning this dictum. In the sixth century, John Philoponos had demonstrated by an experiment that the contrary was true. Galileo approached the problem by using the principles of deductive reasoning and mathematics rather than by direct experiment.

He considered two possibilities in the case of a uniformly accelerated motion starting from rest: (1) that the speed was proportional to the distance fallen, (2) that it was proportional to the elapsed time. The first led to an apparent contradiction, so he accepted the second, the now familiar law that the velocity equals the acceleration times the time: $v = At$. Then, making use of the well-known proof that a uniformly accelerated body moves through a distance s in any time t equal to the distance it would have fallen in the same time t with the average velocity, he derived the equivalent of the law: $s = \frac{1}{2}At^2$.

As a check, Galileo proposed an experiment on an inclined plane. This test was a means of "diluting gravity," so that one could study the relatively slow rolling motion by timing it with a water clock. The test depended on Galileo's important theorem of the composition of motions. A body moving down an inclined plane, in the Galilean scheme, has two components: a horizontal or forward motion, and a vertical or falling motion. Each is independent of the other. By making a rough check with an inclined plane, he demonstrated that the law $s = \frac{1}{2}At^2$ seemed to hold along the inclined plane. From this he inferred that it also held for freely falling bodies.

Here we have a typical example of Galileo's method in physics: Imagine the conditions of a given situation, make a mathematical formulation and derive the reasonable consequences, then make a rough check, if it seems necessary, to be sure that the result is correct. His experimental test involved a brass ball rolling in a groove. He measured the time for different distances, at varying angles of inclination of the grooved board. In "experiments near an hundred times repeated," Galileo found that the times agreed with the law, with no differences "worth mentioning." His conclusion that the differences were not "worth mentioning" only shows how firmly he had made up his mind beforehand, for the rough conditions of the experiment would never have yielded an exact law. Actually the discrepancies were so great that a contemporary worker, Père Mersenne could not reproduce the results described by Galileo, and even doubted that he had ever made the experiment.

Once Galileo had satisfied himself that he knew the law of falling bodies, he wished to apply it. He knew full well that the law would work precisely only in an ideal situation—one in which there was no resisting medium—but he nevertheless decided to apply it to falling bodies in air, since he observed that the effect of the air resistance was small for a heavy body such as a cannon ball.

Keeping in mind that motion in air departs slightly from the ideal case, Galileo next applied his principles to the problem of determining the trajectory of a projectile. According to the Galilean analysis, a projectile has two independent components of motion, horizontal and vertical, like the ball on the inclined plane. If fired horizontally from a gun, it moves forward the same distance in every second if we disregard the small factor of air resistance. As it emerges from the barrel it also begins to fall toward the earth. During the first second it will fall 16 feet; during the second second, 48 feet; during the third, 80 feet, and so on. Hence the path of the shell will be a parabola. Here was a brand new discovery that was of the utmost practical importance in the new science of artillery-ranging.

Implicit in Galileo's analysis was another brand-new idea: the principle of inertia. While he did not state it explicitly, in his assumptions about the movement of the projectile he made use of the theorem that a body will continue in uniform motion in a straight line unless acted on by an outside force. Galileo introduced the revolutionary concept, contrary to all older physics, that uniform motion in a straight line is physically equivalent to a state of rest, thereby transforming the science of mechanics from a static to a kinematic basis.

These new principles gave the first complete explanation of the mechanics of the Copernican universe. Now one could explain why a stone dropped from a tower would fall at the base of the tower even though the earth had moved while the ball fell. One could also understand for the first time why a stone dropped from the masthead of a moving ship would fall at the foot of the mast in spite of the movement of the ship. Galileo pointed out that the stone partakes of the ship's forward motion before it is dropped, and this forward motion continues unchanged while the stone falls because the forward and the downward motions are independent. Consequently an observer on such a boat could not tell from this experiment whether the boat was at rest or in uniform motion. In other words, an observer cannot distinguish between a state of rest and of uniform motion save with regard to an observable external system of reference. This is the principle of Galilean relativity. He observed: "In respect to the Earth, to the Tower, and to our selves, which all as one piece move with the diurnal motion together with the stone, the diurnal motion is as if it had never been."

At this point the reader may ask: What about the story of the famous experiment in which Galileo dropped two balls of unequal size and weight from the Leaning Tower of Pisa? At some time and place, he did drop two unequal weights and found that they did not hit the ground with the great difference that Aristotle had predicted. But it appears from modern scholarship that he never did so, at least publicly, from the Pisan tower.

Galileo worked out his physics by thought, by correct reasoning and mathematics, not by induction from experiments. During his days at Pisa, before he went to Padua, he wrote: "But, as ever, we employ reason more than examples (for we seek the causes of effects, and they are not revealed by experiment)." Galileo liked to use what we may call "thought experiments," imagining the consequences rather than observing them directly. Indeed, when he described the motion of a ball dropped from the mast of a moving ship, in his *Dialogue on the Two Great Systems of the World,* he then had the Aristotelian, Simplicio, ask whether he had made an experiment, to which Galileo replied: "No, and I do not need it, as without any experience I can affirm that it is so, because it cannot be otherwise."

To confute the supposed results of Aristotelian logic Galileo made a frontal attack on Aristotelians. For example, he pointed out that "it may be possible, that an artist may be excellent in making organs, but unlearned in playing on them, thus he might be a great logician, but unexpert in making use of logick; like as we have many that theorically understand the whole art of poetry, and yet are unfortunate in composing but mere four verses; others enjoy all the precepts of Cinci, and yet know not how to paint a stoole. The playing on the organs is not taught by them who know how to make organs, but by him that knows how to play on them; poetry is learnt by continual reading of poets: limning is learnt by continual painting and designing: demonstration from the reading of books full of demonstrations, which are the mathematical onely, and not the logical."

As for Aristotle's appeal to the experience of the senses, Galileo asks: "And doth he not likewise affirm, that we ought to prefer that which sense demonstrates, before all arguments, though in appearance never so well grounded? and saith he not this without the least doubt or hesitation?" To which Simplicio, the Aristotelian, replies, "He doth so." Then, says Galileo, ". . . you shall argue more Aristotelically, saying, the heavens are alterable, for that so my sense telleth me, than if you should say, the heavens are unalterable, for that logick so perswaded Aristotle. Furthermore, we may discourse of coelestial matters much better than Aristotle; because, he confessing the knowledg thereof to be difficult to him, by reason of their remoteness from the senses, he thereby acknowledgeth, that one to whom the senses can better represent the same, may philosophate upon them with more certainty. Now we by help of the telescope, are brought thirty or forty times nearer to the heavens, than ever Aristotle came; so that we may discover in them an hundred things, which he could not see, and amongst the rest, these spots in the Sun, which were to him absolutely invisible; therefore we may discourse of the heavens and Sun, with more certainty than Aristotle."

Galileo's writings abound with references to the facts of experience, of direct observation. In this sense, Galileo built his science on a somewhat empirical basis. But he was in no sense such an empiricist as the 19th-century writers attempted to make him out. He was not a careful experimenter, though he was a keen observer, and it is only the fallacy of writing history backwards that has made us visualize him as the patient investigator who only reluctantly drew conclusions after long test. The latter picture describes a much later kind of scientific man, of whom the prototype may well have been Robert Boyle.

Galileo's greatest general contribution was the idea that mathematics was the language of motion, and that change was to be described mathematically, in a way that would express both its complete generality and necessity, as well as its universality and applicability to the real world of experience. While Galileo ridiculed the numerology aspect of Platonism, he declared in the opening pages of the *Dialogue*: "I know perfectly well that the Pythagoreans had the highest esteem for the science of number and that Plato himself admired the human intellect and believed that it participates in divinity solely because it is able to understand the nature of numbers. And I myself am well inclined to make the same judgment." That nature herself "loves the integers" was shown in Galileo's discovery that a falling body moves so that its speeds after successive seconds are in the ratio of whole numbers 1, 2, 3. . . . The distances fallen in successive seconds are in the ratio of the odd numbers 1, 3, 5 . . . . The most important influence on Galileo's thinking undoubtedly was Archimedes, but whereas the latter had constructed a geometry of rest, Galileo built a geometry of motion.

The net result of Galileo's lifework was to adduce new evidence for the Copernican theory of the solar system, and to provide the mechanical rationale of its operation. One evidence of the success of this activity was the hostility his work aroused. In the evening of his life he was brought into conflict with the Roman Inquisition. Galileo took the point of view, as expressed in his famous letter to the Grand Duchess Cristina, that the Holy Scriptures did not have the teaching of science as their ultimate aim. He argued that the language of the Bible was not to be taken literally. Thus when the sun was described as moving around the earth, this did not imply the truth of the geocentric system, but was merely an expression in everyday language. (In the same way we still speak of the sun rising and setting.) From this point of view, Galileo held that one could accept the Copernican system while remaining a good Catholic and without in any way impugning the Scriptures.

Had Galileo remained at Padua under the rule of Venice,

which held herself independent of papal jurisdiction, he would never have had to face the Inquisition. But with the fame attendant on his initial discoveries with the telescope, he chose to move to Florence. There is a vast and readily available literature on Galileo's trial and condemnation, which will not be discussed in this chapter confined to his scientific work. It is true that Galileo was never put to torture during his stay in the prison of the Inquisition. But the knowledge that others had been tortured there, and that not too long before Giordano Bruno had been burned alive, surely had its effect upon him. He was a man of 69 in poor health. Three physicians attempting to avert the trial had testified in 1633: "All these symptoms are worthy of notice, as under the least aggravation they might become dangerous to his life." The poor man, formerly eager for combat with those who would deny the new truths, was now crushed by the action of the Holy Office of the Church to which he had ever been faithful. Upon repeated examination, he "confessed":

"I, Galileo Galilei, son of the late Vincenzio Galilei of Florence, aged seventy years, being brought personally to judgment, and kneeling before you, Most Eminent and Most Reverend Lords Cardinals, General Inquisitors of the Universal Christian Commonwealth against heretical depravity, having before my eyes the Holy Gospels which I touch with my own hands, swear that I have always believed, and, with the help of God, will in future believe, every article which the Holy Catholic and Apostolic Church of Rome holds, teaches, and preaches. But because I have been enjoined, by this Holy Office, altogether to abandon the false opinion which maintains that the Sun is the centre and immovable, and forbidden to hold, defend, or teach, the said false doctrine in any manner . . . I am willing to remove from the minds of your Eminences, and of every Catholic Christian, this vehement suspicion rightly entertained towards me, therefore, with a sincere heart and unfeigned faith, I abjure, curse, and detest the said errors and

heresies, and generally every other error and sect contrary to
the said Holy Church; and I swear that I will never more in
future say, or assert anything, verbally or in writing, which
may give rise to a similar suspicion of me; but that if I shall
know any heretic, or any one suspected of heresy, I will de-
nounce him to this Holy Office, or to the Inquisitor and
Ordinary of the place in which I may be. I swear, moreover,
and promise that I will fulfil and observe fully all the penances
which have been or shall be laid on me by this Holy Office. But
if it shall happen that I violate any of my said promises, oaths,
and protestations (which God avert!), I subject myself to all
the pains and punishments which have been decreed and
promulgated by the sacred canons and other general and particular constitutions against delinquents of this description.
So, may God help me, and His Holy Gospels, which I touch
with my own hands, I, the above named Galileo Galilei, have
abjured, sworn, promised, and bound myself as above; and, in
witness thereof, with my own hand have subscribed this present
writing of my abjuration, which I have recited word for word."

One can only wonder at the indomitable spirit that enabled
Galileo—shamed, confined, ill, his major work placed on the
Index of Prohibited Books—to complete his last major work, *The
New Sciences*, the publication of which had to be arranged sur-
reptitiously. And today we may also wonder whether the fight for
freedom of belief has yet been truly won. For we can repeat
Galileo's tragic declaration: "Philosophy wants to be free!"

ISAAC NEWTON

by I. Bernard Cohen

THE MIND and personality of Isaac Newton challenge any historian. Newton was a strange, solitary figure, and the wellsprings of his behavior were hidden even from his contemporaries. A biographer of his time compared Newton to the River Nile, whose great powers were known but whose source had not been discovered. Nevertheless, the few facts we have about his early life do allow some speculation about Newton's character and development.

He was born prematurely, a physical weakling. It is said that he had to wear a "bolster" to support his neck during his first months, that no one expected him to live. Newton later was fond of saying that his mother had said he was so tiny at birth that he could have been put into a quart mug.

Newton's father died three months before he was born. When the boy was less than two years old, his mother remarried, and he was turned over to his aged grandmother. He lived on an isolated farm, deprived of parental care and love, without the friendly companionship and rivalry of brothers and sisters. The late Louis T. More, author of the best-known modern biography of the man, held that much of Newton's "inwardness" could be attributed to his lonely and unhappy childhood.

Born in 1642, Newton grew up in an era when England was still tasting the "terrrors of a protracted and bitter civil war." Raiding and plundering parties were common. His grandmother was "suspected of sympathy to the royal forces." In the face of these real terrors and "the frights of his imagination," he could not have received much comfort from his grandmother or the hired laborers on the farm. Naturally enough, as More observed, the boy turned to "the solace of lonely meditation" and developed a strong habit of self-absorption. A girl who knew him in his youth described him as a "sober, silent, thinking lad" who "was never known scarce to play with the boys abroad, at their silly amusements."

He evidently overcame his physical weakness by the time he reached school age, for a schoolmate reported that Newton challenged a bully who had kicked him in the belly to a fight and "beat him till he would fight no more"—winning out because he had "more spirit and resolution." The bully stood high in the class, and Newton was so determined "to beat him also at his books" that "by hard work he finally succeeded, and then gradually rose to be the first in the school."

When Newton was 14, his mother took the boy back into her home, her second husband having died. She conceived the idea of making him a farmer, but the experiment proved an unqualified failure. Newton found farming totally distasteful. Instead of attending properly to his chores, he would read, make wooden models with his knife, or dream. Fortunately for science, his mother gave up the attempt and allowed him to prepare for Cambridge University.

At the age of 18, Newton entered Trinity College. In his early years at the University he was not outstanding in any way. Then he came under the influence of Isaac Barrow, a professor of mathematics and an extraordinary man. He was an able mathematician, a classicist, an astronomer and an authority in the field of optics. Barrow was one of the first to recognize Newton's genius. Soon after his student had taken a degree, Barrow resigned his professorship so that Newton might have it. Thus at 26 Newton was established in an academic post of distinction and was free to pursue his epoch-making studies.

He had already sown the seeds of his revolutionary contributions to three distinct fields of scientific inquiry: mathematics, celestial mechanics and physical optics. After his graduation from the University he had returned to his home at Woolsthorpe for

920
5

18513

BERNARDA
BRYSON

18 months of work which can fairly be described as the most fruitful 18 months in all the history of the creative imagination. Newton's subsequent life in science consisted to a large degree in the elaboration of the great discoveries made during those "golden" months. What Newton did at Woolsthorpe is best stated in his words:

"In the beginning of the year 1665 I found the method for approximating series and the rule for reducing any dignity [power] of any binomial to such a series [i.e., the binomial theorem]. The same year in May I found the method of tangents of Gregory and Slusius, and in November [discovered] the direct method of Fluxions [i.e., the elements of the differential calculus], and the next year in January had the Theory of Colours, and in May following I had entrance into the inverse method of Fluxions [i.e., integral calculus], and in the same year I began to think of gravity extending to the orb of the Moon . . . and having thereby compared the force requisite to keep the Moon in her orb with the force of gravity at the surface of the earth, and found them to answer pretty nearly. . . ."

As a by-product of his analysis of light and colors, which he had shyly kept to himself, Newton invented a reflecting telescope, to free telescopes from the chromatic aberration of refracting lenses. He made a small version of his new telescope for the Royal Society of London, and was shortly elected, at the age of 30, as a Fellow of the Royal Society, the highest scientific honor in England.

Newton was understandably overwhelmed by his sudden public recognition. He had been loath to announce his discoveries, but within a week after his election to the Society he asked permission to communicate an account of the "philosophical discovery" which had induced him "to the making of the said telescope." With a disarming lack of false modesty, he said that in his judgment he had made "the oddest, if not the most considerable detection, which hath hitherto been made in the operations of nature."

Newton's letter to the Royal Society, "containing his new theory of light and colours," was sent to London on February 6, 1672. This paper can claim a number of "firsts." It was Newton's initial publication; it founded the science of spectroscopy, and it marked the beginning of a sound analysis of color phenomena. Briefly, what Newton showed is that a prism separates white light into its component colors, associated with specific indices of refraction, and that a second prism can recombine the dispersed light and render it white again. These magnificent experiments provided a new departure for the formulation of theories about the nature of color. Yet the paper did not win for Newton the universal applause that he had sought. The Royal Society was bombarded with letters disputing Newton's conclusions. Some of the objectors were unimportant, but others were men of stature: Christian Huygens, Robert Hooke. With astonishing patience, Newton wrote careful letters answering each objection. But he won over only one of his opponents—the French Jesuit Father Pardies.

The controversy had an acid effect on Newton's personality. He vowed that he would publish no further discoveries. As he wrote later to Leibnitz: "I was so persecuted with discussions arising from the publication of my theory of light, that I blamed my own imprudence for parting with so substantial a blessing as my quiet to run after a shadow." And yet he did later continue to publish; he wanted the applause of the scientific world. This ambivalence was not overlooked by Newton's enemies. The astronomer John Flamsteed, who broke with Newton, described him as "insidious, ambitious, and excessively covetous of praise, and impatient of contradiction. . . . I believe him to be a good man at the bottom; but, through his nature, suspicious."

At Cambridge Newton was the very model of an absent-minded professor. His amanuensis, Humphrey Newton (no relative), wrote that he never knew Newton "to take any recreation or pastime either in riding out to take the air, walking, bowling, or any other exercise whatever, thinking all hours lost that were not spent in his studies." He often worked until two or three o'clock in the morning, ate sparingly and sometimes forgot to eat altogether. When reminded that he had not eaten, he would go to the table and "eat a bite or two standing." Newton rarely dined in the college hall; when he did, he was apt to appear "with shoes down at heels, stockings untied, surplice on, and his head scarcely combed." It was said that he often delivered his lectures to an empty hall, apparently with as much satisfaction as if the room had been full of students.

After the controversy, Newton withdrew from the public eye as a scientist. He served the University as its representative in Parliament and worked away in private at chemistry and alchemy, theology, physics and mathematics. He became acquainted with Leibnitz, but refused to give his great contemporary any exact information about his discoveries in mathematics. Today it is generally agreed that the calculus was discovered more or less independently by both Newton and Leibnitz, but the two men and their partisans quarreled acrimoniously over priority, and Newton accused Leibnitz of plagiarism. Newton conceived a jealous proprietary interest in every subject he studied, and almost every achievement of his creative life was accompanied by some quarrel.

In 1684 came the famous visit to Newton by the astronomer Edmund Halley. He had a problem concerning the gravitational attraction between the sun and the planets. Halley and Hooke had concluded from Johannes Kepler's accounting of planetary motions that the force of attraction must vary inversely with the square of the distance between a planet and the sun. But they had been unable to prove their idea. "What," Halley asked Newton, "would be the curve described by the planets on the supposition that gravity diminished as the square of the distance?" Newton answered without hesitation: "An ellipse." How did he know that? "Why," replied Newton, "I have calculated it." These four words informed Halley that Newton had worked out one of the most fundamental laws of the universe—the law of gravity. Halley wanted to see the calculations at once, but Newton could not find his notes. He promised to write out the theorems and proofs. Under Halley's insistent urging he completed a manuscript for the Royal Society. Thus was born the *Philosophiae Naturalis Principia Mathematica*, known ever since simply as the *Principia*.

Just before its publication a crisis arose when Hooke laid claim to the inverse-square law. Newton threatened to withdraw the climactic chapters of his work, but Halley mollified him and the great classic went to press intact. Halley's credit in this enterprise is enormous. He not only got Newton to write the work but also saw it through the press and paid the costs of publication, although he was not a wealthy man.

The *Principia* is divided into three "books." In the first Newton laid down his three laws of motion and explored the consequences of various laws of force. In the second he explored motion in various types of fluids; here he was somewhat less successful, and much of his work had to be revised in the succeeding decades. In the third he discussed universal gravitation and showed how a single law of force explains at once the falling of bodies on the earth, the motion of our moon or of Jupiter's satellites, the motions of planets and the phenomenon of tides.

One of the most vexing problems for Newton was to find a rigorous proof that a sphere acts gravitationally as if all its mass were concentrated at its center. Without this theorem, the whole theory of gravitation would rest on intuition rather than precise calculation. For instance, in the simple case of an apple falling to the ground—the occasion of the central idea of gravitation according to Newton's own account—what is the "distance between" the earth and the apple? Here the calculus came into play. Newton considered the earth as a collection of tiny volumes of matter, each attracting the apple according to the inverse-square law of gravitation. Then he summed up the individual forces and showed that the result was the same as if the earth were a point mass, as if all the matter of the earth were shrunk into a tiny region at its center.

Newton suffered some kind of "nervous breakdown" after the completion of the *Principia*. He complained that he could not sleep, and said that he lacked the "former consistency of his mind." He wrote angry letters to friends and then apologized; he protested bitterly to John Locke, for example, that the philosopher had attempted to "embroil him with women."

In 1696 Newton abandoned the academic life for the position of Warden, later Master, of the Mint. Honors for his scientific achievements continued to come to him: he was knighted in 1705 and served many years as president of the Royal Society. But the last quarter century of his life produced no major contributions to science. Some say that his creative genius had simply burned out. Others argue that after having founded the science of physical optics, invented the calculus and shown the mechanism of the universe, there just wasn't anything left for him to do in the realm of science.

Although he made no important discoveries, Newton's last years were not barren of ideas. Now famous and honored, he felt secure enough to offer many public speculations on scientific problems. He suggested various possible hypotheses as to the "cause" of gravitation and speculated on the nature of the "ether," the size of the constituent units of matter, the forces of electricity and magnetism, the cause of muscular response to the "commands of the will," the origins of sensation, the creation of the world, the ultimate destiny of man. In the century after Newton, physical experimenters followed up many of his bold speculations.

Newton is often described as the inaugurator of the "Age of Reason." Alexander Pope expressed the sentiment of his time in the famous lines:

> *Nature and Nature's laws lay hid in night:*
> *God said, Let Newton be! and all was light.*

But the late Lord Keynes called attention to another side of
Newton: his quest for an answer to the riddle of existence, his
intense interest in alchemy, occult philosophy and religious
studies, his unorthodox theological views. Anyone who reads the
nonscientific writings of Newton, or even the speculations he published in the *Opticks* toward the end of his life, will not be wholly
satisfied with Pope's famous couplet. He will, perhaps, prefer the
summary by William Wordsworth, who wrote of Newton:

> . . . *with his prism and silent face,*
> . . . *a mind forever*
> *Voyaging through strange seas of thought, alone.*

ROBERT HOOKE
by E. N. da C. Andrade

THE NAME of Robert Hooke is known to every student of physics and engineering by Hooke's law (mechanical strain is proportional to the stress). This law, with the consequences Hooke deduced from it, certainly is an achievement of the first importance —sufficient to entitle its originator to a sure place in the history of science. But the law that bears his name constitutes only a small part of Hooke's claim to greatness. He made contributions of fundamental value to every branch of science known in his day. Scientists who have studied his work, or aspects of it, have expressed astonished admiration for his versatile genius and the range of his discoveries. However, his achievements are not as widely known as they should be.

Robert Hooke was born on July 18, 1635, in the village of Freshwater on the Isle of Wight, just off the south coast of England. His father was curate there and lived in a little house which was still standing at the beginning of the present century. Robert was a weakly boy from birth, and all through his life his health varied from indifferent to miserable. Even as a youngster he suffered from severe headaches, almost certainly due to chronic inflammation of his frontal sinuses. From the diaries he kept in his middle age we know that he was plagued with catarrh, with indigestion so troublesome that he gratefully noted any meal that happened to agree with him, with giddiness, with insomnia and with fearful dreams when he slept. In considering the irritability with which he is sometimes reproached, it is well to remember this background of chronic suffering.

Nor was Hooke well favored in looks for making his way in the world. No portrait of him exists, but we know from contemporary descriptions that he was lean, bent and meanly ugly, with a wide, thin mouth and a sharp chin. Samuel Pepys referred to Hooke's unpromising appearance in his diary. After a visit to the Royal Society on February 15, 1665, Pepys wrote: "Above all, Mr. Boyle to-day was at the meeting, and above him Mr. Hooke, who is the most, and promises the least, of any man in the world that ever I saw."

When Hooke was 13, his father died. Somehow the boy managed to become an apprentice to the famous painter Sir Peter Lely in London. But the odor of the oil paints made his headaches worse, and he soon left to go to school at Westminster, where he won the regard of the famous headmaster, Dr. Busby, who remained his friend for life. Hooke's father had left him 100 pounds, which went far in those days. At the age of 18 he entered Oxford University with a decent knowledge of Latin and Greek and of the elements of geometry. He had acquired considerable ability as a craftsman in wood and metal, skill as a draftsman (judging by drawings which he made a little later) and sufficient musical ability to win a position as a chorister in Christ Church, one of the Oxford colleges. With the chorister's stipend and work as a servant to a certain Mr. Goodman, he supported himself.

At Oxford there was a small band of brilliant young men keenly interested in experimental science, then a new study. Among these were Christopher Wren and Robert Boyle, both of whom were to have decisive influences on Hooke's career. Boyle, eight years older than Hooke, was a man of means and position— the seventh son and fourteenth child of the "great" Earl of Cork. It was later said of Boyle that he was "the father of chemistry and brother of the Earl of Cork." About 1655, while Hooke was still a student at Oxford, Boyle engaged him as assistant in his experimental work. The air pump described in Boyle's earliest scientific book was designed and made by Hooke, and there are good grounds for believing that "Boyle's law" was really due to Hooke.

Hooke's first publication, in 1661, was a little book dealing

mainly with surface-tension phenomena, especially the rise of liquids in capillary tubes. He did not go far toward explaining these phenomena, but his book is full of acute observation and the experimental spirit. For instance, he recognized that the floating of small bodies on a liquid surface and the rise of oil in a lampwick and of the sap in a tree were due to the same agency that caused the liquid to rise in the fine tubes.

Hooke's first major invention, concerned with the balance wheel for watches, occasioned the first of the acrimonious disputes that were to embitter much of his working life and his relations with some of his contemporaries. The history of the watch episode is involved and obscure. Before Hooke's day, watches kept time by means of a swinging bar which bounced to and fro under the impulses of the teeth of the escape wheel. They were notoriously inaccurate; in fact, Shakespeare had used watches of his day, known as "Nuremberg eggs," to exemplify unreliability.

> A woman, that is like a German clock,
> Still a repairing, ever out of frame,
> And never going aright; being a watch . . .

There seems no doubt that Hooke conceived the fundamental idea of a spring to control the oscillations of a balance wheel in a watch, and that he drafted a patent for this device before 1660. It appears probable that a few years later he invented the spiral spring, which was introduced later (in 1675) by Christian Huygens. Hooke failed, however, to publish an account of this discovery, explaining afterward that he had put off doing so on account of a dispute with the backers of his patent. After the news of Huygens' invention, Hooke submitted his claim for priority to the Royal Society. The Society did not support him. Its secretary at the time was one Oldenburg, a great intriguer, to whom Huygens had consigned the English patent rights for his invention. Oldenburg, an enemy of Hooke, admitted that the latter had "made some watches of this kind" before 1675, but contended that they did not work—a matter about which he can scarcely have had personal knowledge.

The English authority A. R. Hall, who has investigated the question, recently summarized Hooke's inventions in chronometry as follows: "We can only admire the penetration with which he went to the heart of the difficulties: the remontoir, the independent balance, the detent escapement were all features of the first successful chronometers, and they are all suggested in Hooke's contrivances, crudely, but clearly and originally. If he had included a means of temperature compensation, he would have grasped all the essential principles of the chronometer." The anchor escapement of pendulum clocks also is generally attributed to Hooke, but here the evidence in his favor seems insufficient. The whole story of Hooke's performance in this episode of the watch—his comprehensive and clear-sighted solution of fundamental difficulties, his haste, his incomplete records—is typical of much of his work.

When the Royal Society received its Charter in 1662, it decided to appoint Hooke as its curator. His duty was to provide "three or four considerable experiments" every time the Society met, which was once a week! He did, in fact, produce an extraordinary diversity of experiments, mostly original, for the Society. Hooke received no pay as curator for two years, and he had to make a living somehow in the meantime. He must have been prodigiously busy. In 1665 he published his great work *Micrographia,* which alone would have sufficed to put his name among the very great in science. Pepys, no scientist but a man of sound judgment and wide interests, records that he sat up until two o'clock in the morning reading the volume—"the most ingenious book that ever I read in my life." In scientific circles, both in England and on the Continent, the book made a great impression and established Hooke's name.

The *Micrographia* places Hooke among the great founders of microscopic study in biology—in the company of Anton van

Leeuwenhoek, Marcello Malpighi and Nehemiah Grew. In this work Hooke described the first practical compound microscope. It consisted of a hemispherical objective lens and a large plano-convex eyepiece, of which only the center was used. A third lens could be inserted at the top of the cylindrical tube to act as a field lens, but this Hooke used only occasionally when he wanted to see much of the object at once. The focusing was effected by means of a screw cut on the eyepiece extension. Hooke discussed the defects of the instrument in quite a modern manner and later proposed the use of an immersion objective.

Proof of the excellence of the instrument and of the genius and perspicacity of the observer is given by the plates of some 60 microscopic objects, all of which he drew by his own hand. They record a number of fundamental discoveries in the world of living things: for example, he described the compound eye of the fly, observed the metamorphosis of the gnat larva and gave a description of the structure of feathers which remained the standard delineation for some 200 years. His figures of the louse, the silverfish insect and the flea (magnified to a length of 16 inches) are extraordinary in their accurate detail. Fungi and the sting of the nettle and of the bee are other subjects on which he made pioneering observations. In describing the structure of cork he used the word "cell" for the first time in its biological sense. Hooke turned the microscope not only on the living world but on the inanimate. He was the first to use it to examine metals —the point of a needle, the edge of a razor, the tiny spheres of steel struck off by a flint. He observed and depicted the beautiful crystals of snow.

Hooke was, then, a great pioneer in microscopy, distinguished alike as a designer of the instrument and its adjuncts, as an observer and as an interpreter of what he saw. But the *Micrographia*, in spite of its title, was by no means confined to microscopy. It records fundamental work in many branches of science. In it Hooke described the first refractometer for liquids, the first wheel barometer, a sealed alcohol thermometer and an indicating hygrometer which measured the moisture of the atmosphere by means of the beard of a wild oat, whose natural twist varies with the dampness of the air. Hooke was the first to propose as zero the freezing point of water—"common distilled water, that is so cold that it just begins to freeze and shoot into flakes." He devised the first examples of almost all the other common meteorological instruments used today—a wind gauge, a self-measuring rain gauge and a "weather clock" which registered automatically, by punches in a paper strip, the readings of the various meteorological instruments. Members of the Royal Society saw the latter instrument work, but it was frequently out of order, which is scarcely surprising.

Hooke was indeed the founder of scientific meteorology. He was the first to point out clearly that a rapid fall in the barometer presaged storms, to explain the polar circulation of the atmosphere and to ascribe the weather to physical forces governed primarily by the sun's radiation and the rotation of the earth. He put forward a scheme for making systematic meteorological records.

The *Micrographia* does not include Hooke's meteorological theories, but it contains a host of other significant discoveries and theoretical suggestions, most of which were never followed up. He proved by ingenious experiments that thermal expansion was a general property of liquids and solids. He put forward clearly the mechanical theory of heat, saying that it was "nothing else but a very *brisk* and *vehement agitation* of the parts of the body." In support of this idea he showed that mechanical friction gives rise to heat, and that the sparks struck from steel are spherical particles of the metal—evidence that they have been molten. He demonstrated that wood heated in a sealed vessel would not burn in the absence of air, and then put forward the theory (later adopted by the English chemist John Mayow without acknowledgment) that combustible bodies burned because air contained a "dissolving" substance, "like, if not the very same, with that which is fixed in *Salt-peter*" (that is, oxygen): the substance was used up in the combustion, so that fresh supplies of air were continually necessary. His remarks on respiration show a like grasp of the essentials. To realize Hooke's genius it is only necessary to read other contemporary speculations on these subjects.

Starting with an examination of quartz crystals in flint, he was led to consider crystal structure as a general property exhibited by various substances, among which he specified salts and metals. He then proceeded to build with spherical bullets some models of crystals which look remarkably modern. In particular he stated that rock salt "is compos'd of a texture of *Globules,* placed in a *cubical* form. . . ."

Considering the colors of thin plates—flakes of mica, films of air between glass sheets, soap films—Hooke shrewdly concluded that these colors were produced by the co-operation of light reflected from the front and the back of the film. His theory of light was that it was produced by a very rapid vibration in the luminous body, the waves being carried by an all-pervading ether. Many features of his theory of light and color are obscure, but much correct perception lies in these speculations, which occupy only a few pages. We know that Isaac Newton read them carefully.

The work concludes with some pages on astronomical matters —unexpected, perhaps, in a book on the microscope. Hooke for the first time pointed out the refracting effect of the atmosphere on light reaching us from heavenly bodies. He also reported two experiments he had made to see how the craters on the moon might have been formed. In one he let bullets fall into a mixture of pipe clay and water. In the other he noted how the last bubbles broke the surface in a pot of wet powdered alabaster as it ceased to boil. In both cases he obtained pits like the craters of the moon. These two experiments precisely illustrate the two leading theories today: that the craters were made either by falling meteorites or by volcanic eruptions.

This remarkable book by a young man of 29 gives a picture of a mind bursting with new and astonishingly correct ideas on all aspects of science, and of a superb experimenter. Its publication happened to coincide with a major change in England and in Hooke's life. The Great Plague of 1665 and the Great Fire of 1666 destroyed much of London and its life. Hooke helped his friend Christopher Wren in the rebuilding of the city. Hooke was made City Surveyor, which relieved him, probably for the first time, of financial anxiety. Within a week after the Fire ended, Hooke laid before the Royal Society a model for rebuilding the city on a rectangular pattern, as adopted later in New York! He was, incidentally, quite a good architect and designed several well-known London buildings.

Hooke's scientific activity never ceased. In 1674 he published an account of a systematic attempt to observe the parallaxes of stars. To measure angular distances in the heavens he devised a new quadrant which was the first instrument with telescopic sights and a screw adjustment ever made. It was an immense advance over the open-sight instruments of his contemporary, Hevelius of Danzig. It is to be particularly noted that Hooke not only designed the improved instrument but was perfectly clear as to what its advantages were. He found out by measurement that the resolving power of the naked eye was only about a minute of arc and realized that the telescope greatly increased this resolving power.

Hooke was the supreme instrument-maker of his time. In the same publication he described, with detailed illustrations, a clock-driven equatorial telescope to follow the stars. An incidental feature of his astronomical instruments was the universal, or "Hooke's," joint so widely used today. Apparently Hooke never actually built a clock-driven telescope; the first one was constructed in France some 70 years later.

In writing of Hooke it is hard to avoid piling up a catalogue of discoveries. We cannot list them all here. But a word must be said about his work entitled *Lectures de Potentia Restitutiva, or*

Of Spring, which appeared in 1678. Hooke's law and its implications were here expounded. He showed that the vibrations of any body in which the restoring force was proportional to the displacement, that is, of any elastic body, must have the same period whatever the amplitude—a capital discovery. From vibrations he proceeded to form a general, if necessarily crude, kinetic theory of matter, conceiving that motion of its particles accounted for many phenomena.

In 1677, Oldenburg having died, Hooke was appointed secretary to the Royal Society. In that capacity he soon wrote to Newton asking him to contribute a paper. The two men had previously been involved in controversy, exacerbated by Oldenburg, over the nature of light, but Hooke's letter now was courteous and led to a correspondence. However, it ended in hostility. Hooke had published in 1674 these principles: firstly, that all celestial bodies had a gravitational attraction toward their centers; secondly, that all bodies continued to move in a straight line except insofar as they were pulled aside by some force; thirdly, that the gravitational attraction fell off with the distance according to some law which he did not then know. Newton had already reached these conclusions himself, but he had not published a word or spoken of them to anyone, and Hooke's proposals were entirely independent. In 1680 Hooke wrote a letter to Newton asking what form the orbits of the planets would have if it was assumed that gravitational attraction was in inverse proportion to the square of the distance. If Hooke himself had been able to deduce mathematically the consequences of his principles where planetary orbits were concerned, he would have solved the great problem of the solar system which it was Newton's glory to settle. How near he came, with his instinctive sense of scientific truth!

When Hooke learned, just before publication of Newton's *Principia* six years later, that the book contained a demonstration of the solar system based on the principles he had put forward, without any acknowledgment to him, he was much irritated. It appears that all he wanted was a mention in the preface or some such civility. But Newton, an equally irritable man, was highly incensed by Hooke's protest. He omitted any mention of Hooke, not only from the *Principia* but also from the *Opticks*, published after Hooke's death. Hooke, who lacked not generosity but only tact, deserves all sympathy.

He gave up the secretaryship in 1682 but continued to deliver papers to the Royal Society on everything from the nature of memory to comets. In 1687 the death of his niece, who had lived with him for several years, came as a great shock. A few years later his wretched health finally broke down entirely. He lingered on, however, until 1703. He had a decent funeral, attended by all the Fellows of the Royal Society then in town. But it seems a symbolic commentary on this unhappy man that the site of his grave is unknown.

Two years after his death the *Posthumous Works of Robert Hooke* appeared as a volume of some 400,000 words. The collection was prepared from manuscripts, mostly of lectures, that he had left unpublished. These extraordinary papers establish Hooke as a great geologist and a pioneer evolutionist, among other things. He recognized fossils as a record of the past life of the globe. After pointing out that coins, medals or documents can be forged, he said of fossil shells: "These Characters are not to be counterfeited by all the Craft in the World, nor can they be doubted to be, what they appear, by any one that will impartially examine the true appearance of them: And tho' it must be granted, that it is very difficult to read them, and to raise a Chronology out of them, and to state the intervalls of the Times, wherein such, or such Catastrophies and Mutations have happened, yet 'tis not impossible. . . ." Compare this with the fairy tales written by his contemporaries on the subject.

One could go on for pages noting discoveries by Hooke, any one of which should have made his name remembered, and many of which have been credited to later men. Let us take a single day in the Royal Society. At the meeting of July 27, 1681, it is recorded: "Mr. Hooke showed his new-contrived aperture for long telescopes, which would open and close just like the pupil of a man's eye, leaving a round hole in the middle of the glass of any size desired; which was well approved of. He shewed an experiment of making musical and other sounds by the help of teeth of brass-wheels; which teeth were made of equal bigness for musical sounds, but of unequal for vocal sounds." Here are, firstly, the iris diaphragm, usually supposed to be a nineteenth-century invention, and, secondly, a superior version of the acoustical instrument known as Savart's wheel, after a Frenchman who is credited with inventing it in 1820. Hooke also showed a third trifle, his helioscope, all recorded in the minutes of the same day.

I have deliberately avoided a systematic classification of Hooke's work, for the chronological story tells more faithfully and more vividly how one discovery, invention and prediction after another tumbled out of this extraordinary man. As John Ward very truly observed in 1740: "Had he been more steady in his pursuits, and perfected one discovery before he entered upon another, he might perhaps in some cases have done greater service to the public, and prevented what often gave him uneasiness, the fear of losing credit of them by others, who built upon his foundation."

Hooke, sick, overworked, often cheated, the object of envy and attack by lesser men, made many enemies, but note that some of the great figures of the period were his firm friends—his headmaster Busby, John Evelyn, Thomas Sydenham and Christopher Wren, for example. For Wren and for Boyle he always expressed the greatest admiration. He was, if irritable, also fearless, upright, quick to thank for any kindness shown and quick to forgive injuries by great men whose work he admired. L. T. More, in his biography of Newton, expressed the wish that Newton, "in the full plenitude of his fame, could have shown more tolerance and a greater sympathy" for Hooke, "that brave mind and spirit, housed in a suffering body."

Hooke was hasty, impatient with fools and intolerant of obliquity, which it is perhaps safe to resent in the small but unwise to take amiss in the influential. "He had," his friend and editor R. Waller wrote, "a piercing Judgment into the Disposition of others, and would sometimes give shrewd Guesses and smart Characters," which is a dangerous diversion. He lacked the smooth approach, the adroitness, the discrimination of motives and the concealment of antipathy that are so essential to worldly success. He was also, alas, sensitive—a grave fault. No doubt everyone believes that in our times Hooke would have been better treated. Perhaps.

LAPLACE

by James R. Newman

HISTORIANS OF SCIENCE have rightly called the Marquis de Laplace the Newton of France. He earned the title for his immense work on celestial mechanics, which capped the labors of three generations of mathematical astronomers and produced a universal principle that has been applied to almost every field of physics. Biographers have found Laplace no less interesting—though less impressive—as a person than as a scientist. He was a man of curiously mixed qualities: ambitious but not unamiable, brilliant but not above stealing ideas shamelessly from others, supple enough to be by turns a republican and a royalist in the tempestuous time in which he lived—the era of the French Revolution.

Pierre Simon de Laplace was born at Beaumont-en-Auge, a Normandy village in sight of the English Channel, on March 23, 1749. The facts of his life, of the earlier years especially, are both sparse and in dispute. Most of the original documents essential to an accurate account were burned in a fire which in 1925 destroyed the château of his great-great-grandson the Comte de Colbert-Laplace; others were lost during World War II in the bombardment of Caen. Many errors about Laplace's life have gained currency: that his father was a poor peasant, that he owed his education to the generosity of prosperous neighbors, that after he became famous he sought to conceal his "humble origins." Recent researches by the mathematician Sir Edmund Whittaker seem to show that whatever Laplace's reasons for reticence about his childhood, poverty of his parents was not among them. His father owned a small estate and was a syndic of the parish; his family belonged to the "good bourgeoisie of the land." One of Laplace's uncles was a surgeon, another a priest. The latter, a member of the teaching staff of the Benedictine Priory at Beaumont, where Laplace had his first schooling, is said to have awakened the boy's interest in mathematics. For a time it was thought that Laplace would follow his uncle's profession as a priest, but at the University of Caen, which he entered at the age of 16, he soon demonstrated his mathematical inclinations. He wrote a paper on the calculus of finite differences which was published in a journal edited by Joseph Louis Lagrange, the great mathematician, 13 years Laplace's senior, with whom he was later to collaborate.

When Laplace was 18, he set out for Paris. He carried enthusiastic letters of recommendation to Jean le Rond d'Alembert, the most prominent mathematician of France. D'Alembert ignored them; Laplace, not an easy fellow to put off, thereupon wrote him a letter on the general principles of mechanics which made so strong an impression that d'Alembert at once sent for the precocious young man and said: "Monsieur, as you see, I pay little enough attention to recommendations; you had no need of them. You made your worth known; that is enough for me; my support is your due." A short while later d'Alembert procured for him an appointment as professor of mathematics in the Ecole Militaire of Paris.

Laplace's rise was rapid and brilliant. He submitted to the Academy of Sciences one memoir after another applying his formidable mathematical capabilities to the outstanding questions of planetary theory. "We have never seen," said a spokesman for the usually imperturbable savants of the Academy, "a man so young present in so short a time so many important memoirs on such diverse and difficult problems."

One of the main problems Laplace ventured to attack was the perturbations of the planets. The anomalies of their motion had long been known; the English astronomer Edmund Halley

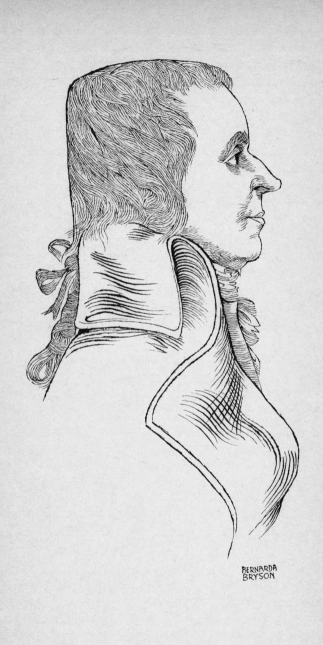

BERNARDA
BRYSON

had noted, for instance, that Jupiter and Saturn over the centuries alternately lagged behind and were accelerated ahead of their expected places in a peculiar kind of orbital horse race. The application of Newton's theory of gravitation to the behavior of the planets and their satellites entailed fearful difficulties. The famous three-body problem (how three bodies behave when attracting one another under the inverse square law) is not completely solved today; Laplace tackled the much more complex problem of all the planets cross-pulling on one another and on the sun.

Newton had feared that the planetary melee would in time derange the solar system and that God's help would be needed to restore order. Laplace decided to look elsewhere for reassurance. In a memoir described as "the most remarkable ever presented to a scientific society," he demonstrated that the perturbations of the planets were not cumulative but periodic. He then set out to establish a comprehensive rule concerning these oscillations and the inclination of the planetary orbits. This work bore on the fate of the entire solar system. If it could be shown that disturbances in the machinery were gradually overcome and the status quo restored—a kind of self-healing and self-preserving process analogous to the physiological principle which Walter Cannon has called homeostasis—the future of the cosmic machine, and of its accidental passenger, man, was reasonably secure. If, however, the disturbances tended to accumulate, and each oscillation simply paved the way for a wilder successor, catastrophe was the inevitable end. Laplace worked out a theoretical solution which seemed to fit observation, showing that the outcome would be happy, that the changes of the solar system merely "repeat themselves at regular intervals, and never exceed a certain moderate amount." The period itself is of course tremendously long; the oscillations are those of "a great pendulum of eternity which beats ages as our pendulums beat seconds."

Thus Laplace's theorems gave assurance of the reliability of the stellar clockwork of the universe; its peculiar wobbles and other irregularities were seen to be minor, self-correcting blemishes which in no sense threatened the revolutions of the engine as a whole. Indeed, Laplace regarded the anomalies as a boon to astronomers. He wrote in the *Mécanique céleste*: "The irregularities of the two planets appeared formerly to be inexplicable by the law of universal gravitation; they now form one of its most striking proofs. Such has been the fate of this brilliant discovery, that each difficulty which has arisen has become for it a new subject of triumph—a circumstance which is the surest characteristic of the true system of nature."

Two reservations about this work have to be noted. Laplace's solution did not completely prove the stability of the solar system. His solution would be valid for an idealized solar system undisturbed by tidal friction or other force; but the earth is now known, as it was not in Laplace's day, to be a nonrigid body subject to deformation by tidal friction, which thus acts as a brake on its motion. The effect is very small but acts always in one direction. Consequently we cannot conclude, as Laplace did, that nature arranged the operations of the celestial machine "for an eternal duration, upon the same principles as those which prevail so admirably upon the Earth, for the preservation of individuals and for the perpetuity of the species."

The second point concerns Laplace's failure to mention his indebtedness to Lagrange. Almost everything that Laplace accomplished in physical astronomy owes a debt to Lagrange's profound mathematical discoveries. It is impossible in many instances to separate their contributions. Lagrange was the greater mathematician; Laplace, for whom mathematics was only a means to an objective, was primarily a mathematical physicist and astronomer. Others have severely censured Laplace for his lack of acknowledgment of his collaborator's contributions, but Lagrange, obviously a saintly soul, did not; the two always remained on the best of terms.

Laplace's *Mécanique céleste* appeared in five immense volumes between 1799 and 1825. He described its scope as follows:

"We have given, in the first part of this work, the general principles of the equilibrium and motion of bodies. The application of these principles to the motions of the heavenly bodies has conducted us, by geometrical reasoning, without any hypothesis, to the law of universal attraction; the action of gravity, and the motion of projectiles, being particular cases of this law. We have then taken into consideration a system of bodies subjected to this great law of nature; and have obtained, by a singular analysis, the general expressions of their motions, of their figures, and of the oscillations of the fluids which cover them. From these expressions we have deduced all the known phenomena of the flow and ebb of the tide; the variations of the degrees, and of the force of gravity at the surface of the earth; the precession of the equinoxes; the libration of the moon; and the figure and rotation of Saturn's rings. We have also pointed out the cause why these rings remain permanently in the plane of the equator of Saturn. Moreover, we have deduced, from the same theory of gravity, the principal equations of the motions of the planets; particularly those of Jupiter and Saturn, whose great inequalities have a period of above 900 years."

Napoleon, on receiving a copy of the *Mécanique céleste*, protested to Laplace that in all its vast expanse God was not mentioned. The author replied that he had no need of this hypothesis. Napoleon, much amused, repeated the reply to Lagrange, who is said to have exclaimed: "Ah, but it is a beautiful hypothesis; it explains many things."

To mathematicians the work is especially memorable. The Irish mathematician William Rowan Hamilton is said to have begun his mathematical career by discovering a mistake in the *Mécanique céleste*. George Green, the English mathematician, derived from it a mathematical theory of electricity. Perhaps the greatest single contribution of the work was the famous Laplace equation:

$$\frac{\partial^2 u}{\partial x^2} + \frac{\partial^2 u}{\partial y^2} + \frac{\partial^2 u}{\partial z^2} = 0$$

Laplace's expression is a field equation, which is to say it can be used to describe what is happening at every instant of time at every point in a field produced by a gravitational mass, an electric charge, fluid flow and so on. Another way of saying this is that the equation deals with the value of a physical quantity, the potential, throughout a continuum. The potential function u, introduced in the first instance as a purely mathematical quantity, later acquired a physical meaning. The difference between the values of the potential function at two different points of a field measures the amount of work required to move a unit of matter from one of these points to the other; the rate of change of potential in any direction measures the force in that direction.

By giving u different meanings (e.g., temperature, velocity potential and so on) the equation is found to have an enormous range of applications in the theories of electrostatics, gravitation, hydrodynamics, magnetism, sound, light, conduction of heat. In hydrodynamics, where u is the velocity potential (distance squared divided by time), the rate of change of potential is the measure of the velocity of the fluid. The equation applies to a fluid which is incompressible and indestructible; if as much fluid flows out of any tiny element of volume as flows in, the potential function satisfies Laplace's equation. A rough explanation of why this equation serves as an almost universal solvent of physical problems is that it describes a characteristic economy of natural behavior—"a general tendency toward uniformity so that local inequalities tend to be smoothed out." Thus a metal rod heated at one end tends to become of uniform temperature throughout; a solute in a liquid tends to distribute itself evenly.

The *Mécanique céleste* is a book whose difficulties are proportional to its bulk. Laplace made no concession to the reader. He bridged great gaps in the argument with the infuriating phrase "it is easy to see." The United States mathematician and astronomer Nathaniel Bowditch, who translated four of the volumes into English, said he never came across this expression "without feeling sure that I have hours of hard work before me to fill up the chasm." Laplace himself, when required to reconstruct some of his reasoning, confessed he found it not at all *"aisé à voir"* how his conclusions had been reached. Nor is it a modest or entirely honorable writing. "Theorems and formulae," wrote Agnes Mary Clerke, the noted historian of astronomy, "are appropriated wholesale without acknowledgment, and a production which may be described as the organized result of a century of patient toil presents itself to the world as the offspring of a single brain." The biographer Eric Temple Bell has remarked that it was Laplace's practice to "steal outrageously, right and left, wherever he could lay his hands on anything of his contemporaries and predecessors which he could use."

For those unable to follow the formidable abstractions of the *Mécanique* Laplace wrote in 1796 the *Exposition du système du monde,* one of the most charming and lucid popular treatises on astronomy ever published. In this masterpiece Laplace put forward his famous nebular hypothesis (which had been anticipated by Immanuel Kant in 1755). Its gist is that the solar system evolved from a rotating mass of gas, which condensed to form the sun and later threw off a series of gaseous rings that became the planets. While still in the gaseous state the planets threw off rings which became satellites. The hypothesis has had its ups and downs since Kant and Laplace advanced it. In Laplace's theory revolution in a retrograde direction by a member of the solar system was impossible; yet before Laplace died Sir William Herschel found that the satellites of Uranus misbehaved in this way, and others have since been discovered. Yet the theory was an intellectual landmark, and much of its basic reasoning is still accepted by some cosmologists as valid for astronomical aggregates larger than the solar system.

Another subject upon which Laplace bestowed his attention,

both as a mathematician and as a popularizer, is the theory of probability. His comprehensive treatise *Théorie analytique des probabilités* described a useful calculus for assigning a "degree of rational" belief to propositions about chance events. Its framework was the science of permutations and combinations, which might be called the mathematics of possibility.

The theory of probability, said Laplace, is at bottom nothing more than common sense reduced to calculation. But his treatise seemed to indicate that the arithmetic of common sense is even more intricate than that of the planets. No less a mathematician than Augustus de Morgan described it as "by very much the most difficult mathematical work we have ever met with," exceeding in complexity the *Mécanique céleste*.

Laplace's contributions to probability are perhaps unequaled by any other single investigator; nevertheless the *Théorie analytique,* like the *Mécanique,* failed to acknowledge the labors of other mathematicians, on which many of its conclusions depended. De Morgan said of Laplace: "There is enough originating from himself to make any reader wonder that one who could so well afford to state what he had taken from others, should have set an example so dangerous to his own claims."

In a companion work, the *Essai philosophique sur les probabilités,* presenting a nontechnical introduction to the laws of chance, Laplace wrote a passage which is regarded as the most perfect statement of the deterministic interpretation of the universe, a symbol of that happy and confident age which supposed that the past could be described and the future predicted from a single snapshot of the present:

"We ought then to regard the present state of the universe as the effect of its anterior state and as the cause of the one which is to follow. Given for one instant an intelligence which could comprehend all the forces by which nature is animated and the respective situation of the beings who compose it— an intelligence sufficiently vast to submit these data to analysis—it would embrace in the same formula the movements of the greatest bodies of the universe and those of the lightest atom; for it, nothing would be uncertain and the future, as the past, would be present to its eyes. The human mind offers, in the perfection which it has been able to give to astronomy, a feeble idea of this intelligence. Its discoveries in mechanics and geometry, added to that of universal gravity, have enabled it to comprehend in the same analytical expressions the past and future states of the system of the world. Applying the same method to some other objects of its knowledge, it has succeeded in referring to general laws observed phenomena and in foreseeing those which given circumstances ought to produce. All these efforts in the search for truth tend to lead it back continually to the vast intelligence which we have just mentioned, but from which it will always remain infinitely removed. This tendency, peculiar to the human race, is that which renders it superior to animals; and their progress in this respect distinguishes nations and ages and constitutes their true glory."

Together with the great chemist Antoine Lavoisier, Laplace engaged in experiments to determine the specific heats of a number of substances. They designed the instrument known as Laplace's ice calorimeter, which measures heat by the amount of ice melted, a method employed earlier by the Scottish chemist Joseph Black and the German Johann Karl Wilke.

Laplace prospered financially and politically; Lavoisier died on the guillotine. In 1784 Laplace was appointed "examiner to the royal artillery," a lucrative post and one in which he had the good fortune to examine a promising 16-year-old candidate named Napoleon Bonaparte. The relationship was to blossom forth 20 years later, much to Laplace's advantage. With Lagrange, Laplace taught mathematics at the Ecole Normale, became a member and then president of the Bureau of Longitudes, aided in the introduction of the decimal system and suggested, in keeping with the reform spirit of the Revolution, the adoption of a new calendar based on certain astronomical calculations.

There is some reason to believe that for a brief period during the Revolution Laplace fell under suspicion; he was removed from the commission of weights and measures. But he managed not only to hold on to his head but to win new honors. He had a knack for riding the waves of his turbulent era. Under the Republic he was an ardent Republican and declared his "inextinguishable hatred to royalty." The day following the 18th Brumaire (November 9, 1799), when Napoleon seized power, he shed his Republicanism and formed an ardent attachment for the first consul, whom he had helped earlier to form a Commission for Egypt. Almost immediately Napoleon rewarded Laplace with the portfolio of the Interior. The evening of his appointment the new minister demanded a pension of 2,000 francs for the widow of the noted scholar Jean Bailly, executed during the Terror, and early the next morning Madame Laplace herself brought the first half-year's income to "this victim of the passions of the epoch." It was a "noble beginning," as Laplace's protégé François Arago wrote, but it is hard to discover any other noble accomplishment gracing Laplace's ministerial career. His tenure of office was brief—six weeks. Napoleon wrote tartly of Laplace's shortcomings in his St. Helena memoirs: "He was a worse than mediocre administrator who searched everywhere for subtleties, and brought into the affairs of government the spirit of the infinitely small." But to soothe the hurt of his dismissal the deposed minister was given a seat in the Senate and in 1803 became its Chancellor.

Historians have amused themselves describing Laplace's skill in running with the hare and hunting with the hounds. The neatest evidence appears in his introductions to successive editions of his books. He inscribed the first edition of the *Système du monde* in 1796 to the Council of Five Hundred, and in 1802 prefixed the third volume of the *Mécanique céleste* with a worshipful paean to Napoleon, who had dispersed the Council. Laplace dedicated the 1812 edition of the *Théorie analytique des probabilités* to "Napoleon the Great"; in the 1814 edition he suppressed this dedication and wrote "that the fall of empires which aspired to universal dominion could be predicted with very high probability by one versed in the calculus of chances." Napoleon had made Laplace a count; this gave him the opportunity to join in the 1814 decree of forfeiture banishing the man who had made him a count. When the Bourbons returned, Laplace was one of the first to fall at their feet; for this genuflection he received a marquisate.

Laplace was not an evil or a malicious man. He gave a hand up to many younger scientists. At his country home in Arcueil he surrounded himself with "adopted children of his thought": Arago, an astronomer and physicist; the physicist Jean Biot, noted for his investigations of the polarization of light; Baron Alexander von Humboldt, the celebrated German naturalist and traveler; Joseph Gay-Lussac, the great chemist and physicist; Siméon Poisson, the brilliant mathematician. Biot related that after he had read a paper on the theory of equations, Laplace took him aside and showed him "under a strict pledge of secrecy papers yellow with age in which he had long before obtained the same results." Having soothed his ego, Laplace told the young man to say nothing about the earlier work and to publish his own.

The almost universal admiration for Laplace's scientific genius did not mitigate the widespread distrust inspired by his political adaptability. The more tolerantly cynical of his contemporaries referred to his "suppleness." The stock appraisal is to compare him to the Vicar of Bray. The Vicar, an accommodating man who was twice a Papist and twice a Protestant, is said to have defended the charge of being a time-server by replying: "Not so, neither, for if I changed my religions, I am sure I kept true to my principle, which is to live and die the Vicar of Bray." Laplace could have made similar answer.

About his family life and personal habits there is a strange lack of information. Laplace's marriage with Charlotte de Courty de Romanges, contracted in 1788, was apparently a happy one. They had a daughter and a son, Emile, who rose to the rank of general in the artillery. In later years Laplace passed much of his time at Arcueil, where he had a house next to the chemist Count de Berthollet. There in his study, where the portrait of Racine, his favorite author, hung opposite that of Newton, he pursued his studies with "unabated ardor" and received "distinguished visitors from all parts of the world." He died on March 5, 1827, a few days before his 78th birthday. Illustrious men are required to say deathless things on their deathbeds. Laplace is said to have departed after expressing the reasonable opinion, "What we know is very slight; what we don't know is immense." De Morgan, observing that "this looks like a parody on Newton's pebbles," claimed to have learned on close authority that Laplace's very last words were: "Man follows only phantoms."

PART 2 THE NEW WORLD SYSTEM

I. WILLIAM ROWAN HAMILTON
by Sir Edmund Whittaker

II. G. F. FITZGERALD
by Sir Edmund Whittaker

Sir Edmund Whittaker continued active and productive as a scientist and scholar until his death in his eighty-third year in 1956. He was not only an eminent mathematician but was associated in his long career with a remarkable galaxy of great modern scientists. He studied mathematics at Cambridge under Arthur Cayley and Sir George Stokes; as a Fellow of Trinity College he worked with A. N. Whitehead, Bertrand Russell, Sir J. J. Thomson and Lord Rutherford; as a young officer of the British Association for the Advancement of Science he came to know personally the distinguished theoretical physicist George Francis Fitzgerald; among his students over the years were G. H. Hardy, Sir James Jeans, Sir Arthur Eddington, H. W. Turnbull and Sir Geoffrey Taylor. In 1906 Whittaker was appointed Royal Astronomer of Ireland, and to the same chair of astronomy at the University of Dublin that had been occupied by William Rowan Hamilton. His most famous pupil there was Eamon de Valera, then a promising young mathematician. When Whittaker left Ireland for the chair of mathematics at the University of Edinburgh, de Valera wrote him that his greatest ambition was to translate Whittaker's *Modern Analysis* and *Analytical Dynamics* into the Celtic language. Outside of mathematics and physics his activities were chiefly in the fields of religion and philosophy. He was a Catholic and devoted considerable attention to the relation between science and theology.

WILLIAM ROWAN HAMILTON

by Sir Edmund Whittaker

Aᴏᴛᴇʀ ɪsᴀᴀᴄ ɴᴇᴡᴛᴏɴ, the greatest mathematician of the English-speaking peoples is William Rowan Hamilton, who was born in 1805 and died in 1865. His fame has had some curious vicissitudes. During his lifetime he was celebrated but not understood; after his death his reputation declined and he came to be counted in the second rank; in the twentieth century he has become the subject of an extraordinary revival of interest and appreciation.

About his ancestry there is not much to be said. His father was a Dublin solicitor who defended the outlawed Irish patriot Archibald Hamilton Rowan and obtained a reversal of his sentence. From Rowan, who acted as sponsor at the baptism of the infant William, the boy received his second Christian name. The child was not brought up by his own parents. When he was about a year old, they decided to entrust his education to Mr. Hamilton's brother James, a clergyman settled at Trim, a small town 30 miles north of Dublin. Young William lived in Trim, with occasional visits to Dublin, until he was of age to enter the University.

Whether the credit must be given to his uncle's methods of education or to his own natural gifts, it is recorded that by the age of three William could read English easily; at five he was able to read and translate Latin, Greek and Hebrew; at eight he had added Italian and French; before he was 10 he was studying Arabic and Sanskrit. At the age of 14 he wrote a letter in Persian to the Persian ambassador, then on a visit to Dublin.

The boy loved the classics and the poets, but at the age of 15 his interests, and the course of his life, were completely changed when he met one Zerah Colburn, an American youngster who gave an exhibition in Dublin of his powers as a lightning calculator. "For a long time afterwards," wrote Hamilton later, "I liked to perform long operations in arithmetic in my mind; extracting the square and cube root, and everything that related to the properties of numbers." William resolved upon a life of mathematics. "Nothing," he declared, "so exalts the mind, or so raises a man above his fellow-creatures, as the researches of Science. Who would not rather have the fame of Archimedes than that of his conqueror Marcellus? . . . Mighty minds in all ages have combined to rear the vast and beautiful temple of Science, and inscribed their names upon it in imperishable characters; but the edifice is not completed; it is not yet too late to add another pillar or another ornament. I have yet scarcely arrived at its foot, but I may aspire one day to reach its summit."

In his diary there presently appeared such entries as "read Newton's *Life*" and "began Newton's *Principia*." At the age of 16 he made the acquaintance of Laplace's *Mécanique céleste*. (An entry in his journal around this time recounted: "We have been getting up before five for several mornings—that is, my uncle and I; he pulls a string which goes through the wall and is fastened to my shirt at night.") In 1823, preceded by rumors of his intellectual prowess, "Hamilton the prodigy" entered Trinity College at Dublin. There his progress was brilliant, not only on the examinations but also in original research. When he was only 21 years old he submitted to the Royal Irish Academy a paper entitled "A Theory of Systems of Rays" which in effect made a new science of mathematical optics.

In this paper Hamilton's aim was to remodel the geometry of light by establishing one uniform method for the solution of all problems in that science. He started from the already established principles that a ray of light always travels by the path that takes the least time (according to the wave theory) or the least "action" (according to the corpuscular theory) in going from one point to another; this is true whether the path is straight or bent

by refraction. Hamilton's contribution was to consider the action (or time) as a function of the positions of the points between which the light passes, and to show that this quantity varied when the co-ordinates of these points varied, according to a law which he called the law of varying action. He demonstrated that all researches on any system of optical rays can be reduced to the study of this single function. Hamilton's discovery of this "characteristic function," as he called it, was an extraordinary achievement of scientific genius. He had originally projected it when he was 16 and he brought it to a form approaching completeness in his twenty-first year.

The communication of the paper was soon followed by a great change in Hamilton's circumstances. The chair of professor of astronomy at Trinity College, which paid an annual salary of 250 pounds and conferred on its occupant the title of Royal Astronomer of Ireland, was vacated in 1826 when its holder, the Reverend John Brinkley, was appointed to the Bishopric of Cloyne, once held by the great philosopher George Berkeley. Hamilton was elected as Brinkley's successor a few months later. The election of an undergraduate to a professorial chair was an astonishing event, and it led to some curious consequences. For instance, the Royal Astronomer was by virtue of his office an examiner for the Bishop Law Prize, a mathematical distinction open to candidates of junior bachelor standing, and thus came to pass the anomalous proceeding of an undergraduate examining graduates in the highest branches of mathematics.

While everyone acknowledged the unprecedented honor of Hamilton's appointment to the chair, opinion was sharply divided as to whether he was wise to have accepted it. In another year or two he would undoubtedly have been elected a fellow of Trinity College, with better financial and other prospects. What determined his choice was the consideration that the royal astronomership was practically a research appointment, involving very little in the way of fixed duties, while a fellow was required to become a clergyman and must soon have developed into a tutor and lecturer, with duties occupying most of his time. To be sure, the research equipment of the astronomical observatory was poor in the extreme, but what really was in the minds both of Hamilton and of the electors was not astronomy but an arrangement by which he could continue the theoretical researches of which the paper on "Systems of Rays" was such a glorious beginning.

Hamilton did have the duty of giving a course of lectures on astronomy. In these it was his custom to discuss the relations of astronomy to physical science in general, to metaphysics and to all related realms of thought. His lectures were so poetic and learned that they attracted crowded audiences of professors and visitors as well as his class of undergraduates; when in 1831 there was some talk of his being transferred to the chair of mathematics, the Board insisted that he remain where he was. As inducement the Board raised his salary to 580 pounds a year and gave him permission to devote his research principally to mathematics.

In 1832 Hamilton announced to the Royal Irish Academy a remarkable discovery in optics which followed up his theory of systems of rays. It had been known for some time that certain biaxial crystals, such as topaz and aragonite, gave rise to two refracted rays, producing a double image. Augustin Fresnel of France had worked out the rules of double refraction. Now Hamilton, investigating by his general method the law of Fresnel, was led to conclude that in certain cases a single ray of incident light in a biaxial crystal should give rise to not merely two but an infinite number of refracted rays, forming a cone, and that in certain other cases a single ray within such a crystal would emerge as a different cone. He therefore proposed from theory two new laws of light, which he called internal and external conical refraction. They were soon verified experimentally by his friend Humphrey Lloyd, a Dublin physicist.

In 1834 Hamilton, then 29, wrote to his uncle: "It is my hope and purpose to remodel the whole of dynamics, in the most extensive sense of the word, by the idea of my characteristic function." He proceeded to apply this principle to the motion of systems of bodies, and in the following year he expressed the equations of motion in a form which showed the duality between the components of momentum of a dynamical system and the co-ordinates of its position. Only a century later, with the development of quantum theory, did physicists and mathematicians fully realize the importance of this duality.

In 1835 Hamilton received the honor of knighthood, and two years later he was elected president of the Royal Irish Academy. But his private life was less happy. Upon becoming a professor he had set up house with three of his sisters at the Dunsink Observatory on a hill five miles from Dublin. At the age of 26 he fell in love with Helen Maria Bayly, the daughter of a former rector in County Tipperary. She at first refused to entertain his proposal of marriage but ultimately accepted him, and the wedding took place on April 9, 1833. He had remarked in a letter to a friend on her "extreme timidity and delicacy"; these qualities were only too fully confirmed after the marriage. Lady Hamilton bore two sons and a daughter in six years, but she found herself unequal to the work of home administration and left Dunsink for two years to live with a married sister in England. She returned in 1842, but things became no better. Hamilton henceforth had no regular times for his meals, and he began to use alcoholic stimulants to a dangerous extent.

When I held Hamilton's chair, to which I had the honor of being appointed in 1906, many years after his death, I met many people who had known him. The countryside was full of stories about him. One of them concerns his administration of the 17 acres of farmland around Dunsink Observatory, of which the Royal Astronomer has control. Hamilton, who was town-bred, knew nothing of farming, but in order to supply his household with milk he bought a cow. After some time, in the ordinary course of nature, the yield of milk began to fall off. Hamilton went to consult a neighboring farmer. The farmer, knowing with whom he had to deal, said that the cow, as the solitary occupant of 17 acres, was suffering from loneliness. Thereupon Hamilton inquired whether it would be possible to provide her with companions, and the farmer graciously agreed, in recognition of a payment by Hamilton, to allow his cattle to graze on the rich pastures of Dunsink.

In spite of the unfavorable conditions of his life, Hamilton's scientific work went on. In 1843 he made a great discovery—the calculus of quaternions.

He was led to this discovery by long thought on the problem of finding a general rule for computing the fourth proportional to three straight-line segments when the directions of those lines were taken into account. A line segment with a specified direction is called a vector. It was well known that a vector in a plane could be represented by a complex number; that is, a number formed of both real and imaginary numbers, or $x + y\sqrt{-1}$. (The square root of -1, an imaginary number, is usually written i, so that the expression becomes $x + yi$.) If we represent real numbers by distances on the x axis of a graph, then multiplication of any number by -1, changing it to the negative number, may be thought of as rotating the line segment 180 degrees, while multiplication by i, the square root of -1, may be thought of as a 90-degree rotation (see illustration opposite). Thus imaginary numbers are represented on the y axis, and i may be considered a unit on that axis, or a "unit vector." Any vector in a plane may then be specified by a complex number giving its x and y components. Such a pair of numbers, known as a doublet, obeys the same algebraic laws as a single number: doublets can be added, subtracted, multiplied and divided according to the usual rules. Thus it is possible to calculate the fourth proportional to three vectors in a common plane: $V_1 : V_2 = V_3 : x$.

Hamilton conjectured that in three-dimensional space a vector might be represented by a set of three numbers, a triplet, just

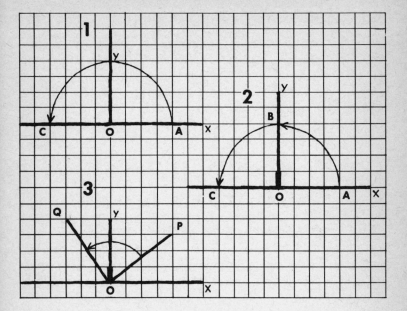

Complex number, made up of a real number and an imaginary one, the square root of −1, is used to describe the length and direction of a line segment. When complex numbers are added, subtracted or multiplied, the process is equivalent to a geometrical operation, e.g., rotation. In the diagram numbered 1 the line segment OA, representing the number +4, is multiplied by −1, which changes it to the line segment OC, or −4. Thus multiplication by −1 is equivalent to rotation through 180 degrees. In diagram 2 multiplication by −1 is done in two steps, i.e., multiplication by $\sqrt{-1}$ and by $\sqrt{-1}$ again. (The square root of −1 is usually written i.) Consequently multiplication by i can be considered rotation through 90 degrees. This leads to the idea of measuring imaginary distances on the y axis, as is indicated by making i the "unit vector" on that axis. Diagram 3 demonstrates that multiplication by i has the effect of a 90-degree rotation even if the starting point is not the x axis. The line segment from point O (x = 0, y = 0) to point P (x = 4, y = 3) is represented in complex-number notation as $4 + 3i$. Multiplying this number by i gives $4i + 3i^2$, or $3 − 4i$. The latter number represents the line segment OQ (x = −3, y = 4), or a 90-degree rotation of the line OP.

as a vector in a plane was expressed by a doublet. He sought to find the fourth proportional by multiplying triplets, but encountered difficulties. The younger members of the household at Dunsink shared affectionately in the hopes and disappointments of their illustrious parent as the investigation proceeded. William Edwin (aged nine) and Archibald Henry (eight) used to ask at breakfast: "Well, Papa, can you multiply triplets?" Whereto he was obliged to reply, with a sad shake of the head, "No, I can only add and subtract them."

One day, while walking from Dunsink into Dublin, Hamilton suddenly realized the answer: the geometrical operations of three-dimensional spaces required for their description not triplets but *quadruplets*. To specify the operation needed to convert one vector into another in space, one had to know four numbers: (1) the ratio of the length of one vector to the other, (2) the angle between them, and (3) the node and (4) the inclination of the plane in which they lie.

Hamilton named the set of four numbers a quaternion, and found that he could multiply quaternions as if they were single numbers. But he discovered that the algebra of quaternions differed from ordinary algebra in a crucial respect: it was *noncommutative*. This word calls for some explanation. When we multiply 2 by 3 we obtain the same product as when we multiply 3 by 2. This *commutative* law of multiplication, as it is called, is embodied in the algebraic formula ab = ba. It applies to imaginary numbers as well as to real numbers. It does not, however, hold for the calculus of quaternions, because the latter describes geometrical operations such as rotations. The illustration opposite shows why. It represents three mutually perpendicular axes, the y and z axes lying in the plane of the paper and the x axis extending toward the reader. The characters i, j and k represent unit vectors along the x, y and z axes respectively. Multiplication by i is defined as a 90-degree counterclockwise rotation in the plane of the paper; multiplication by j and k, as rotations in planes perpendicular to that plane. Now multiplication of j by

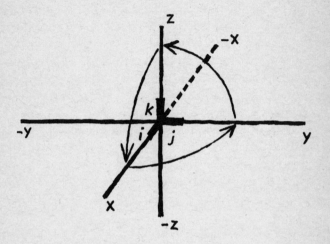

Noncommutative algebra is used to represent geometrical operations in three dimensions. A vector in three dimensions is represented in a system of co-ordinates with three mutually perpendicular axes (x points toward the reader, y and z are in the plane of the page) in terms of the unit vectors i, j and k. Multiplication by i is arbitrarily defined as meaning a rotation of 90 degrees in the plane perpendicular to the i vector, i.e., the plane of y and z. Multiplication by j and k are similarly defined, as indicated by the arrows. Now it can be seen that multiplication $i \times j$ has the effect of rotating j into k. On the other hand, the multiplication $j \times i$ has the effect of rotating i into $-k$. So $i \times j = k$, and $j \times i = -k$. In other words, the multiplication is noncommutative: $i \times j$ does not equal $j \times i$.

i rotates j to k; that is, $ij = k$. But multiplication of i by j rotates i to $-k$; that is, $ji = -k$. Thus ij does not equal ji.

The surrender of the commutative law was a tremendous break with tradition. It marked the beginning of a new era. The news of the discovery spread quickly, and led, in Dublin at any rate, to a wave of interest among people of rank and fashion like the later boom in general relativity in London, when Lord Haldane invited Einstein to meet the Archbishop of Canterbury at luncheon. Hamilton was buttonholed in the street by members of the Anglo-Irish aristocracy with the question: "What the deuce are the quaternions?" To satisfy them he published the delightful *Letter to a Lady*, in which he explained that the term "occurs, for example, in our version of the Bible, where the Apostle Peter is described as having been delivered by Herod to the charge of four quaternions of soldiers. . . . And to take a lighter and more modern instance from the pages of *Guy Mannering*, Scott represents Sir Robert Hazelwood of Hazelwood as loading his long sentences with 'triads and quaternions.'"

From this time until his death 22 years later, Hamilton's chief interest was to develop the new calculus. They were mostly sad and lonely years, owing to the frequent illnesses and absences of his wife. He worked all day in the large dining room of the Observatory house, into which from time to time his cook passed a mutton chop. (After his death scores of mutton chop bones on plates were found sandwiched among his papers.)

Hamilton's discovery was quickly followed by other new algebras, such as the theory of matrices, which is likewise noncommutative. Thus he started a glorious school of mathematics, though it was not to come into full flower for another half-century. I remember discussing in 1900 with Alfred North Whitehead whether quaternions and other noncommutative algebras had much of a future as regards applications to physics. Whitehead remarked that while all the physics then known could be treated by ordinary algebra, it was possible that new fields in physics might some day be discovered for which noncommutative algebra would be the only natural representation. In that very year this anticipation was started on the road to fulfillment. Max Planck introduced the quantum h, the beginning of the quantum theory. Now h is a quantum of action, and action was a central conception in Hamilton's system of dynamics. Thus the Hamiltonian ideas on dynamics began to come into prominence. But very slowly. When my book *Analytical Dynamics* was published in 1904, I was criticized severely for devoting a large part of it to such topics as the co-ordinates–momentum duality, action and other Hamiltonian ideas. The critics called them mere mathematical playthings.

The good work went on, however. The discovery of special relativity brought quaternions to the fore, because Arthur Cayley of Cambridge University had shown in 1854 that quaternions could be applied to the representation of rotations in four-dimensional space. His result yielded a particularly elegant expression for the most general Lorentz transformation. Moreover, the new discoveries again emphasized the importance of action, which preserves its form in different reference systems and is therefore fundamental in relativity physics.

Meanwhile, the workers in quantum theory were coming to realize that Hamilton's dynamical conceptions must form the basis of all rules of quantification. And in 1925 the other side of his work—his noncommutative algebra—was brought into quantum theory by Werner Heisenberg, Max Born and Pascual Jordan, who showed that the ordinary Hamiltonian equations of dynamics were still valid in quantum theory, provided the symbols representing the co-ordinates and momenta in classical dynamics were interpreted as operators whose products did not commute.

Time has amply vindicated Hamilton's intuition of the duality between generalized co-ordinates and generalized momenta. This was strikingly shown in 1927, when Heisenberg discovered the principle of uncertainty, which is usually stated in this way: the more accurately the co-ordinates of a particle are determined, the less accurately can its momentum be known, and vice versa, the product of the two uncertainties being of the order of Planck's constant h.

Quantum-mechanical workers have generally tended to regard matrices rather than quaternions as the type of noncommutative algebra best suited to their problems, but the original Hamiltonian formulas keep on cropping up. Thus the "spin matrices" of Wolfgang Pauli, on which the quantum-mechanical theory of rotations and angular momenta depends, are simply Hamilton's three quaternion units i, j, k. Arthur Conway has shown that quaternion methods may be used with advantage in the discussion of P. A. M. Dirac's equation for the spinning electron. Hamilton's formulae of 1843 may even yet prove to be the most natural expression of the new physics.

G. F. FITZGERALD

by Sir Edmund Whittaker

In the last years of the nineteenth century, when I was a very young man, I was one of the secretaries of the mathematical and and physical section of the British Association for the Advancement of Science, and so I came to know one of the most regular attenders and prominent speakers at its annual meetings, the eminent physicist George Francis FitzGerald of Dublin.

While I knew well the Oxford and Cambridge mathematicians and physicists, in the midst of whom I lived, it was only at the British Association gatherings that one had an opportunity of meeting the Irishmen. (It is amazing, incidentally, how many great mathematicians and physicists of the nineteenth century sprang from the Anglo-Irish stock: there were William Rowan Hamilton, Humphrey Lloyd, George Gabriel Stokes, Lord Kelvin, George Salmon, Joseph Larmor and FitzGerald.) FitzGerald fascinated me. He was an arresting figure—bearded, with piercing eyes, and strikingly handsome. His ample gray locks gave him a venerable appearance, though in fact he was not yet 50 when he died in 1901. "He reminded me," said one of his nonscientific colleagues, "of the bust of some Greek philosopher, which we cannot look upon without that instinctive feeling of respect which intellect and character command among civilized men."

FitzGerald's father was the Right Reverend William FitzGerald, Bishop of Cork and the most distinguished prelate of the former Established Church. His mother was a sister of George Johnstone Stoney, a well-known mathematician and physicist, to whom we are indebted for the word "electron." Young Fitz-Gerald was educated at home. It is surprising how many of the privately tutored sons of cultured parents are later recognized as men of genius; a conspicuous living example is Bertrand Russell. Why this should be so, I shall not inquire. A cynic might say that the tendency of school education is to make everybody second-rate, and the reason why schooling does no harm to most boys is that they would never be more than second-rate in any case. FitzGerald was certainly fortunate in his private tutor, who was the sister of George Boole, the creator of symbolic logic.

At the age of 16 he entered the University of Dublin, where he took a brilliant degree in mathematics and experimental science in 1871. In those days there were no Ph.D. courses, and the next step for one who wanted to continue his education was to read for a fellowship. At Dublin the candidate was expected to make a profound study of the illustrious Frenchmen Joseph Lagrange, Pierre Laplace, Siméon Poisson and Jean Fourier, as well as of the great Dublin mathematical physicists Hamilton and James MacCullagh. FitzGerald read deeply in their writings, and was attracted also to the metaphysical works of the Irish philosopher George Berkeley. He succeeded in obtaining a fellowship in 1877, and in 1881 was elected to Dublin's professorship of natural and experimental philosophy.

Until this time there had been no teaching of practical physics in Dublin. The first university physical laboratory intended for the instruction of ordinary students was, so far as I know, that opened by Professor P. G. Tait in Edinburgh in 1868, though at Glasgow William Thomson (afterwards Lord Kelvin) had for some years used his best honors students as research assistants. The Cavendish professorship at Cambridge was not created until 1871. FitzGerald, on his appointment to the chair at Dublin, persuaded the Board of Trinity College to assign to him an unused chemical laboratory. There he began classes in experimental physics.

But FitzGerald himself was by choice primarily a theoretical worker, and it was to theoretical problems that he turned his main attention. The question that concerned him was the ether.

BERNARDA
BRYSON

He accepted Newton's celebrated dictum: "To suppose that one body may act upon another at a distance through a vacuum, without the mediation of anything else, . . . is to me so great an absurdity, that I believe no man, who has in philosophical matters a competent faculty for thinking, can ever fall into." Fitz-Gerald, like Descartes, was convinced that space, even interplanetary space, is occupied by a medium which, though imperceptible to the senses, is capable of transmitting force and exerting effects on material bodies immersed in it. This medium, the ether, must therefore possess mechanical properties. Were these properties those of a solid, a liquid or a gas?

Descartes had suggested that the ether was constituted of extremely fine particles continually in motion and everywhere pressing upon or colliding with one another. In the following century the French-Swiss scientist George Louis LeSage had considered it as composed of an infinite number of very small, rapidly moving corpuscles, so small that not more than one out of every hundred of them meets another corpuscle during millions of years. Ethers of this kind more or less resembled a gas as pictured in the kinetic theory, and natural philosophers of the seventeenth and eighteenth centuries were inclined to regard the ether as a kind of gas permeating all bodies and filling interplanetary space; they likened the propagation of light in the ether to that of sound in a gas. But early in the nineteenth century this theory was faced by an insuperable objection. Thomas Young discovered in 1817 that the vibrations of light are executed at right angles to the direction of propagation, whereas the vibrations of sound are in the same direction as its propagation. Thus the analogy between sound and light broke down in an essential feature. Some change in the conception of the ether was necessary, and this was provided in 1821 by Augustin Fresnel. He suggested that the ether behaved not like a gas but like an elastic solid: its resistance to attempts to distort its shape accounted for transverse vibrations.

The phenomena so far considered in connection with the ether were those of gravitation and light. But there are other physical effects which can be transmitted through a so-called vacuum or the ether: namely, electricity and magnetism. As early as 1800 Young had remarked: "Whether the electric ether is to be considered the same with the luminous ether, if such a fluid exists, may perhaps at some future time be discovered by experiment." Fifty years later Michael Faraday wrote: "It is not at all unlikely that if there be an aether, it should have other uses than simply the conveyance of radiation." When electrical effects were considered, however, the most satisfactory kind of ether seemed to be a liquid. Lord Kelvin showed that a bar magnet has properties resembling those of a straight tube immersed in a perfect fluid, the fluid entering at one end and flowing out by the other. If like ends of two such tubes are presented to each other, they attract; unlike ends repel. The forces are thus diametrically opposite in direction to those of magnets, but in other respects the laws of mutual action between these tubes and between magnets are precisely the same.

When FitzGerald attacked the problem of the ether, he did not sink into the crude materialism that characterized all these theories. He regarded the medium as *sui generis*, not necessarily capable of being described in terms of any familiar kind of matter. Indeed, he remarked as early as 1878 that James Clerk Maxwell's electromagnetic theory, if it "induced us to emancipate ourselves from the thralldom of a material aether, might possibly lead to most important results in the theoretic interpretation of nature."

FitzGerald brought two dominant motives to bear on the investigation: first, the conviction that a single ether must suffice to explain all physical phenomena, and secondly, a firm belief in the truth of Maxwell's electromagnetic theory of light. Maxwell had published his theory in 1861 to 1864, but for more than 20 years it was not widely accepted. FitzGerald was one of its earliest and stoutest champions. He realized that the ether needed to have both the properties of a liquid and the properties of a solid, and these apparently contradictory requirements he succeeded in satisfying.

His starting point was a theory of matter which had been proposed by Lord Kelvin. Kelvin had pointed out that the mutual interaction of atoms might be illustrated by the behavior of smoke rings, which after approaching each other closely are observed to rebound. He had suggested that many of the properties of atoms, including the conservation of matter, might be explained by the hypothesis that they were constituted of vortex rings in a perfect fluid. He conceived the idea of a "vortex-sponge"—a mass of fluid in which rotating and nonrotating portions were finely mixed together.

FitzGerald saw that the concept of a vortex-sponge would solve his problem. For vortex-filaments in a perfect fluid are types of motion that possess permanent individuality throughout all changes, and their presence gives the fluid a certain stiffening, so to speak. They perform the same kind of function as the steel bars embedded in reinforced concrete: the fluid remains still a fluid, but a finite morsel of it would resist distortion. From the point of view of its fine structure, it would be a liquid, but from the point of view of its coarse structure, it would have some of the properties of a solid.

It was now necessary to identify the electric and magnetic vectors of Maxwell's theory with features of the vortex-sponge. Since vorticity in a perfect fluid cannot be created or destroyed, FitzGerald reasoned that an electric field was a modification of the system in which the vortex motion was polarized. Long vortex-filaments might be bent spirally about axes parallel to a given direction. When filaments were bent in a spiral form the fluid would have more energy than when they were straight, and the increase in energy could be measured by a vector parallel to their directions. The presence of a single spiral filament in the fluid would bend the surrounding parallel straight ones, and

81

from this action a model of magnetic force could be constructed. FitzGerald went on to study the dynamics of a vortex-sponge, and showed that the density of energy was the sum of the square of two quantities which might be interpreted as the electric and magnetic intensities. It will be noticed that electromagnetic phenomena in this ether are essentially statistical in character, since they depend on its coarse structure.

FitzGerald wrote many memoirs developing Maxwell's electromagnetic theory; it was he who first gave what are commonly called the Maxwell–Lorentz equations, which connect the electric and magnetic vectors with the positions and motions of the charges. He applied the Maxwellian theory to the rotation of the plane of polarization of light by reflection from a magnet and to problems such as the electric and magnetic fields due to a moving charge; the Faraday magnetic rotation of light and its relation to the Zeeman effect; the Kerr effect; and the generation of radiant energy by a small electric current, in which the current-strength is varied according to a simple periodic law. The electric oscillators he proposed were closely akin to those used a few years later by Heinrich Hertz in his historic experimental demonstration of the existence of electric (Hertzian) waves.

Yet FitzGerald doubtless will always be best known as the discoverer of the "FitzGerald contraction." He devised this hypothesis to explain a very puzzling result which the U. S. physicists A. A. Michelson and E. W. Morley had found in trying to measure the velocity of the earth relative to the ether. With an interferometer they had compared the time of travel of light over a fixed distance in the direction of the earth's motion and at right angles to this direction. It was expected that the optical lengths of these paths would be different, but no difference could be observed. This suggested that the ether was carried along with the earth—a supposition hard to reconcile with the theory of astronomical aberration and other known facts. Discussing this dilemma one day with Oliver Lodge in Lodge's study in Liverpool, FitzGerald suddenly remarked that it would be solved if one could assume that the apparatus automatically contracted in the direction of the earth's motion. Following up this idea, he calculated that the contraction must be measured by the ratio $\sqrt{(1 - v^2/c^2)}$ to 1, with v representing the earth's velocity relative to the ether and c, the velocity of light.

The Irish mathematician Joseph Larmor shortly afterward pointed out that clocks, as well as rods, must be affected by motion; to put the matter somewhat loosely, a clock moving with velocity v must run slower in the same ratio as the length of the rod contracts. Larmor's assertion has had a remarkable experimental verification recently in the observation of the rate of disintegration of mesons, the particles produced in cosmic rays. According to Larmor's theory, to a stationary observer the rate of disintegration of a meson should appear to be slower, the faster the meson is moving. This was found in 1941 to be actually the case.

The discoveries that the length of a rigid rod and the indications of a clock are not absolute properties of the rod and the clock, but depend on their motion, made it possible to explain the failure of all the experiments that had been made for the purpose of determining the velocity of the earth relative to the ether. They also led directly to the modern theory of relativity, which may be said to have begun with the discovery of the FitzGerald contraction in 1892. Unhappily FitzGerald died in 1901, barely missing the momentous outcome of the revolution in the philosophy of physics which he had started.

PART 3 WHAT IS FIRE?

I. PRIESTLEY *by Mitchell Wilson*

A novelist, physicist and one-time industrial researcher, Mitchell Wilson has made a name for himself as one of the few literary "regional" writers in the field of science and technology. Born in New York City in 1913, he felt an equal pull toward literature and science while at New York University and Columbia University. For a time the balance was tipped toward science by a good physics teacher. Wilson did graduate work under I. I. Rabi, became an assistant to Enrico Fermi, doing some early work on the meson, and in 1940 joined the research staff of the Columbian Carbon Company, working on thin films and high-frequency heating. All the while he was also striving to be a writer, selling his first story to *Cosmopolitan* in 1939 and regularly to the "slicks" thereafter, in addition to doing several mystery novels. In 1944 he found he had to make a choice between research and writing. The first product of his commitment to the latter was *Live with Lightning*, a novel which won critical acclaim as the story of how it is to be a physicist in these times.

II. LAVOISIER *by Denis I. Duveen*

Denis I. Duveen is the president of a soap company. A chemist, he was born in London in 1910, graduated from Oxford University in 1929 and did research in organic chemistry at the College de France. He came to the United States in 1948, having been, during World War II, technical assistant to the director of an explosives factory run by the British Ministry of Supply. Duveen maintains a scholarly interest in the history of chemistry. A general collection of alchemical and early chemical works which he assembled is now at the University of Wisconsin. Duveen has what is probably the most extensive collection of Lavoisier's printed works and manuscripts, and recently collaborated in publishing a full bibliography of the great chemist's writings. His nonscientific hobby is big-game fishing.

PRIESTLEY

by Mitchell Wilson

O<small>N MONDAY MORNING</small>, June 9, 1794, the Philadelphia newspaper the *American Daily Advertiser* greeted the arrival of a refugee from England:

> "It must afford the most sincere gratification to every well-wisher to the rights of man, that the United States of America, the land of freedom and independence, has become the asylum of the greatest characters of the present age, who have been persecuted in Europe, merely because they have defended the rights of the enslaved nations.
> "The name of Joseph Priestley will be long remembered among all enlightened people; and there is no doubt that England will one day regret her ungrateful treatment of this venerable and illustrious man. . . ."

The illustrious chemist's flight across the Atlantic to the New World came at the end of a career of embroilment not only in science but also in the social turmoil of his uneasy time. Thirty years earlier Priestley, as a young clergyman, had come to a London teeming with fops, highwaymen, industrious apprentices and geniuses. He was then 30 years old, slender, with delicate, almost feminine features. For an ordained minister he dressed with somewhat worldly elegance. He had gaiety, a quiet wit, and enjoyed his growing reputation as a writer on religious matters. He had a genteel poverty that he took for granted; he also had an incorruptible moral courage.

He had come to London to meet the famous philosopher from the American Colonies, Benjamin Franklin, who was at the height of his fame as a scientist. Franklin's experiments with lightning had made him an almost Mephistophelean figure to his European contemporaries. People believed that he was capable of producing a thunderbolt at will, and the very benignity of his bearing made him the more terrible. Although he had been sent to London to plead the cause of the colonies, Franklin found it diplomatic to live the life of a visiting scientist rather than that of a political emissary.

Priestley was a theological polemicist on behalf of what was then considered radical doctrine: Unitarianism. The son of a weaver in the small town of Leeds, he had been orphaned and had been adopted by an aunt, a strong-minded woman of independent temper. She had raised him in an atmosphere of free religious discussion. Because his health was fragile, he had had little formal schooling but had taught himself French, Latin, algebra and geometry. His aunt's influence had turned him to the ministry; he taught at an academy, married a sympathetic, intelligent woman when he was 28 and became a popular writer on theological subjects. No one was less suited to the name of traitor and anti-Christ that was to be fastened on him.

Priestley's visits to Franklin's salon in London, which occurred shortly after his marriage, resulted in a new turn of his career. Up to that time he had taken only an educator's interest in science. Casually he suggested to Franklin that someone ought to write a popular book on electricity; Franklin urged him to do so. From this came Priestley's brilliant work *The History and Present State of Electricity*, which he finished within a year. In writing it he was led to investigate for himself certain disputed points of electrical theory. As it happened, he had a natural flair for research and made some original discoveries, one of which was the fact that carbon is an excellent conductor of electricity.

The book was so successful that a year after its appearance Priestley was elected to the Royal Society.

This taste of science was all that was needed to start him on a

new life, but it was an accident that led him to chemistry. In Leeds he lived next to the public brewhouse of Jakes and Nell. The odoriferous product of fermentation permeated his house and became the object of his first researches.

Chemistry was still dominated by the ideas of alchemy. Matter was supposed to be made up of a *prima materia* modified by four elements—earth, fire, air and water. By Priestley's day these original Aristotelian elements had been elaborated into various kinds and orders. Earth was differentiated into three varieties—mercurial, vitreous and combustible. There were, in addition to the elements, four spirits—sulfur, mercury, arsenic and sal ammoniac. There were also six bodies—gold, silver, copper, lead, tin and iron. And the "soul" of all matter was phlogiston; by virtue of it, combustible bodies burned.

Priestley set out to make one of the varieties into which air had been divided—"fixed air" (actually carbonic-acid gas, or carbon dioxide). It was commonly thought that sea scurvy was due to an insufficient supply of "fixed air" in the human system. Priestley worked out a method of producing this gas from chalk and sulfuric acid, and he charged water with it by leading the gas through a flexible tube containing traps for impurities. Thus he invented soda water. Priestley explained his method to Lord Sandwich, the First Lord of the Admiralty, and after an investigating commission had given its approval, two shops were set up with his apparatus to supply the Navy. The Royal Society was so impressed with Priestley's achievement that it awarded him the Copley medal, its highest honor in chemistry. The product also won commercial recognition. A Mr. Bewley bottled and sold the preparation under the following formula:

"To prepare Mr. Bewley's julep dissolve three drachms of fossil alkali in each quart of water, and throw in streams of fixed air till the alkaline taste be destroyed. This julep should not be prepared in too large quantities, and should be kept in bottles very closely corked and sealed. Four ounces of it may be taken at a time, drinking a draught of lemonade or water acidulated with vinegar or weak spirit of vitriol, by which means the fixed air will be extricated in the stomach."

Priestley's next scientific project was less happy. The Royal Navy had yielded to the plea of astronomers to send a vessel to observe a lunar eclipse in the South Pacific; the Navy had been looking for an excuse to dispatch an innocent-looking expedition to these waters, and so it outfitted a collier under the command of Captain James Cook, allowed the periwigged scientists to go aboard, and sent it off with sealed orders to Cook to afford the astronomers every opportunity to make observations and then proceed on his true mission: to chart and claim the land mass in the South Pacific known as Terra Incognita Australis. Priestley, eager to go along, was commissioned chaplain to the crew. But at the last moment he was barred from the voyage because his radical theological writings had earned him enemies who charged that he would subvert the men on the expedition.

Priestley resumed his experiments in gas chemistry ("pneumatic chemistry"), which he was to report eventually in his classic *Experiments and Observations on Different Kinds of Air.* His apparatus had the elegance of true simplicity. His method was to place the reaction material in a glass flask partly filled with mercury. He would invert the flask in a trough filled with mercury so that each vessel became a sort of Torricellian barometer. If the chemical reaction generated gas, the additional pressure would push down the mercury level within the flask. On the other hand, if the reaction absorbed one of the gases in the enclosed atmosphere, the mercury level would rise. Thus the change in gas volume was easy to measure. To heat substances in the flask Priestley used the rays of the sun focused by a lens.

Priestley's first discovery was his greatest: the production and isolation of oxygen. He heated what was then called *mercurius calcinatus* (mercuric oxide) and found that the salt gave off four to five times its own volume of gas. When he fed a sample of this gas into an enclosed flask in which a candle was burning, the candle "burned in this air with a remarkably vigorous flame. . . . I had got nothing like this remarkable appearance from any [other] kind of air . . . the candle burned with splendor . . . and a piece of red-hot wood *sparkled* in it . . . and consumed very fast. . . ."

Later Priestley learned that mice lived much longer in his new gas than in an equal volume of ordinary air. In a closed container a burning candle or a live animal somehow "injured" the air so that the flame or the animal soon expired. Priestley realized that he had discovered a way to "restore" the vital element lost from the air. He next found out how nature maintained this element in air. He wrote:

"I have been so happy as by accident to have hit upon a method of restoring air which has been injured by the burning of candles, and to have discovered at least one of the restoratives which Nature employs for this purpose. It is *vegetation*.

"On the 17th of August, 1771, I put a sprig of mint into a quantity of air in which a wax candle had burned out, and found that on the 27th of the same month, another candle burned perfectly well in it. This experiment I repeated without the least variation in the event, not less than eight or 10 times in the remainder of the summer. . . ."

Priestley elaborated the experiment to remove as many extraneous details as possible in order to arrive at the simplest general statement. He demonstrated that the remarkable ability to restore air was not peculiar to mint, for spinach, "springs of balm" and the weed called groundsel had the same effect. He concluded: "Plants, instead of affecting the air in the same manner with animal respiration, reverse the effects of breathing and tend to keep the atmosphere sweet and wholesome when it is become noxious in consequence of animals either living and breathing, or dying and putrefying in it."

Priestley, who was so radical in his theological and political beliefs, was extremely conservative as a scientific theorist. He unquestionably accepted and clung to the theory of phlogiston, one of the last remnants of alchemy, and his prestige kept it alive far longer than it deserved. Hardly understanding what he was doing, Priestley isolated for the first time not only oxygen and carbon dioxide but also ammonia ("alkaline air"), nitrogen, nitric oxide, carbon monoxide, sulfur dioxide ("vitriolic acid air") and other substances.

Now recognized as a man of genius in science, Priestly was invited to join the famous Lunar Society in Birmingham, whose members and guests included some leading scientists of the day— the astronomer Sir William Herschel, the engineer John Smeaton, the botanist Erasmus Darwin, the inventor James Watt. The dozen or so members met at one another's homes each month on the Monday nearest to the full moon. Meetings began with dinner about two o'clock in the afternoon and went on until eight in the evening, when the brilliant moon gave light by which to walk home. Soon after Priestley joined, a member wrote to a friend:

"We have long talked of phlogiston without knowing what we talked about: but now that Dr. Priestley hath brought the matter to light we can pour that element out of one vessel into another; can tell how much of it by accurate measurement is necessary to reduce a calx into contact with any visible thing. In short, this goddess of levity can be measured and weighed like other matter. For the rest, I refer you to the doctor himself."

Priestley spent the next 10 years or so in Birmingham, happily busy not only in chemistry but also writing on education and ethics. Though an undeviating monarchist, he publicly expressed sympathy with the objectives of the American colonists during the Revolutionary War. Priestley might have escaped punishment for this, as many Englishmen did, had he not also come out boldly for the separation of church and state in England and supported the cause of the French Revolution.

His biographer T. E. Thorpe has remarked that "great as Priestley's merit is as an experimentarian philosopher, his greater claim on our regard and esteem rests upon his struggles and his sufferings in the cause of civil, political and religious liberty."

On Bastille Day in 1791 Priestley joined a small group of his friends in a quiet celebration of the event in Birmingham. For five days before the celebration a group of hotheads and bigots had distributed pamphlets and broadsides accusing those who planned to attend the dinner of treason, and threatening Priestley and his family with hanging. Ignoring the threats, Priestley and his friends had their dinner at noon in a private dining room without interference, but in the evening trouble began. A hysterical mob put the two dissident churches in Birmingham to the torch and set out to burn down Priestley's house and lynch him and his family. A female neighbor of Priestley's gave this description of what happened when news of the mob's approach arrived and her father went out to try to halt it:

> "Arriving at Dr. Priestley's gate before the mob, he stationed himself withinside until the mob came up, and then addressed them, endeavoring to induce them, by fair words and money, to desist and return home. They seemed inclined to listen, till one more loud than the rest, and who had the appearance of a ringleader cried out, 'Don't take a sixpence of his money: in the riots of '80 in London a man was hanged for only taking sixpence!' and began to fling stones. My father, then finding it rashness to brave two or three hundred men, turned his horse and rode . . . off."

While Priestley and his family took refuge with friends, the howling crowd looted his house, scattered his papers, battered down the walls and made a bonfire of the debris. Several hours later the mob went in pursuit of Priestley. He and his family escaped in a coach with only a few minutes to spare. They reached London after a week of roundabout traveling.

In London many people were shocked at the news, but many more felt that where there was smoke there must be fire: the Priestleys must be disloyal. A servant of a family living on the same street asked for her release because she dreaded being so near the infamous Dr. Priestley. Members of the Royal Society began to cut Priestley dead. His sons could not be placed anywhere, and the young men sailed to America. England was entering that 30-year period of repression which was to send shiploads of political noncomformists to Botany Bay or to the gallows.

After two years in London Priestley, realizing that he would never be able to live and work in peace in England, decided to follow his sons to Pennsylvania. In the new nation he became a welcome visitor of George Washington in retirement. He preached to a congregation that included President John Adams, and became a close friend of Thomas Jefferson. However, he refused a professorship and later the presidency of the University of Pennsylvania, preferring to live quietly. His favorite son died, and shortly afterward his wife, who had never recovered from the shock of the Birmingham riots.

But Priestley's American exile was not entirely passive. He demonstrated and explained his marvelous experimental techniques to James Woodhouse, John Maclean and Robert O'Hare, the pioneer U. S. chemists who began the process of forging that science which more than any other was to lead the way in exploring and exploiting the wealth of the American frontier.

LAVOISIER

by Denis I. Duveen

ANTOINE LAURENT LAVOISIER is universally known as the founder
of modern chemistry, but this achievement tells only a small part
of the story of his life. Had Lavoisier never performed a chemical
experiment, he would still deserve a prominent place in history.
He was a many-sided genius who pioneered not only in chemistry
but also in physiology, scientific agriculture and technology, and
at the same time was a leading figure of his era in finance, economics, public education and government. Few men in history
have busied themselves in so many fields with such powerful
effect as this brilliant and charming Frenchman.

Lavoisier was born in Paris on August 26, 1743, the only son
of well-to-do parents. His mother died while he was still young,
and he was brought up with loving care by his father and a
maiden aunt. His father wanted him to become a lawyer; Antoine
dutifully completed his legal education and obtained a license
to practice, but he had shown his predilection for science by
choosing to do his undergraduate work at the Collège Mazarin,
where he studied astronomy, botany, chemistry and geology with
famous masters. After law school he quickly turned to science
again. Within three years, at the age of 25, he was elected to the
Royal Academy of Sciences, as a result of his work in helping to
prepare a geological atlas of France, his chemical research on
plaster of Paris and his recognition with a special gold medal for
plans submitted in a royal competition to improve the street lighting of Paris.

Now resolved on a career of scientific research, Lavoisier first
arranged to assure himself of sufficient financial means. He
bought a share of the Ferme Générale, the private company

97

that collected taxes for the King. This association was highly profitable to Lavoisier throughout his life, but it was to bring him to the guillotine.

At 28 Lavoisier married Marie Anne Pierrette Paulze, the 14-year-old daughter of a leading member of the Ferme. Although it was a marriage of convenience, arranged by the father to save his daughter from pressure in high places to marry an elderly and dissolute count, the union between Lavoisier and his child bride was to prove a happy success. Marie set about learning Latin and English to translate scientific works for her husband, who had little knowledge of foreign languages. She translated two important books by the Irish chemist Richard Kirwin and supplied Lavoisier with résumés of papers published by Joseph Priestley, Henry Cavendish and other contemporary British chemists. Her translations and footnotes show that she herself achieved more than a superficial knowledge of chemistry. As a hostess Marie made the Lavoisier home a popular meeting place for French and foreign scientists; as an accomplished artist she sketched and engraved plates for his books; she helped him in the laboratory as his secretary, taking notes on many of his experiments. After Lavoisier's execution she edited and printed for private circulation his last uncompleted work, compiled in prison, *Mémoires de Chimie*. It seems a poor reward that her life after Lavoisier was made bitter by an unhappy, short marriage to Count Rumford, who was a renowned scientist and inventor but also a careerist and adventurer.

Lavoisier's work in chemistry is a textbook classic which can be quickly reviewed. In 1772, at the age of 29, he began to study combustion and the "calcination" (oxidation) of metals. He observed that sulfur and phosphorus gained weight when they burned, and he supposed that they absorbed air. The key to the explanation of his own observations came when Joseph Priestley discovered "dephlogisticated air" (oxygen). Lavoisier soon showed that it was this substance, to which he gave the name

BERNARDA
BRYSON

oxygen, that was absorbed by metals when they formed "calces," i.e., oxides. He proceeded to replace the century-old "phlogiston" theory (that substances burned because of an escape of phlogiston) with the correct view that combustion is a chemical combination of the combustible substance with oxygen. Lavoisier could not explain the production of fire, and he introduced the term *calorique* to describe the *élément impondérable*—heat. The complete explanation of combustion and heat was not to come until the theory of entropy was developed in the nineteenth century. Nonetheless Lavoisier, in collaboration with the great physicist Pierre Simon de Laplace, made studies of the heat evolved in combustion which laid the foundation of thermochemistry.

Lavoisier's theory at first failed to account for the combustion of "inflammable air" (hydrogen), evolved when metals were dissolved in acids. Here it was a discovery by Cavendish that gave Lavoisier the clue he needed. Cavendish learned that the burning of inflammable air produced pure water. Lavoisier extended his experiments and concluded that water was a compound of the two gases we now call oxygen and hydrogen. He recognized immediately that this fact supplied a keystone for the building of a whole new edifice of chemistry.

The new chemistry was quite readily accepted. It called for revision of the list of elements and a new system for naming substances; Lavoisier, with other leading French chemists, composed a new terminology, and with minor revisions it is still used today.

Lavoisier's keen interest in combustion led him naturally to respiration. There are those who say that his work in this field justifies his being called the founder of physiology and biochemistry. Certainly he brought order out of chaos. Many had guessed that all life depended on a vital ingredient in the atmosphere; Priestley and others had demonstrated by experiment that breathing animals exhausted the air of a necessary factor. It was left to Lavoisier to show the purely chemical nature of the role played by oxygen, or as it was first called, vital air, in respiration and combustion. He was the first to show that animal heat is produced by a slow process continually occurring in the body and consisting of a form of slow combustion. To demonstrate this experimentally, he planned and carried out with Laplace a series of elegant experiments. They worked with guinea pigs. By accurately measuring the animals' intake of oxygen and output of carbon dioxide and heat—the latter with an ice calorimeter they invented—they laid the foundation of the science of calorimetry. As an extension of this work Lavoisier later collaborated with Armand Seguin in a program of research which established the facts of basal metabolism. The apparatus he designed for this work is the direct ancestor of the equipment used today in determining basal metabolism.

Lavoisier's scientific research was frequently interrupted by calls for technical assistance from the government. One of these was to remedy a shortage of gunpowder. France was suffering from a scarcity of saltpeter, an essential constituent of gunpowder, which was produced by an inefficient licensed monopoly. Called upon for advice by the comptroller general of finance, Lavoisier suggested the formation of a government-owned Régie des Poudres. He was appointed as one of the four administrators of this agency and proceeded to institute new and efficient methods of production. Within three years he raised France's annual production of gunpowder from 714 tons to 1,686 tons. It can be said that Lavoisier's efforts contributed to the success of the American Revolution, for without the gunpowder supplied the colonists by France the outcome might have been different.

The Régie des Poudres provided Lavoisier with a home and a scientific laboratory at the Arsenal, where he spent his happiest and most productive years. But two episodes in this experience illustrate the hazards to which a scientist may be exposed in government service. On one occasion Lavoisier, his wife and three associates undertook to experiment with potassium chlorate as a possible new explosive. The experiments produced a laboratory explosion which killed two of the party, but the Lavoisiers escaped unharmed. Lavoisier reported the affair to the King's Minister in lofty terms which well illustrate his character: "If you will deign, Sir, to engage the King's attention for a moment with an account of this sad accident and the dangers I faced, please take the opportunity to assure His Majesty that my life belongs to him and to the state, and that I shall always be ready to risk it whenever such action may be to his advantage, either by a resumption of the same work on the new explosive, work which I believe to be necessary, or in any other manner."

The second exposure was political. In 1789, when the Revolutionists had taken control of Paris, the Administration of Powders decided to ship 10,000 pounds of low-quality industrial gunpowder out of the city and replace it with better-quality musket powder. The move alarmed the populace; Lafayette, who was in charge of munitions and had not been informed of the shipment, ordered it returned to the Arsenal. The local commune investigated the powder administrators on charges of treason, and although the inquiry exonerated them, public clamor for Lavoisier's arrest did not abate until the powder was restored to the Arsenal.

Like Thomas Jefferson, whom he resembled in many ways, Lavoisier had a keen and personal interest in agriculture. He inherited from his father a farm at Le Bourget, and soon afterward he also acquired a large agricultural estate near the town of Orléans. Here he himself farmed about 370 acres and leased 865 acres to sharecroppers. It was his habit to spend the sowing and harvest seasons at the farm, and to keep close account of the crop yields and costs by double-entry bookkeeping. Farmer Lavoisier soon decided that crop yields were intimately connected with the amount of manure used on the fields. He then carefully calculated the optimum balance of cattle to acreage of pasture and cultivated land for a mixed farm. His studies of the requirements of various cash crops and of cattle were highly practical and successful. He was able to record with satisfaction that in 14 years he had doubled his yield of wheat and quintupled the size of his herd of cattle.

Lavoisier was active in the Agricultural Society of Paris and in the official Administration of Agriculture, of which he was one of the five original members and the guiding light. He represented the third estate in the Provincial Parliament of Orléans, where he was the prime mover of almost all the subjects discussed and decisions taken. His reports, which dominate the printed proceedings of the Parliament, dealt not only with matters strictly agricultural but also with such varied subjects as public assistance for orphans and widows, steps to found a savings bank in Orléans, the abolition of the hated *corvée* (the obligation to repair the roads of a parish), tax reforms, the preparation of a mineralogical map of the district and the establishment of workhouses for the poor. He expressed his social creed in these words: "Happiness should not be limited to a small number of men; it belongs to all." Lavoisier was a physiocrat—devoted to the belief that all wealth stemmed from the land and that individual liberty was the most sacred right of man.

Scientifically a pioneer, politically a liberal, sociologically a reformer, Lavoisier was orthodox in his views on finance. In the new republic of 1789 he was elected to the presidency of the Discount Bank which was eventually to become the Bank of France. In a lucid and discerning address he noted with disquiet that inflation had set in. Three years later Lavoisier presented a report to the National Assembly on the lamentable state of the finances of the country. A recent appraisal of Lavoisier's exposition by an expert calls it superb. This report was printed by Lavoisier's friend Pierre S. Du Pont, whom he had financed in the publishing business and whose young son, Irénée, was an apprentice bookkeeper under Lavoisier at the Arsenal. When Irénée, after the Du Pont family's emigration to the United States, established the great gunpowder works in Delaware, he wanted to name the factory Lavoisier Mills, but the family finally settled on E. I. Du Pont de Nemours.

Lavoisier's famous treatise on political economy, *On the Land Wealth of the Kingdom of France,* is an important one in the history of economics. He had started it before the Revolution, but the National Assembly considered it so useful afterward that it ordered the paper printed in 1791. Lavoisier argued that a sound system of taxation could be founded only on exact knowledge of the country's agricultural production, and he collected data from all the provinces of France. His figures on production, consumption and population were the first reliable national statistics ever made available. Lavoisier recommended that France found an institution to gather and study all forms of economic data—not only on agriculture, but also on industry, population, capital and so on.

As a member of a committee established by the National Assembly in 1791 to advise the government on important questions concerning trades and crafts, Lavoisier proposed a national system of public education. He stressed that education of the people was a good investment from the state's point of view, and that free education should rightfully be available to all irrespective of sex and social position. He proposed the establishment of four kinds of schools: primary, elementary arts, institutes, and 12 national high schools, located in the 12 largest cities of France. He also suggested the creation of four national societies, to advance mathematics and the physical sciences, technical applications of science, the moral and political sciences, and literature and the fine arts.

Lavoisier took an active part in a little-known French attempt to establish an ambitious system of higher education in the new United States republic in 1788. The moving spirit of this project was Alexandre Marie Quesnay de Beaurepaire, grandson of a famous French philosopher, economist and court physician. Quesnay proposed a college, to be located in Richmond, the new capital of Virginia, which would be international in scope. The French Academy appointed a commission, which included Lavoisier, to study the question, and the commissioners made a favorable report, which it is reasonable to assume Lavoisier wrote, considering his propensity for taking the responsibility of drafting reports in all such situations.

Quesnay's academy was actually built in Richmond, but it never got a real start, probably because of the revolutionary overturn of France in the following year. It was in this very building that the Constitution of the United States was formally ratified. It later became a theater, burned down in 1811, was rebuilt, and today is in use as a church.

One of the first targets of the French Revolution—after the royal family—was the tax-collecting Ferme Générale, whose members had always borne odium as bloodsuckers who battened on the people. In 1791 the National Assembly finally suppressed the Ferme and ordered a detailed statement of its accounts. Delays in producing these accounts inflamed the Revolutionary Committee, and on November 14, 1793, arrest of all the Farmers-General was ordered. When Lavoisier heard of the decree, he went into hiding and tried to have the order reversed, on the grounds of his valuable scientific work for his country. But these attempts were fruitless, and after a few days he surrendered himself.

The Farmers-General were locked up in their former offices, where they finished the rendering of a final accounting in January, 1794. Their accounts showed quite clearly that the tax gatherers had acted throughout in complete conformity with the law.

The Terror, however, was entering upon its most extreme phase, and the Farmers-General were not to escape. New charges were preferred, accusing them of various abuses—levying excessive rates of interest, adulterating tobacco with excessive moisture (thus undermining smokers' health), and the like. In the heated atmosphere of the times the Farmers' accusers had no difficulty in getting a decree ordering their trial before the Revolutionary Tribunal. This was tantamount to a death sentence. At one o'clock in the morning of May 8, 1794, each of the prisoners was handed an almost illegible copy of the charges against him, and at 10 o'clock the same morning they were brought before the Tribunal for trial. Here a difficulty arose, for the Tribunal had jurisdiction only over counterrevolutionary activity, of which the Farmers-General had not been accused. But the Tribunal president, Jean Baptiste Coffinhal, disposed of the difficulty by charging the jury to ask themselves whether it had been shown that the Farmers had taken part in a plot against the people by various misdeeds, including supplying the enemies of the Republic with money illegally withheld from the Treasury—a charge which had not been mentioned in the indictment or supported by any evidence during the trial. The jury unanimously returned a verdict of guilty, and the convicted men were duly guillotined before nightfall.

So died France's greatest scientist. Joseph Louis Lagrange, the great mathematician, said the next day: "It required only a moment to sever that head, and perhaps a century will not be sufficient to produce another like it."

PART 4 MAGNETISM AND ELECTRICITY

I. BENJAMIN FRANKLIN *by I. Bernard Cohen*

In Widener Library at Harvard University, I. Bernard Cohen now occupies the crowded study of his teacher and predecessor in his professorship in the history of science, the late George Sarton. Its shelves are filled from floor to ceiling with the most comprehensive collection of writings on the history of science—books, monographs, pamphlets, manuscripts—to be found anywhere in the world. A biographical note on Cohen appears at the beginning of Part 1.

II. MICHAEL FARADAY *by Herbert Kondo*

A member of the research staff of *The American People's Encyclopedia,* Herbert Kondo is a student of the history of physics. He was born in New York City in 1924, attended the University of Florida, and received an M.A. in cultural history in 1951 at the University of Chicago. A radar technician during the war, he has also studied physics and mathematics at the Illinois Institute of Technology, and works in electronics as a hobby. He has picked up a reading knowledge of French, Spanish, German and Sanskrit. His study of Faraday grew out of an investigation of the history of the theory of relativity.

III. JOSEPH HENRY *by Mitchell Wilson*

In addition to *Live with Lightning,* cited in the biographical note on page 85, Mitchell Wilson has written two novels, *My Brother, My Enemy,* on the tragic life of a pair of American inventors, and *The Lovers,* an interlude played against the background of Martha's Vineyard, where the author lives. Wilson feels that technology and its men now form the background and hard core of American living, as authentic as the Western plains and mountains of an earlier tradition. His most recent book, a work of nonfiction, is *American Science and Invention,* a big, handsome pictorial history published by Simon and Schuster in 1954.

IV. JAMES CLERK MAXWELL
by James R. Newman

Between 1940, when *Mathematics and the Imagination* went to press, and 1956, James R. Newman took time from other pursuits, detailed in the biographical note at the beginning of Part 1, to survey the literature of mathematics, beginning with the Rhind papyrus (1700 B.C.). The product of this labor, *The World of Mathematics,* in four volumes priced at $20.00, was published by Simon and Schuster in 1956. Even those merchandisers were surprised when sales ran over 100,000 boxed sets.

BENJAMIN FRANKLIN
by I. Bernard Cohen

ALTHOUGH almost every aspect of Benjamin Franklin's career has been subjected to the microscopic examination of critical scholarship, his place in the history of science, as described in books on American history, remains curiously distorted. In his own lifetime, Franklin was generally acknowledged by contemporary scientists to be one of the truly great scientific luminaries of the age. Joseph Priestley declared that Franklin's book on electricity bade fair "to be handed down to posterity as expressive of the true principles of electricity; just as the Newtonian philosophy is of the true system of nature in general." Franklin was awarded every scientific honor that his contemporaries had the power to bestow. One review of his book, comparing Franklin's writings with Newton's famous *Principia Mathematica,* averred that "the experiments and observations of Dr. Franklin constitute the *principia* of electricity, and form the basis of a system equally simple and profound."

Most writers today either stress Franklin's practical inventions or deny altogether his claim to a place among the great founders of pure science. Typical of the latter point of view is an article that appeared recently in the journal *Science,* wherein the author declared that the only reason Franklin is sometimes said to be a great scientist and is occasionally listed in the company of the truly great, such as J. Willard Gibbs and A. A. Michelson, is that he was important in American political history!

All too many discussions of Franklin's scientific career center upon the one contribution that almost everyone knows about: his proof, by the experiment of flying a kite during a storm, of the hypothesis that lightning is an electrical discharge. Some, indeed, would deny him even this distinction. The author of an article in a learned journal not long ago argued that the story of the lightning kite had been made out of whole cloth by spinners of legends—despite the fact that Franklin published an account of that experiment, which other scientists then repeated, in the leading scientific journal of the day.

But let us forget the kite. It was a comparatively unimportant episode in Franklin's career. It was not the first experiment he designed to test the hypothesis of the electrical nature of the lightning discharge. Neither was it the first experiment that proved this hypothesis, nor was this particular hypothesis original with Franklin. Benjamin Franklin's place in the history of science rests on surer foundations, among them the vast accumulation of new facts of nature that he uncovered by his extraordinary skill in designing and executing experiments, plus his genius in constructing the first satisfactory unitary theory of electrical·action. Furthermore, his consummate success gave the art of experimentation itself a new dignity that was wanting in the eighteenth century. The principles of electricity that he expounded in his book *Experiments and Observations on Electricity Made at Philadelphia in America* are part of the very fiber of electrical theory today. We constantly pay Benjamin Franklin an honor of which we are probably not even aware when we use the words "plus" and "positive," or "minus" and "negative," "electrical battery," and a host of other terms that Franklin was the first to apply to electrical phenomena.

Franklin's treatise on electricity was one of the most widely reprinted scientific books of the mid-eighteenth century. There were five editions printed in English, three in French, one in Italian, one in German. So great was Franklin's scientific reputation that he was elected a Fellow of the Royal Society and awarded its Copley Medal for his experiments in electricity, and in 1773 he was elected one of the eight "foreign associates" of the Royal Academy of Science in Paris. In an age in which scientific accomplishment was esteemed perhaps even more than in our own, Franklin's book was widely studied and his name was on every tongue.

BERNARDA
BRYSON

Franklin first became acquainted with the subject of electrical science sometime around 1744. Between 1747 and 1751 he made his major discoveries and began to win scientific acclaim. Contrary to the supposed general rule that the great discoveries in physics are made by men in their twenties and thirties, Franklin began his scientific work at about the age of 40; he had previously been too busy earning a living to devote much time to scientific pursuits. Having been successful in the world of affairs and now finding the pursuit of truth congenial to his tastes and gifts, he decided, as he tells us in his autobiography, to give up his business and to spend his time making experiments. No sooner had he retired from business, however, than a great national crisis arose and he put aside his scientific research in order to participate in the defense of Philadelphia. From then on until he died, he pursued his research only in his spare time. His city, colony and nation never ceased to require his services. At 81 years of age, when his work at Paris was finished and he was ready to come home to America, Franklin wrote to his most intimate scientific correspondent, the Dutch physician Jan Ingen-Housz, that he was once more a free man "after fifty years in public affairs." He hoped that his friend would come with him to America, where "in the little remainder of my life . . . we will make plenty of experiments together." Alas, even this was to be denied him, for ahead there lay not days of joyful interrogation of nature but the trying and tedious work of the Constitutional Convention. Long before, Franklin had been forced to choose between the role of a quiet philosopher and a "public man." He had decided the issue without hesitation, saying: "Had Newton been pilot of but a single common ship, the finest of his discoveries would scarce have excused, or atoned for his abandoning the helm one hour in time of danger; how much less if she carried the fate of the Commonwealth."

As we read these lines today, we cannot help thinking of our own scientists who, during the late war, gave up their own individual research to serve the nation. But there is a fundamental difference between their problem and Franklin's. In Franklin's day the one outstanding American scientist, the only one with a world-wide reputation, found that he could serve his country best by going abroad to plead its cause, rather than by applying his scientific skills to devising new instruments of destruction. Yet such was Franklin's stature in science—for he was the Newton of his age—that some suspected that the man who dared to tame the lightning bolts of Jove had turned his talents to the perfection of a new and terrible weapon. "The natural philosophers in power," wrote Horace Walpole in 1777, "believe that Dr. Franklin has invented a machine of the size of a toothpick case, and materials that would reduce St. Paul's to a handful of ashes."

Benjamin Franklin made scientific contributions in many fields, including pioneer studies of heat conduction, the origins of storms, and so on, but his most significant work was done in electricity. He worked in electrostatics—the science of electricity at rest or moving in sudden swift surges. Before Franklin, the known facts of this subject were meager and their explanation was inadequate. When he left the field, a whole new set of observed data had been entered in the record and the Franklinian theory of electrical action had unified the known facts, preparing the way for the progress of the future.

Franklin's theory of electrical action is simple and straightforward. It is based on the fundamental idea that there is "common matter," of which the bulk of bodies is composed, and "electrical matter," or, to use other eighteenth-century terms, "electric fluid" or "electric fire." In its normal state, every body contains a fixed amount of the electric fluid. But a body may, under certain conditions, gain an excess of the electric fluid or lose some of its normal complement of it. In such a state a body is "electrified" or "charged." In the first case, when there is an excess of the fluid, said Franklin, let us call the charge "positive" or "plus," indicating that something has been added to it; in the second case, let us call it "minus" or "negative," indicating that something has been lost. When we rub a piece of glass with a silk rag, the glass acquires an excess of the electric fluid and becomes charged plus. Franklin insisted that electricity was not "created" by friction, as many of his contemporaries believed, but rather was redistributed by the act of rubbing. If the glass gains an excess of fluid, the silk must lose the very same amount, thereby gaining a negative charge of the same magnitude. Today we call this principle the law of conservation of charge.

Franklin illustrated his theory by the following experiment. He placed two experimenters on insulated glass stools, one man charged plus and the other minus. When the two experimenters touched hands, both lost their charge because the excess of one supplied the deficiency of the other. If a third uncharged experimenter touched either of the charged ones, he drew a spark or got a shock, because he had relatively more electric fluid than the man charged minus, and less than the man charged plus.

This was a simple, dramatic demonstration of Franklin's contention that electricity is a single fluid. The late J. J. Thomson, discoverer of the fundamental properties of moving electrons, wrote only a few years ago: "The service which Franklin's one-fluid theory has rendered to the science of electricity by suggesting and coordinating researches can hardly be overestimated."

To understand the application of Franklin's theory, let us follow him through two series of significant experiments. The first begins with one of the many facts first discovered by Franklin and now part of the basic data of the science—the "wonderful effect of pointed bodies, both *drawing off* and *throwing off* the electric fire." Franklin found that if a pointed conductor such as a needle is brought into the neighborhood of a charged insulated body, the needle will draw off the charge; but it will do so only if it is grounded, that is, in contact with the hand or a grounded wire. If the needle is inserted in wax, a nonconductor or insulator, it will not draw off the charge. He also found that if you try to charge a metal object with a jagged edge or point, the object will "throw off the charge" as fast as you put it on. He discovered further that a charged object could be discharged by sifting fine sand on it, by breathing on it, by bringing a burning candle near it, or by surrounding it with smoke.

For at least 50 years before Franklin's research, people had speculated that lightning was probably electrical. But what distinguished Franklin from his predecessors was the fact that he was able to design an experiment to test this hypothesis. He made a small model showing how a discharge might take place between two electrified clouds or between a cloud and the earth. He then pointed out that since a small pointed conductor could draw off the charge from an insulated charged body in his laboratory, a large pointed conductor erected in the ground might very well draw the electricity from passing clouds. This suggested to his active mind that "the knowledge of this power of points might be of use to mankind, in preserving houses, churches, ships, &c., from the stroke of lightning, by directing us to fix on the highest parts of those edifices, upright rods of iron made sharp as a needle, and gilt to prevent rusting, and from the foot of those rods a wire down the outside of the building into the ground, or down around one of the shrouds of a ship, and down her side till it reaches the water."

The experiment which Franklin proposed to test his hypothesis was described by him in these words: "On the top of some high tower or steeple, place a kind of sentry-box . . . big enough to contain a man and an electrical stand. From the middle of the stand let an iron rod rise and pass bending out of the door, and then upright 20 or 30 feet, pointed very sharp at the end. If the electrical stand be kept clean and dry, a man standing on it when such clouds are passing low, might be electrified and afford sparks, the rod drawing [electric] fire to him from a cloud. If any danger to the man should be apprehended (though I think there would be none) let him stand on the floor of his box, and now and then bring to the rod the loop of a wire that has one end fastened to the leads, he holding it by a wax handle; so the sparks, if the rod is electrified, will strike from the rod to the wire, and not affect him."

This famous "sentry-box experiment" was first performed in France on May 10, 1752, by a man named Dalibard, who had translated Franklin's book into French at the request of the great naturalist Georges de Buffon. (King Louis XV was so fascinated by Franklin's book that he ordered some of the experiments it described to be performed in his presence.) The experiment was soon repeated in England. Glowing testimonials to the Philadelphia scientist speedily increased in number. An enterprising British manufacturer advertised for sale a ready-made machine "for making the Experiment by which *Franklin's* new theory of Thunder is demonstrated." Franklin did not make the experiment himself because he thought that a very high building would be necessary and he was waiting for the completion of the high spire on Christ Church in Philadelphia. After the book was published, but before he had heard from Europe of Dalibard's successful execution of the experiment, the kite project occurred to him as a good substitute and he carried it through.

Franklin devised other experiments and instruments to test the charge of clouds, of which one of the most interesting was a pair of bells located in his study. One of the bells was grounded by a rod going into the earth and the other was connected with a rod ending in a point on the roof. A little ball hung between them. Whenever an electrified cloud passed overhead, the ball was set in motion and rang the bells. Franklin's careful studies soon showed him that clouds may be charged either plus or minus, and he concluded, therefore, that lightning probably goes from the earth to a cloud at least as often as from a cloud to the earth— an idea which has been confirmed only in our own time by such research as that of B. J. F. Schonland and his associates in South Africa.

Franklin's studies of lightning and his invention of the lightning rod brought him universal fame, but the scientists of his day were perhaps even more impressed by his analysis of the electrical condenser, which set the seal to his scientific reputation.

In the form that the eighteenth century knew it, the condenser was a glass jar coated on the outside with metal foil and filled with metal shot, water or metal foil. It was fitted with a wooden cover into which a rod ending in a knob was inserted. From the lower end of the rod a metal chain depended, going down into the water or shot. This device, invented in the late 1740s, was known as a "Leyden jar," because one of its several independent discoverers, Pieter van Musschenbroek, was a professor in Leyden. The essential feature of a condenser is the placement of an insulator or dielectric (e.g., air, glass, wax or paper) between two conducting surfaces in close contact with it. In the first Leyden jar the inner conductor was water, the dielectric was the glass and the outer conductor was a man's hand. Musschenbroek developed his version of it while carrying out some experiments with an electrical machine which charged a whirling glass globe by rubbing it against an experimenter's hands. The charge was transferred to a gun barrel, from the end of which hung a wire that was partly immersed in a round glass vessel filled with water. When Musschenbroek held the vessel in his right hand and attempted to draw a spark from the gun barrel with his left hand, he "was struck with such violence that my whole body was shaken as by a thunderbolt . . . in a word, I thought it was all up with me."

The condenser was a wonderful instrument. By making it bigger and bigger, the shocks it could give were made stronger and stronger. Apparently, somehow or other electricity accumulated in it, and through some little-understood aspect of its construction, it could hold more electricity than anything else of its size. The electric fluid or fluids must, it was thought, be condensed in it. Musschenbroek wrote a letter describing this experiment which was published in the *Mémoires* of the French Academy of Sciences. It ended with the famous statement that he would never again receive such a shock, even if he were to be offered the kingdom of France! For such ignoble sentiments he was publicly rebuked by Priestley, who called him a "cowardly professor" and contrasted him with the "magnanimous Mr. Boze, who with a truly philosophic heroism worthy of the renowned Empedocles, said he might die by the electric shock, that the account of his death might furnish an article for the memoirs of the French Academy of Sciences." Then, referring to one Richman, who had just been killed while performing a variation of Franklin's sentry-box experiment, Priestley concluded, "But it is not given to every electrician to die the death of the justly envied Richman."

All the electricians of Europe wondered what made the Leyden jar work. "Everybody," wrote Priestley, "was eager to see, and, notwithstanding the terrible account that was reported, to *feel* the experiment." In France the new device provided a means of satisfying simultaneously the court's love of spectacles and the great interest in science. One hundred and eighty soldiers of the guard were made to jump into the air with a greater precision than soldiers of the guard displayed in any other maneuvers. Seven hundred monks from the Couvent de Paris, joined hand to hand, had a Leyden jar discharged through them all. They flew up into the air with finer timing than could be achieved by the most glorified corps of ballet dancers. From one end of the world to the other, traveling demonstrators of electrical phenomena made fortunes.

Franklin's step-by-step analysis of the vexing problem of the condenser showed him to be a great master of the technique of scientific experimentation. He found that the inner conductor is always charged in the opposite sign to the outer conductor and that the amount of charge given to both is the same. In other words, after charging of the jar, one of the two conductors gains the exact quantity of "electric fluid" that the other loses. "There is really no more electric fire in the [Leyden] phial after what is called its *charging*, than before, nor less after its *discharging*," Franklin wrote. To prove it, he affixed a wire to the lead coating of a Leyden jar and placed it so that it was near the knob leading to the water inside the jar, but not near enough to produce a spark when the jar was charged. He then placed the jar on an insulating stand, a block of wax, and suspended a small cork on a string between the wire and the knob. The cork, he noted, "will play incessantly from one to the other, 'til the bottle is no longer electrized." In other words, the cork carried the charge from the plus conductor to the minus until equilibrium was restored.

Most important of all, Franklin showed that "the whole force of the bottle, and power of giving a shock, is in the GLASS ITSELF." How would *you*, reader, go about finding "wherein its strength lay"? Every student knows today that the only way to proceed is to test the instrument one element at a time, and to find the role played by each. But this apparently simple rule was not taken for granted in the time of Franklin, as can readily be seen in the fact that his contemporaries failed to make the kind of analysis that Franklin now proceeded to carry out.

He charged a Leyden jar that stood on glass and carefully drew out the cork with its wire that hung down into the water. Then he took the bottle in one hand, and brought the other hand near its mouth. "A strong spark came from the water, and the shock was as violent as if the wire had remained in it, which shewed that the force did not lie in the wire." If it was not in the wire, then perhaps it was in the water itself. Franklin recharged the Leyden jar, drew out the cork and wire as before, and carefully poured the water into an empty Leyden jar which likewise stood on a glass insulator. The second jar did not become charged in this process. "We judged then," Franklin wrote, "that [the charge, or force] must either be lost in decanting, or remain in the first bottle. The latter we found to be true; for that bottle on trial gave the shock, though filled up as it stood with fresh unelectrified water from a tea-pot." Apparently the essential element was glass, the insulator between the two conductors. But it remained to be demonstrated whether "glass had this property merely as glass, or whether the form [of the jar] contributed anything to it."

The next part of the experiment involved the invention of the parallel plate condenser. Franklin sandwiched a large piece of glass between two square plates of lead, equal to each other in size but slightly smaller than the glass. When this condenser was charged, he removed the lead plates, which had but little charge, and noted that a small spark could be taken from the glass at almost any point that it was touched. When the two completely uncharged plates were put back in place, one on each side of the glass, and a circuit made between them, "a violent shock ensued." When we demonstrate this phenomenon to students today, we call it the "experiment of the dissectible condenser." We explain it by stating that the dielectric, or glass, has been polarized during charging, i.e., it has become an electret. There are certain types of wax that can be polarized in this way simply by being heated and then cooled. Such an electret will give off little or no charge by itself, but if we put a conductor on two sides of it, we have a charged condenser which can be then discharged like any other. Another fact about such condensers that we teach students today was also discovered by Franklin: the force of the electric shock is greater when the dielectric separating the two conductors is very thin than when it is thick.

Franklin's experiment of the cork that traveled back and forth between the two conductors contained, by the way, the germ of an important idea, although he did not realize it. We know today that a condenser never discharges in one complete stroke, but rather in a series of oscillations—a fact of great importance in radio and modern electronics.

Franklin's extraordinary experiments and his splendid theory marked the beginning of a new era in the subject of electricity. He discovered what is known today as the Faraday effect, namely that the charge on a hollow cylindrical conductor (or a hollow sphere) is on the outside surface only. At first he could not explain this. Later the answer came to him: the "electric fluid" is self-repellent and the symmetry of the conductor causes the fluid to distribute itself on the outside. From this explanation, Frank-

123

lin's friend Joseph Priestley deduced that the law of electrical action must be an inverse square law similar to the law of gravitation. This deduction, although published, was overlooked and had to await rediscovery decades later by Charles Coulomb, when it became known as Coulomb's law.

Yet another advantage of Franklin's theory was the ease with which it lent itself to the making of measurements, by concentrating attention on the amount of "electric fluid" or charge which a body gained or lost. When working with two bodies, it did not matter which one was used, because Franklin's law of conservation of charge meant that the quantity gained by one was exactly the quantity that the other lost. The first electricians to make quantitative measurements—such men as Volta, Bennet, Canton, Cavendish and Henley—built upon the convenient one-fluid theory of Benjamin Franklin, and the law of conservation of charge which follows from it.

It is often said that Franklin was typically American in his approach to science—a utilitarian interested in science chiefly, if not solely, because of its practical applications. It is true that when he had discovered the action of pointed grounded conductors and proved that clouds are electrified, he applied these discoveries to the invention of the lightning rod. But he did not make these discoveries in order to invent a lightning rod! Franklin's inventions were of two kinds. One type was pure gadgetry; in this class were his inventions of bifocal glasses, which required no recondite knowledge of optical principles, and of a device for taking books down from the shelf without getting up from one's chair. The lightning rod, on the other hand, developed from pure scientific research. If Franklin's approach to science had been strictly utilitarian, it is doubtful that he would ever have studied the subject of electricity at all. In the eighteenth century there was only one practical application of electricity, and that was the giving of electric shocks for therapeutic purposes, chiefly to cure paralysis. (Although Franklin on occasion participated in such therapy, he did not believe that the shock itself ever cured a case of paralysis. With shrewd psychological insight, he guessed that the reported cures arose from the desire of the patient to be cured rather than from the passage of electric fluid.)

Franklin studied nature because he wanted to discover her innermost secrets, and he chose electrostatics because chance brought him the instruments with which to study this subject, and because he quickly found out that this was a subject well fitted to his particular talents. In a spirit which might well be emulated by all men engaged in research, he wrote humbly at the end of one of his communications: "These thoughts, my dear friend, are many of them crude and hasty; and if I were merely ambitious of acquiring some reputation in philosophy [i.e., natural philosophy, or science], I ought to keep them by me, 'till corrected and improved by time, and farther experience. But since even short hints and imperfect experiments in any new branch of science, being communicated, have oftentimes a good effect, in exciting the attention of the ingenious to the subject . . . you are at liberty to communicate this paper to whom you please; it being of more importance that knowledge should increase, than that your friend should be thought an accurate philosopher."

With the discovery of electrons, protons and neutrons, many modern writers have argued about whether Franklin's one-fluid theory was or was not closer to the modern conception than the two-fluid theory of his rivals. To my mind, such debates are wholly without value. The value of Franklin's contribution to electricity does not lie in the degree to which it resembles our modern theory, but rather in the effect his researches had in getting us along on the road to our modern theory.

At the time that Franklin undertook his studies, the world of science lay under the spell of Isaac Newton, whose great *Principia* had shown that the motions of the universe could be explained by simple mathematical laws. Newton convinced almost everyone that mathematics and mathematical laws were the only key to the understanding of nature. What many people forgot, however, was that Newton's success in applying mathematical analysis to celestial and terrestial mechanics was possible only because the facts had been accumulated and classified, and were in a state where his great genius could make the first great synthesis of the modern scientific era. But when it came to optics, Newton made no synthesis such as he did for mechanics, nor was he able to reduce his quantitative and qualitative discoveries to the form of general mathematical law. In the field of optics, Newton was but one of the giants upon whose shoulders some later synthesizer was to stand. In contrast with the austere *Principia,* whose motto was *Hypotheses non fingo* ("I frame no hypotheses"), his *Opticks* contained a long set of "queries" in which Newton discussed the possible explanations that might be given to his observed facts. These resemble Franklin's speculations concerning electrical phenomena. In Franklin's time, as with optics in Newton's time, the state of electrical science did not yet permit a full mathematical synthesis. Science required "giants" to uncover the facts of charge, of induction, of grounding and insulation, of the effect of shapes of conductors and so on—giants to build a workable manipulative theory to unify these facts and to draw attention to essential elements that might be measured. Franklin's success paved the way for the mathematical theorists of the nineteenth century.

But, even more, his mastery of the technique of experimentation, his successful and consistent explanations in terms of a simple physical conceptual scheme, and the many new and curious facts of nature he revealed, gave experimental science a new dignity in the eyes of his eighteenth-century contemporaries. The French philosopher Diderot wrote, in his essay on the interpretation of nature, that Franklin's book on electricity, like the works of the chemists, would teach a man the nature of the experimental art and the way to use the experimental research to draw back the veil of nature without multiplying its mysteries.

This was the sense, then, in which Franklin's contemporaries believed him to be the new Newton, and this was the first great contribution made by America to the mind of science. In this light, there can be no doubt of Franklin's stature in science, nor that he deserves to stand as the first American scientist.

MICHAEL FARADAY

by Herbert Kondo

MICHAEL FARADAY is celebrated as an experimenter who discovered the induction of electricity. History has more or less overlooked the fact that he was also one of the great founders of modern physics. Indeed, he can be said to be the man who started the revolution which upset the long reign of Newton and rebuilt physics on new theoretical foundations. For Faraday was the first scientist to suggest the modern idea of the field—that concept which was to become a keystone of James Clerk Maxwell's electromagnetic theory, Albert Einstein's general theory of relativity and the twentieth century's progress toward understanding physical reality.

Not the least remarkable thing about all this is that Faraday had little mathematics and no formal schooling beyond the primary grades. To present-day physicists his achievement may well seem incredible. Actually Faraday's ignorance of mathematics contributed to his inspiration. It compelled him, when he looked for an explanation of his electrical and magnetic phenomena, to develop a simple, nonmathematical concept. His deduction of the field theory illustrates two qualities that more than made up for his lack of education: his fantastic intuition and his independence and originality of mind.

Faraday's biographers have emphasized his great intellectual energy and his obsession with his experimental researches. Fortunately for his biographers, he wrote everything down; his notes and jottings were eventually published as a seven-volume diary. Physics and chemistry were the great passion of his life; he cared little for women (although he eventually married) and less for money. He could have made a fortune from his discoveries, but he deliberately dropped every scientific project when it reached the stage of commercial value. Faraday was born in poverty and died in poverty—to him his consuming work was sufficient reward.

A blacksmith's son, Faraday was born near London on September 22, 1791. His family was too poor to keep him in school. "My education," he scribbled in his diary, "was of the most ordinary description, consisting of little more than the rudiments of reading, writing and arithmetic at a common day school. My hours out of school were passed at home and in the streets." At the age of 13 he took a job as errand boy in a bookshop run by a man named Riebau. A year later Riebau apprenticed him as a bookbinder for a term of seven years. Faraday developed a passionate interest in Riebau's books. "Whilst an apprentice," he wrote in his diary, "I loved to read the scientific books which were under my hands, and amongst them Marcet's *Conversations in Chemistry,* and the electrical treatises in the *Encyclopaedia Britannica.*" Faraday went to hear some lectures on chemistry by the world-renowned scientist Sir Humphrey Davy, and took neat and copious notes on them. He promptly applied for a job with the Royal Society and was as promptly rejected.

When Faraday's apprenticeship expired in 1812, he took a position as journeyman bookbinder with a M. de la Roche. But he was unhappy in the job and soon applied to Davy for employment, submitting his lecture notes as proof of his earnestness. Davy, a vain man, was impressed and hired Faraday as a secretary, but after a few months he dismissed the young man and advised him to go back to bookbinding. Not long afterward Davy, reconsidering, hired Faraday as his laboratory assistant.

Henceforth Faraday was to devote nearly all his working hours to research in pure science. After a two-year tour of Europe with Sir Humphrey, he settled down to work in Davy's laboratory. He did experiments in chemistry, electrochemistry and metallurgy which alone would have been sufficient to establish his reputation as a scientist: he discovered benzene, produced the first "stainless steel," was the first to liquefy many gases, discovered

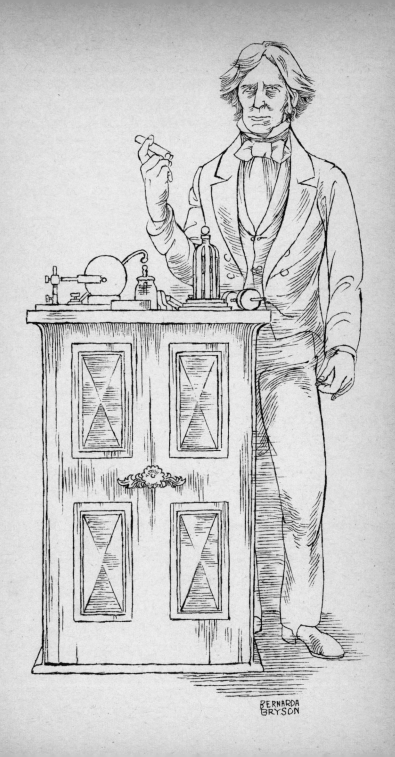

BERNARDA
BRYSON

the laws of electrolysis and the magnetic rotation of the plane of polarized light. But we are interested here in his main work—electromagnetism.

In 1820 the Danish physicist Hans Christian Oersted had announced his discovery of a relation between magnetism and electricity. He had found that a continuous current in a wire caused a deflection of a magnetic needle placed close to it. Oersted suggested that a magnetic field surrounded the wire conductor, acting in circles around the wire and perpendicular to it. In the following year the Frenchman André Marie Ampère substituted another current-carrying wire for the magnetic needle and found a magnetic force of attraction or repulsion in the two wires, depending on the direction of current flow.

Davy and Faraday, though absorbed in chemical researches, promptly became interested in the new electromagnetic discoveries. They repeated the experiments for their own satisfaction. At the same time the noted English scientist William Hyde Wollaston suggested to Davy the possibility that the magnetic field might produce rotation. Faraday interpreted this to mean the rotation of a wire about its own axis. He failed to find such a result, but he soon established for himself—whether independently or after hearing of Oersted's theory—the circular and perpendicular action of a magnetic field about a conductor. He therefore reasoned that if a magnetic pole were free to move, it should rotate about the conductor, and that the opposite also should be true; the conductor itself should be able to revolve about a magnetic pole.

Faraday at once undertook the famous experiments which were to lead to discovery of the basic principle of the electric motor. In his first experiment he bent a copper wire into the curved shape of a carpenter's brace; one end of the wire was stuck through a cork and floated in a basin of mercury, and the other end was connected to a battery by way of an inverted silver cup. Then he placed a bar magnet within the curved part of the wire. When current passed through the wire-mercury circuit, the curved wire swept around until it hit the fixed magnet. Faraday next modified the experiment so that the wire could revolve without obstruction around the magnet. He used a straight piece of wire with one end sticking into a cork floating in the mercury container. The passing of a current through the wire made it revolve continuously around the magnet. When the direction of the current was reversed, the wire revolved in the opposite direction. Faraday's own rough, simplified sketches of these two experiments are shown in the drawings at the top of the facing page.

He now went on to perform the opposite experiment to see whether a magnet would turn around a fixed conductor. This time the bar magnet (loaded at the bottom end with platinum) floated free in the mercury and the wire was fixed. As he had expected, the magnet did revolve around the current-carrying wire.

When Faraday published the results of these experiments, he was at once charged with having used Wollaston's idea without credit. Actually Faraday had misinterpreted Wollaston's sugges-

Sketches from Faraday's diary show the progression of his electromagnetic experiments. The sketch at top left shows how he bent a wire conductor into a curve, floating one end on a cork in mercury, then put a bar magnet in the curve, causing the wire to swivel around it, in the first demonstration of electromagnetic rotation. He next fixed the magnet upright in a bowl of mercury, as shown in the sketch at top right, to allow the floating conductor to revolve completely around it—the principle of the electric motor. In 1831, winding two coils of wire A and B on an iron ring and connecting A with a battery, as shown in the sketch at middle left, he caused an intermittent current to flow in B, thus discovering electrical induction. By plunging a magnet in and out of a hollow cylinder and coil connected to a galvanometer, as in the sketch at middle right, he showed that current may be induced by the relative motion of a conductor and a magnetic field—the principle of the electric generator. Faraday's sketch at the bottom of the page shows how he rotated a copper disc between the poles of the Royal Society's compound magnet, thereby inducing a continuous current—the birth of the dynamo.

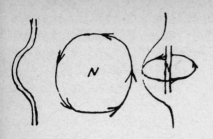
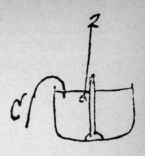
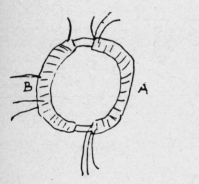
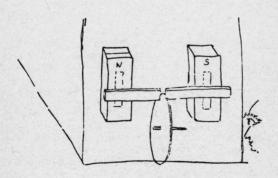

tion to mean rotation of a wire about its own axis; his experiments and findings were his own. In time the misunderstanding cleared up, and Faraday was nominated for membership in the Royal Society. Wollaston supported his candidacy, but Davy voted against him, possibly from jealousy. Nonetheless, he was elected in 1824.

Faraday now dropped his electromagnetic experiments and returned to chemistry. But an irrepressible idea remained on his mind. If an electric current could yield magnetism, could not a magnet produce electricity? In 1824 and again in 1825 he tried to induce current in a wire by placing a magnet near it, but these attempts failed. He did not yet appreciate the central importance of motion in the phenomena that Oersted had demonstrated. It was the motion of the electric current in the wire that produced magnetism. To obtain the reverse effect the magnet had to be moved in relation to the conductor.

In 1831 Faraday suddenly ended his chemical researches and gave himself fully to the problem that was preying on his mind. Within a single day—August 29, 1831—he found an answer that put him on the right track. His reasoning this time started from the analogy of electrostatic induction. It was known that a charged body could induce an electric charge on another body placed near it. Perhaps a current-carrying wire could induce a current in another wire placed close to it. To test this Faraday set up an astonishingly crude apparatus, illustrated by his center sketches on the preceding page. Here, from his diary, is his own account of the famous experiment:

"I have had an iron ring made (soft iron), iron round and 7/8ths of an inch thick, and ring six inches in external diameter. Wound many coils of copper round, one half of the coils being separated by twine and calico; there were three lengths of wire, each about 24 feet long, and they could be connected as one length, or used as separate lengths. By trials with a trough each was insulated from the other. Will call this side of the ring A. On the other side, but separated by an interval, was wound wire in two pieces, together amounting to about 60 feet in length, the direction being as with former coils. This side call B.

"Charged a battery of ten pairs of plates four inches square. Made the coil on B side one coil, and connected its extremities by a copper wire passing to a distance, and just over a magnetic needle (three feet from a wire ring), then connected the ends of one of the pieces on A side with battery: immediately a sensible effect on needle. It oscillated and settled at last in original position. On breaking connection of A side with battery, again a disturbance of the needle."

Faraday noted that when the circuit was closed, the needle deflected in one direction; when it was broken, the needle moved in the opposite direction. But there was no deflection while electricity was flowing in the first coil.

At last he had obtained electricity from magnetism. But he was disappointed. He had expected the current in the primary coil to induce a continuous current in the secondary coil; instead, it produced only momentary impulses at the instant when the primary circuit was closed or broken. Nonetheless, he felt intuitively that he was near success. He wrote to a friend: "I am busy just now again on electromagnetism, and I think I have got hold of a good thing, but can't say. It may be a weed instead of a fish that, after all my labor, I may at last have pulled up."

Faraday continued his experiments, and on October 17, 1831, he performed one which showed that he had caught a very big fish indeed. In this, his simplest and most famous experiment, he wound a coil, the ends of which were connected to a galvanometer, around a hollow paper cylinder. When he thrust a bar magnet quickly into the cylinder, the galvanometer needle was deflected. It moved again, but in the opposite direction, when he withdrew the magnet. Actually it made no difference whether he moved the magnet or the coil; in either case he got an induced current in the wire. It was now clear beyond doubt that what produced the current was the relative motion of the conductor and the magnetic field.

Thus Faraday discovered the basic principle of the electric generator. From this experiment it was but a step to the induction of a continuous electric current. Eleven days later Faraday achieved it with the arrangement shown in the bottom drawing on page 133. Using the compound magnet of the Royal Society, he concentrated the polar strength by placing two small six-inch magnets at the ends of the large poles. Between these poles he rotated a copper disk on a brass axle. On the edge of the disk he spaced two copper contacts at different distances from the poles, connected by wires to a galvanometer. Rotating the disk, he obtained a more or less steady deflection of the needle—"more or less" because he had a hard time holding the contacts.

Faraday performed many other experiments in electromagnetic induction, but for the most part they were variations of these basic ones. His first experiment, with the iron ring, had given the world the first electric transformer; the one just described produced the first dynamo.

Faraday reported his results to the Royal Society within a month and later published these papers as the first part of his *Experimental Researches in Electricity,* rearranging the order of many of his experiments in a way that has confused historians.

As soon as the results were published, the question of priority was again raised. The United States physicist Joseph Henry had already discovered self-induction, and Leopoldo Nobili and Cavalière Antinori of Italy had claimed credit for the discovery of electromagnetic induction even before Faraday published his results. But the Italians had performed their experiments after hearing of Faraday's, and Faraday was able to prove his priority.

Faraday was not satisfied with having discovered electromagnetic induction; he wanted to know why it occurred. Unable to approach the subject mathematically, he resorted to a physical model: the familiar phenomenon of the way that iron filings on a sheet of paper arrange themselves in a pattern of lines about a magnet. Why in lines? Faraday proposed the idea that the space surrounding the magnet was filled with lines of force. The magnetic force was manifest as invisible lines in a state of tension—like stretched rubber bands—and the iron filings arranged themselves by magnetic attraction along these lines.

Faraday did not stop there. He filled *all* space with lines of force, and outlined the revolutionary concept that space was pervaded by various kinds of force: magnetic, electric, radiant, thermal and gravitational. The lines indicate everywhere both the direction and the strength of the force under consideration. For example, on a bar magnet the direction of the lines of force is from positive to negative or from north to south pole, and the number of lines of force proceeding from a magnetic pole indicates its strength at any given place. They are more dense near the magnet than they are farther away in space. Similarly the amount of electricity a body possesses is determined, according to Faraday, by the number of lines of force proceeding from it. The lines of force all terminate some place, either on another body close by, or on the walls of a room, or on the planets in space. At each terminal point there is a quantity of electricity equal in amount but opposite in charge to that on the original body.

Faraday reasoned that the lines-of-force theory explained how a current is induced in a conductor: it is induced whenever the conductor cuts across magnetic lines of force. He discovered that the velocity of the movement was important. "If a wire move slowly," he wrote, "a feeble current is produced in it, continuing for the time of motion; if it move across the same lines quickly, a stronger current is produced for a shorter time." Strictly speaking, it is not a current which is induced, but a voltage. The current merely results from this voltage.

From the idea that there are lines of force of various kinds in space, Faraday went on to his suggestion that these forces fill all of space. He wrote in his diary in 1846: "All I can say is, that I do not perceive in any part of space, whether (to use the common phrase) vacant or filled with matter, anything but forces and the lines in which they are exerted."

Here we have the historic origin of the field theory. Faraday himself never referred to his system as a "field theory" or a "field concept." In fact he held these ideas tentatively and was ready to discard them if experimental evidence could disprove them.

What is so revolutionary about the field concept? Just this. Up to Faraday physicists had concentrated on the material particle. From the particle concept they attempted to derive all phenomena. Physical processes were explained by laws of Newtonian motion and forces of mutual interaction working upon the particle. Faraday relegated the particle to the background and enthroned in its stead lines of force throughout space. To Faraday what was of critical importance was not the electric or magnetic particles but the space in which they operated. And this is the whole basis of the field concept. In field theory it is the geometric and physical condition of space itself that is fundamental.

Faraday was very clear on this point. In the *Experimental Researches* he wrote: "In this view of the magnet, the medium or space around it is as essential as the magnet itself, being a part of the true and complete magnetic system."

Here we see that Faraday actually held what is today called a dual field theory, one in which both particle and field are fundamental, but in which the field plays the basic and leading role. Thus Faraday was a forerunner of the modern relativistic revolution in physics, and the construction of the field concept must rank as one of the greatest creations of the scientific mind.

Faraday himself did not regard the field idea as a theory distinct from the Newtonian system, but rather as one supplementing it. He did not intend to dethrone the particle concept; that came as a later consequence of his suggestion. He also started the downfall of another important concept—the idea of "action-at-a-distance." Newton assumed, and philosophers long before him had believed, that forces could act over large distances—instantaneously and without the need for any intervening medium. Only in this way, they felt, could the gravitational force between planets and stars be explained.

In the nineteenth century action-at-a-distance had a strong foothold in physics. But Faraday felt that this concept was unsatisfactory and that the assumptions of Newtonian mechanics were inconsistent with electrodynamic phenomena. He did not hesitate to rule out action-at-a-distance or to formulate his own concept. Force requires time for transmission, he said, and the means of conveyance are the lines of force. Wherever possible Faraday performed experiments to prove that the force in question required time. In the case of gravitational force he failed, but he did not waver from his belief that he was correct. Faraday himself did not destroy the action-at-a-distance concept; that was accomplished by Maxwell, who eliminated it from electrodynamics, and by Hendrik Lorentz, whose transformation equations banished it altogether from physics.

In May, 1846, Faraday published an interesting paper on some further speculations, entitled "Thoughts on Ray-Vibrations." In it he foreshadowed the electromagnetic theory of light. "The view which I am so bold as to put forth," he wrote, "considers . . . radiation as a high species of vibrations in the lines of force which are known to connect particles and also masses of matter together. It endeavors to dismiss the ether, but not the vibrations." Shortly thereafter Maxwell developed this "bold" view mathematically and announced his electromagnetic theory. Faraday himself had empirically established a relation between light and magnetism. In a series of brilliant experiments he had demonstrated that a magnetic field could rotate the plane of polarized light.

Faraday had a profound and prophetic belief in the underlying unity of nature and of the laws of physics. He believed that gravitational and electromagnetic forces were somehow related, and that some law or principle must govern this relationship. In 1849 he scribbled in his laboratory book: "Gravity. Surely this force must be capable of an experimental relation to electricity, magnetism, and other forces, so as to bind it up with them in reciprocal action and equivalent effect. Consider for a moment how to set about touching this matter by facts and trial." But the numerous experiments he undertook to show such a relationship all ended in failure. In a sad yet optimistic note, he concluded: "Here end my trials for the present. The results are negative. They do not shake my strong feeling of the existence of a relation between gravity and electricity, though they give no proof that such a relation exists."

He was still at work on this problem 10 years later when he wrote his last paper. He was then in broken health, but had not given up experimenting and musing. He suffered prolonged lapses of memory, and would forgetfully repeat an experiment which he had successfully completed only a short time before. The born-to-poverty, unschooled scientist was now a life professor of the Royal Institution, living at Hampton Court. In 1867 his niece, Miss Reid, wrote to Faraday's close friend Bence Jones: "Dear uncle kept up rather better than sometimes, but oh! there was a pain in seeing afresh how far the mind had faded away. . . . This year we came with a melancholy thought of dear uncle's declining, half-paralyzed state." On August 25, 1867, Michael Faraday died peacefully in his study chair, little realizing the turmoil that was to come over whether the field or the particle is supreme.

JOSEPH HENRY

by Mitchell Wilson

IN THE SPRING of 1837 a small group of men in an English laboratory attempted an impromptu experiment: they had rigged up an electric circuit to carry a very feeble current, and they were trying to draw sparks by closing and opening the circuit. Charles Wheatstone touched together the two pieces of wire that completed the circuit. He drew no spark. Michael Faraday said that Wheatstone was going about it in the wrong way. Faraday made a few adjustments and tried his hand. Still no spark.

A visiting American waited patiently while the two famous "electricians" argued back and forth over the probable cause of failure. As the American listened, he absently coiled a length of wire about his finger in a tight corkscrew. After a few minutes, he remarked that, whenever the two gentlemen were ready, he would gladly show them how to draw a spark. Faraday gave him one of his usual brusque answers, but the American went ahead. He added his little coil to one of the leads, and this time, when he opened the circuit, he drew sparks that were clearly visible.

Faraday clapped his hands with delight and said, "Hurrah for the Yankee experiment! What in the world did you do?"

If Joseph Henry had had Faraday's temper, he might have blurted out, "If you would only read what I publish, and understand what you read, you'd know what you just saw!" Instead the Princeton professor patiently explained the phenomenon of self-induction to the man whom the world had already credited with the discovery of induction.

There was a century and a quarter of time and a world of knowledge between the electrical experiments of Benjamin Franklin and the electromagnetic theory of James Clerk Maxwell.

Much of that knowledge was gathered by one man—Joseph Henry. The time required was only 15 years—1829 to 1844. Yet Henry was a stranger in his own time. His friends mistook his scientific idealism for lack of the American spirit; international science ignored him because he was an American. Not until after he was dead and the contemporaries of his youth were gone did younger men realize that he had been a giant and that the considerable fame he had achieved during the latter half of his life had been for the least of his works. In the end science paid him its greatest tribute by raising him on the pedestal of the lower case: to the electrical units the ampere, the volt, the ohm and the farad was added the henry, the unit of inductance.

During the 25 years before Henry's appearance in science, Alessandro Volta showed how to produce a steady current of electricity, G. S. Ohm found the law that governs the strength of the current and Hans Oersted and Dominique Arago discovered that a current of electricity could create magnetism. Now in the 1820s, a few clear-headed investigators were pondering the question: If electricity created magnetism, did magnetism in turn create electricity? Joseph Henry, a mathematics teacher in a country school in a provincial town in an undeveloped nation, not only found the answer, but went far beyond his predecessors in the depth of his research.

In Henry's background there was nothing to indicate either the extent of his ability or the direction his interest would take. He was born in 1797 near Albany, N.Y., and was raised in poverty. Farm hand and storekeeper's apprentice, he was a dreamy boy who barely knew how to read. When he was 13 his main concern was his pet rabbit. One day the rabbit ran away and Henry pursued it by tunneling into a church. He came up inside a locked room which contained a library of romantic novels. He forgot the rabbit and read the books.

He was so enraptured by the melodrama that the next year,

BERNARDA
BRYSON

when he was sent to Albany to earn a living, the 14-year-old boy made a beeline for the Green Street Theater, where John Bernard was directing his famous company. For two years Joseph Henry was a hard-working, talented apprentice actor.

In his sixteenth year he made his second great discovery. Confined to his room by illness one day, he happened to pick up a book left by a fellow boarder. Even late in life he could still recall the opening paragraph: "You throw a stone or shoot an arrow into the air, why does it not go forward in a line with the direction you gave it? On the contrary, why does flame or smoke always mount upwards although no force is used to send them in that direction?" Joseph Henry had found the world of science.

Henry was never able to make minor decisions. Once he ordered a pair of shoes and from day to day changed his mind as to whether he wanted square or round toes. The exasperated cobbler made the shoes both ways—one was round-toed, the other square-toed. But Henry made important decisions on the spur of the moment. With no background, training or tradition he had decided to go on the stage. Now, with even less reason, he abruptly made up his mind to become a natural philosopher.

Henry walked to the Albany Academy and presented himself as a student. The other boys were years younger and the sons of wealthy families, but Henry lived in a private world where everything seemed possible. Fortunately he had so much talent that the real world took the shape of his private dream.

In seven months of night classes and special tutoring he acquired enough learning to get himself an appointment as a country schoolmaster. In this way he could afford to go on with his studies. Teaching and attending classes at the Academy took more than 16 hours a day, but Henry was in love with his life. Later he gave up teaching and talked his professor of chemistry into making him his assistant to set up experiments for public lectures. Henry's theatrical training had taught him that every demonstration must be foolproof, convincing and as dramatic as

145

possible. This experience contributed to the speed and simplicity which later characterized his own experiments.

When Henry had completed his course at the Academy, he took a job as a surveyor and engineer on the Erie Canal. The days of his poverty seemed ended, and the future was wide open. A man of his training could make a fortune almost anywhere from the seaports of the East to the distant hills of Wisconsin. After a few months, however, he was offered the professorship of mathematics and natural philosophy back in Albany. He felt the country needed advanced teachers even more desperately than engineers. Reluctantly he accepted the post.

Joseph Henry rode back to Albany in 1826. At this time he was a young man of striking appearance: he had curly blond hair, piercing blue eyes and the carriage of an actor. Behind the façade was the basic gift of great investigators—the instinct for reducing ideas to their essential simplicity.

His teaching schedule was heavy; the only time he could steal for research was the summer vacation, when he was permitted to convert one of the classrooms into a laboratory. At the end of August his apparatus was stored away and the benches and desks were returned.

His first work was to build electromagnets along the lines described by William Sturgeon of England. Sturgeon's magnet was a bar of iron coated with shellac, around which was loosely wrapped a length of bare wire. Sturgeon bent his bar into the form of a horseshoe; seven pounds of metal could be lifted into the air when he turned the current on, and just as dramatically dropped when he turned the current off. One summer in the Albany schoolroom Henry built a magnet that could lift one ton. Instead of insulating the iron, Henry had carefully insulated the wire. This allowed him to wrap the wire as closely as he wished, so that he could pack an enormous number of turns along the iron bar. Henry described his device in the *American Journal of Science*, published by Benjamin Silliman of Yale.

146

The experiments on electromagnets led Henry to the problem of generating electricity from magnetism. All the previous investigators, misled by the fact that a steady electric current induced a steady magnetic field, had sought some arrangement by which a steady magnetic field would induce an electric current. The usual test was to wind a length of wire around a piece of magnetized iron, to rub the free ends of the wire together and to look for sparks. Henry's great achievement was to perceive that the answer lay not in a steady magnetic field, but in a magnetic field that was changing.

In the crucial experiment Henry used one of his horseshoe-shaped electromagnets with a straight piece of soft iron, which he called an armature, running between its poles. Around the armature he wound a length of insulated copper wire about 30 feet long and connected its ends to a galvanometer some 40 feet away. Thus he had two coils completely independent of each other, the magnet coil attached to a battery and the other coil only to the galvanometer. He was ready to begin. "I stationed myself near the galvanometer," he wrote later, "and directed an assistant at a given word to . . . connect the . . . battery attached to the magnet." Then the miracle happened. "The north end of the galvanometer needle was deflected 30 degrees, indicating a current of electricity in the wire surrounding the armature."

An instant later Henry must have been disappointed. Even though the current continued to flow through the magnet coil, the needle returned to its zero position. He signaled his assistant to turn the current off. To his amazement the moment the circuit was broken the needle moved again, but in a direction opposite that of the first swing.

Henry soon guessed the reason for this unexpected behavior. It was only while the magnetism in the armature was changing—from zero to its full value as the magnetic circuit was closed, from full value back to zero as the circuit was opened—that anything happened in the secondary coil. He summed up the effect as he understood it in this way: "An instantaneous current in one or the other direction accompanies any change in the magnetic intensity of the iron."

Henry had now established that a current will be induced in any wire in a changing field. He shortly discovered that "any wire" includes the very wire that created the field in the first place. As early as 1829 he had observed the magnetic effect of a current on itself—now called self-induction. It was by making use of this phenomenon that he later confounded Faraday and Wheatstone.

Now this great work, and much more, was done in consecutive summers before 1831; but the first account of it, from which the foregoing quotations are taken, was tragically not written until 1832. Henry knew that he was working on the most difficult problem of his day; he knew that he had solved it before anyone else. But he had never had any personal contact with science as a profession, and the European scientists whose names he knew seemed figures of towering stature. He was therefore reluctant to publish any of his results until he could accumulate an overwhelming mass of data. His modesty was actually the unconscious pride of genius demanding to be accepted on its own terms. In addition, he was terribly pressed for time. There was not a moment to spare for the laborious work of composition.

For the rest of his life he was to regret that he had not publicized his results. "I ought to have published earlier," he said sadly. "I ought to have published, but I had so little time! It was so hard to get things done! I wanted to get out my results in good form, and how could I know that another on the other side of the Atlantic was busy with the same thing?"

The blow fell in May, 1832. Still filled with the confidence that he was years ahead of the world on a great work, he casually picked up a British journal. He read two paragraphs and the magazine slowly fell from his hands: he was years ahead of nobody. Faraday had just reported his independent discovery of electromagnetic induction.

Faraday's 1832 paper was based on results achieved as recently as the previous autumn. Although Henry had been years ahead of Faraday, he now felt that there was no point in publishing his own results at all. He was sick with despair. However, Silliman had heard of Henry's work and continually pressed him to describe it for the *American Journal of Science*. Henry finally sat down and began the series of papers that was to secure his place in history, but only after his death.

Not since the scientific work of Benjamin Franklin had there been such a chance for American science to achieve world distinction. The young republic was particularly sensitive to the European attitude that America had nothing culturally to offer. Instead of sympathizing with Henry, many of his friends blamed him for having failed to publish in time. They called him "irresponsible" and "unpatriotic." There were a few who understood. Instead of punishing him, they increased his opportunities for research by getting him an appointment to the faculty at Princeton University.

While still at Albany, Henry had invented the electrical relay. He used it to create the first electromagnetic telegraph system, anticipating Samuel F. B. Morse by at least five years. Henry's signaling device was a bell. He never published the details of the relay as a separate paper. He lectured on its practical importance, but to him it was merely an adaptation of the much deeper principles he had already propounded. He explained the device to Morse and to Wheatstone, the inventor of the English telegraph, and both men used it freely.

Henry's relay was a horseshoe magnet wound with the wire of the long telegraphic sending circuit. Across the pole pieces of the horseshoe was a movable iron armature, which was pulled toward the magnet each time a current impulse of the signal arrived. As the armature moved up and down it mechanically opened and closed a second circuit which contained its own battery. The second circuit contained either a printing mechanism or the horseshoe coil of still another relay so that the strengthened signal could be sent on again. Except for mechanical details Henry's relay has gone unchanged.

At Princeton he built an enlarged telegraphic device and sent signals over a mile of wire, stating that successive relays would allow him to continue the circuit indefinitely. He continued his researches on induction, achieving a remarkable understanding of the details of the phenomenon. In one page he described what was in effect the principle of the electric transformer: "The apparatus used in the experiment consists of a number of flat coils of copper ribbon. . . . Coil No. 1 was arranged to receive the current from a small battery, and coil No. 2 placed on this, with a glass interposed to insure perfect insulation; as often as the circuit of No. 1 was interrupted, a powerful secondary current was induced in No. 2. . . . The shock, however, from this coil is very feeble, and scarcely can be felt above the fingers." In other words, the current had been increased, but the voltage had been stepped down. "Coil No. 1 remaining as before, a longer coil was substituted for No. 2. With this arrangement the magnetizing power was much less, but the shocks were more powerful." Now he had cut down the current, but stepped up the voltage.

Henry's contemporaries knew so little about electricity and electric circuits that they could find in his work only what they were equipped to understand. To those who read the *American Journal of Science*—and its circulation was extremely small— Henry had simply improved the electromagnet. His fundamental insight into the transformer was entirely missed, and therefore forgotten within a few years. Very few Europeans bothered to read the *American Journal*. A decade after the publication of

Henry's original papers they were reprinted in England, but even then they were only superficially appreciated.

Henry rarely used mathematics in his analysis of physical phenomena. In his time Ohm's law—today taught to high-school students—had not yet been reduced to quantitative terms. Henry's analysis was powerful, but it was qualitative rather than quantitative. Voltages were given a relative measurement by the intensity of the shock felt by the experimenter; current intensities were similarly measured either by chemical means or, when they were very weak, by the acid taste produced in the experimenter's mouth. Henry detected feeble voltages by the shock to his tongue. But even though he dealt only with relative quantities, he was able to arrive at the correct exponential shape of the growth-and-decay curve for current in an inductive circuit.

Henry made his last great contribution to the study of electricity in 1842. In that year he demonstrated the transmission of radio waves. It was half a century before the celebrated experiments of Heinrich Hertz. Henry noticed that the effect of a spark could be detected by a parallel circuit 30 feet away. Spark coils operating on the second floor of his laboratory building magnetized needles in the basement, the induction taking place through 30 feet of air and two layers of 14-inch flooring. The following excerpt from his paper shows he clearly understood that this was a wave phenomenon, and that it was identical with the propagation of light: "It would appear that the transfer of a single spark is sufficient to disturb perceptibly the electricity of space throughout at least a cube of 400,000 feet of capacity; and when it is considered that . . . the spark is [oscillatory] . . . it may be further inferred that the diffusion of motion in this case is almost comparable with that of a spark from a flint and steel in the case of light."

In 1846 Henry's career as a research worker came to an end. The United States Government was seeking a director for the newly founded Smithsonian Institution, and Henry was offered the post. To accept meant that all his time would be devoted to administrative duties. But Henry felt that here was a great opportunity to give American science a cohesive form. Twenty years earlier a sense of duty had caused him to give up a profitable career in engineering. Now he felt it was his duty to give up research in order to act as the first national administrator of science.

By the time Henry was in his fifties, he was considered one of America's leading scientists. But his contemporaries knew him as a scientific administrator: director of the Smithsonian, adviser on science to Abraham Lincoln during the Civil War, the man to whom young inventors like Morse and Alexander Graham Bell went for encouragement. They did not know him as the scientific worker whose 15 years of electromagnetic research was far ahead of its time.

Henry's work as director of the Smithsonian touched many fields. He set up a project to report information about the weather, which later developed into the U. S. Weather Bureau. He persuaded James Lick to found his famous observatory in California. He served on innumerable government advisory boards, including the commission that in the 1850s examined the plans for an ironclad gunboat for the U. S. Navy. Henry was the only commissioner to recommend the design. His advice was disregarded, and, when the Civil War broke out, the design was adopted by the Confederacy in the building of the *Merrimac*.

The meteorological data which Henry collected for the Smithsonian was gathered by telegraph from 500 observers throughout the country east of the Mississippi River. As each telegraphic report came in from a local area, a small round card was pinned in position on a large map of the country. Different colors indicated rain, snow, clear weather or cloudiness. Henry said that storms moved eastward at the rate of 20 to 30 miles per hour, and he successfully taught the usefulness of the weather map to farmers, railroad people and shipping interests.

Henry was the first man to study the relative temperature of sunspots. In 1848 he projected an image of the sun on a white screen. Using a very small thermopile he was able to measure the relative temperature of each point on the projected image. He discovered that the images of the spots were cooler than the areas around them.

The development of the dynamo in the last decade of Henry's life marked the beginning of the use of alternating current. Only then were men able to go back and appreciate the importance of Henry's work. Maxwell's electromagnetic theory of the 1860s pointed up, in retrospect, Henry's statement that the propagation of electricity through space was identical with that of light. Hertz's experiments enabled investigators to look back and understand that Henry himself had been transmitting signals of spark frequency and receiving them on crudely tuned circuits. Henry received full honors only after his death because it took 40 years for men to know enough to appreciate what he had done.

JAMES CLERK MAXWELL
by James R. Newman

JAMES CLERK MAXWELL, the greatest theoretical physicist of the nineteenth century, opened a new epoch of science, and much of what distinguishes our world from his is due to his work. Because his most spectacular discoveries were the fruits of theoretical rather than experimental researches, he is often cited as an outstanding example of a scientist who built his systems entirely with pencil and paper. This notion is false. Maxwell combined a profound physical intuition with a formidable mathematical capacity to gain insights into physical phenomena, never losing sight of the observations to be explained. This blending of the concrete and the abstract was the chief characteristic of almost all his researches.

Maxwell was born in Edinburgh on November 13 in 1831, the same year Michael Faraday announced his famous discovery of electromagnetic induction. Descended of an old Scots family whose members were distinguished no less for their individuality, "verging on eccentricity," than for their talents (they included eminent judges, politicians, mining speculators, merchants, poets, musicians), he was the only son of a member of the Scottish bar who took little interest in the grubby pursuits of an advocate but instead managed his small estates, took part in county affairs and gave loving attention to the education of his son. Maxwell's father was a warm and rather simple man with a nice sense of humor and a practical interest in mechanical contrivances. His mother is described as having a "sanguine, active temperament."

Jamesie, as the boy was called, passed his early childhood on the family estate at Glenlair, two days' carriage ride from Edinburgh. He was a nearsighted, lively, affectionate little boy, as persistently inquisitive as his father and as fascinated by machines. To discover of anything "how it does" was his constant aim. "What's the go of that?" he would ask, and if the answer did not satisfy him, he would add, "But what's the *particular* go of that?" His own first creation was a set of figures for a "wheel of life," a scientific toy which produced the illusion of continuous movement; he was fond of making things with his hands, and in later life knew how to design models embodying the most complex motions and other physical processes.

When Maxwell was nine, his mother died of cancer, the disease that was to kill him 40 years later. Her death brought the father and son even more closely together. The boy began his schooling a year later as a day student at the Edinburgh Academy. His early school experiences were painful. The master, a dryish Scotsman whose reputation as a pedagogue derived from a book he had written on the irregular Greek verbs, expected his students to be orderly, well grounded in the usual subjects and unoriginal. Maxwell was deficient in all these departments. He created something of a sensation because of his clothes, which had been designed by his strong-minded father and included such items as "hygienic" square-toed shoes and a lace-frilled tunic. The boys nicknamed him "Dafty" and mussed him up, but he was a stubborn child and in time won the respect of his classmates even if he continued to puzzle them.

At school Maxwell experienced a gradual awakening of mathematical interests. He wrote his father that he had made a "tetra hedron, a dodeca hedron, and two more hedrons that I don't know the wright names for." In his fourteenth year he won the Academy's mathematical medal and wrote a paper on a method for constructing perfect oval curves with pins and thread. Another prodigious little boy, René Descartes, had anticipated him in this field, but Maxwell's contributions were original. It was a wonderful day for father and son when they heard the boy's paper

156

on ovals read before the Royal Society of Edinburgh by Professor James Forbes. "Met," the father wrote of the event in his diary, "with very great attention and approbation generally."

After six years at the Academy Maxwell entered the University of Edinburgh. He was 16, a restless, enigmatic, brilliantly talented adolescent who wrote not very good but strangely prophetic verse about the destiny of matter and energy:

> When earth and sun are frozen clods,
> When all its energy degraded
> Matter to aether shall have faded. . . .

His friend and biographer Lewis Campbell records that he was completely neat in his person, "though with a rooted objection to the vanities of starch and gloves," and that he had a "pious horror of destroying anything—even a scrap of writing paper." He read voraciously and passed much time in mathematical speculations and in chemical, magnetic and optical experiments. "When at table he often seemed abstracted from what was going on, being absorbed in observing the effects of refracted light in the finger glasses, or in trying some experiment with his eyes—seeing around a corner, making invisible stereoscopes, and the like. Miss Cay [his aunt] used to call his attention by crying, 'Jamesie, you're in a prop [an abbreviation for mathematical proposition].'"

While at Edinburgh, Maxwell regularly attended meetings of the Royal Society, and two of his papers, "On the Theory of Rolling Curves" and "On the Equilibrium of Elastic Solids," were published in the *Transactions*. The papers were read before the Society by others, "for it was not thought proper for a boy in a round jacket to mount the rostrum there." During vacations at Glenlair he wrote long letters reporting his multifarious doings to friends. Many of his letters exhibit an intense interest in moral philosophy, reflecting his social sympathy, his Christian earnestness, the not uncommon nineteenth-century mixture of rationalism and simple faith. It was a period when men still believed that questions of wisdom, happiness and virtue could be studied as one studies optics and mechanics.

In 1850 Maxwell went on to the University of Cambridge. There he became a private pupil of William Hopkins, considered the ablest mathematics coach of his time, who prepared him for the mathematical tripos, the stiff competitive examinations in which the brightest students competed. Hopkins at once recognized the talents of the black-haired young Scotsman, describing him as "the most extraordinary man I have ever met," and adding that "it appears impossible for [him] to think incorrectly on physical subjects." Besides working hard on his studies, Maxwell joined fully in social and intellectual activities at the University. He was elected to the Apostles, a club of 12 members which for many years included the outstanding young men at Cambridge. A contemporary described Maxwell as "the most genial and amusing of companions, the propounder of many a strange theory, the composer of many a poetic *jeu d'esprit*." Not the least strange of his theories related to economy of sleep. He would sleep from 5 in the afternoon to 9:30, read very hard from 10 to 2, exercise by running along the corridors and up and down the stairs from 2 to 2:30 A.M. and sleep again from 2:30 to 7. The dormitory inhabitants were not pleased, but Maxwell persisted in his bizarre experiments. Another of his investigations was a study of the process by which a cat always lands on her feet. He demonstrated that a cat could completely right herself even when dropped upside down on a table or bed from a height of about two inches.

In the summer of 1853 a "sort of brain fever" seized Maxwell. For weeks he was totally disabled, and he felt the effects of his illness long afterward. This episode was undoubtedly an emotional crisis, but its causes remain obscure. All that is known is that his illness strengthened Maxwell's religious conviction—a deep, earnest piety, leaning to Scottish Calvinism yet never completely identified with any particular system or sect. "I have no nose for heresy," he used to say.

In January, 1854, Maxwell took the tripos in the Cambridge Senate House, with a rug wrapped around his feet and legs (as his father had advised) to mitigate the perishing cold. His head was warm enough. He finished second wrangler, behind the noted mathematician Edward Routh. (In another competition at Cambridge, for "Smith's prize," where the subjects were more advanced, Maxwell and Routh tied for first.)

After getting his degree Maxwell stayed on for two years at Trinity, studying, lecturing, taking private pupils and doing some experiments in optics. He designed a top with colored paper disks to study the mixing of colors, and he was able to show that suitable combinations of three primary colors—red, green and blue— produced "to a very near degree of approximation" almost every color of the spectrum. For this work in color sensation he later won the Rumford medal of the Royal Society.

Maxwell's most significant activity during the two postgraduate years at Trinity, however, was his reading of Faraday's *Experimental Researches* and entrance upon the studies of electricity which were to lead to his greatest discoveries. Before he left Trinity, he published his first major contribution, the beautiful paper "On Faraday's Lines of Force." In 1856 Maxwell was appointed to the chair of natural philosophy at Marischal College in Aberdeen; he had applied for the post partly to be near his father, whose health had been failing, but his father died a few days before he obtained the appointment. It was an irreparable personal loss to Maxwell; they had been as close as father and son could be. At Aberdeen Maxwell continued his work on electricity. His teaching load was rather light. Although he took teaching seriously, it cannot be said that Maxwell was a great teacher. With classes that were "not bright" he found it difficult to hit a suitable pace. He was unable to heed himself the advice he once gave a friend whose duty it was to preach to a country congregation: "Why don't you give it them thinner?"

Maxwell's electrical studies at Aberdeen were interrupted by a task which engrossed him for almost two years. He entered a competition for a University of Cambridge prize on the subject of Saturn's rings. Were the rings solid? Were they fluid? Did they consist of masses of matter "not mutually coherent"? The problem was to demonstrate which type of structure adequately explained the motion and permanence of the rings. In a brilliant 68-page essay which Sir George Airy, the Astronomer Royal, described as one of the most remarkable applications of mathematics he had even seen, Maxwell demonstrated that the only stable structure would be one composed of disconnected particles. His essay won the prize and established him as a leader among mathematical physicists.

His research on Saturn excited his interest in the kinetic theory of gases. Maxwell's predecessors in this field—Rudolf Clausius, Daniel Bernoulli, James Joule and others—had been successful in explaining many of the properties of gases, such as pressure, temperature and density, on the hypothesis that a gas is composed of swiftly moving particles. However, in order to simplify the mathematical analysis they had assumed that all the particles of a gas move at the same speed. Maxwell realized that this was an altogether implausible assumption, for collisions among the molecules must give them various velocities. If the science of gases was to be developed on "strict mechanical principles," it was necessary, he said, to incorporate this fact into the mathematical formulation of the laws of motion of the particles.

Maxwell proceeded to examine mathematically the behavior of an assemblage of colliding particles as if they were "small, hard and perfectly elastic spheres acting on one another only during impact." Since the many molecules could not be treated individually, he introduced the statistical method for dealing with them. He supposed that the distribution of velocities among the molecules in a gas would follow the famous bell-shaped frequency curve, which applies to so many phenomena, from the pattern of shots on a target to groupings of men according to height. Thus while the velocity of an individual molecule might elude description, the velocity of a crowd of molecules would not. Having arrived at a quantitative description of the speeds of molecules composing a gas, Maxwell was able to write a precise formula for gas pressure. Curiously enough this expression did not differ from that based on the assumption that the velocity of all the molecules was the same, but at last the right conclusion had been won by correct reasoning. Moreover the generality and elegance of Maxwell's mathematical methods led to the extension of their use into almost every branch of physics.

Maxwell went on to consider another factor which needed to be determined for precise formulation of the laws of gases: namely, the distance a molecule travels, on the average, between collisions—i.e., its mean free path. He reasoned that the mean free path of molecules in a given gas could be measured by the viscosity of that gas. Assume that a gas is composed of groups of molecules with different velocities which slide over one another, thus creating friction. This would account for the viscosity of gases. Now the mean free path of molecules would be related to viscosity in the following way. Imagine two layers of molecules sliding past each other. If a molecule passing from one layer to the other travels only a short distance before colliding with another molecule, the two particles do not exchange much momentum, because near the boundary the difference of velocity between the two layers is small. But if the molecule penetrates deep into the other layer before a collision, the velocity differential will be greater; hence the exchange of momentum between the colliding particles is greater. This amounts to saying that in any gas with high viscosity the molecules must have a long mean free path. Maxwell deduced further the paradoxical fact that the viscosity of a gas is independent of its density, for the increased probability of collisions in a dense gas is offset by the fact that in such a gas a molecule will not travel far into a different layer before colliding. On balance, then, the momentum conveyed across each unit area per second remains the same regardless of density.

Thus Maxwell constructed a mechanical model of a gas as an

assemblage of crowds of particles "carrying with them their momenta and their energy," traveling certain distances, colliding, changing their motion, resuming their travels, and so on. His picture made it possible to account in precise quantitative terms for a gas's various properties—viscosity, diffusion, heat conduction. Altogether it was a scientific achievement of the first rank. The model has since been criticized, on the grounds, for example, that molecules are not hard nor perfectly elastic, like billiard balls, nor is their interaction confined to the actual moment of impact. Yet despite the inadequacies of the model and errors of reasoning, the results, which, as Sir James Jeans said, "ought to have been hopelessly wrong," turned out to be exactly right, and Maxwell's law for the behavior of gases is in use to this day.

The German physicist Ludwig Boltzmann, who recognized at once the significance of these discoveries, set to work refining and generalizing Maxwell's proof. He showed that the Maxwell distribution of velocities was the only possible equilibrium state of a gas. This equilibrium state, as both men realized, is the thermodynamic condition of maximum entropy—the most disordered state, in which the least amount of energy is available for useful work.

The concept of entropy led Maxwell to one of the celebrated images of modern science, namely that of the sorting demon. Increasing entropy is man's fate because we are not very bright. But a demon more favorably endowed could sort out the slow- and fast-moving particles of a gas, thereby changing disorder into order and converting unavailable into available energy. Maxwell imagined one of these small, sharp fellows "in charge of a frictionless, sliding door in a wall separating two compartments of a vessel filled with gas. When a fast-moving molecule moves from left to right, the demon opens the door; when a slow-moving molecule approaches, he (or she) closes the door. The fast-moving molecules accumulate in the right-hand compartment, and slow ones in the left. The gas in the first compartment grows hot and that in the second cold." Thus the demon would thwart the second law of thermodynamics. Living organisms, it has been suggested, achieve an analogous process; as Erwin Schrödinger has phrased it, they suck negative entropy from the environment in the food they eat and the air they breathe.

Maxwell and Boltzmann, working independently and in a friendly rivalry, at first made notable progress in explaining the behavior of gases by statistical mechanics. After a time, however, formidable difficulties arose. For example, they were unable to write accurate theoretical formulas for the specific heats of certain gases (the quantity of heat required to raise the temperature of a body of the gas by a given amount). Explanation of the discrepancies they found had to await the development of quantum theory, which showed that the spin and vibration of molecules were restricted to certain values. But neither quantum theory nor relativity, nor the other modes of thought constituting the twentieth-century revolution in physics, would have been possible had it not been for the brilliant labors of these natural philosophers in applying statistical methods to the study of gases.

In February, 1858, Maxwell wrote his aunt, Miss Cay: "This comes to tell you that I am going to have a wife." "Don't be afraid," he added, "she is not mathematical, but there are other things besides that, and she certainly won't stop mathematics." His bride was Katherine Mary Dewar, daughter of the Principal of Marischal College. Their union became very close: they enjoyed doing things together—horseback riding, reading aloud to each other, traveling—and he even found useful tasks for her in his experimental work. The marriage was childless, but this very fact increased the couple's dependency and devotion.

In the summer of 1860 Maxwell moved to London as professor of natural philosophy at King's College. He remained there for five years. Living in London offered him the opportunity to see something of Faraday, with whom, up to this time, Maxwell had

had only correspondence, and to make the acquaintance of other scientists. He was no solitary. "Work is good, and reading is good, but friends are better," he wrote to his friend Litchfield. Despite social distractions and arduous teaching duties at King's, the five years in London were the most productive of Maxwell's life. He continued his work on gases. In the large garret of his house in Kensington he measured the viscosity of gases and obtained practical confirmation of his theoretical work. (To maintain the necessary temperature a fire had to be kept up in the midst of very hot weather and kettles kept boiling to produce steam which would be allowed to flow into the room. Mrs. Maxwell acted as stoker.) But his major work was in the theory of electricity, from which he had been diverted and to which he now returned.

Faraday's experiments had crowned a century of researches (by Coulomb, Oersted, Ampère and others) which had established many facts about the behavior of electricity and its link with magnetism. They had shown that electric charges attracted and repelled each other according to a law like that of gravitation (in proportion to the product of the charges and in inverse proportion to the square of the distance between the charges); that a current produces a magnetic field, and a moving magnet produces a current; that an electric current in one circuit can induce a current in another.

What absorbed Maxwell was the attempt to explain these phenomena. What was a field? How did electricity and magnetism exert their influence through space? Faraday had suggested a new concept to answer these questions, and it was his idea that excited Maxwell's interest.

Most theorists had pursued the analogy of electricity to gravitation and had sought to explain the phenomena in terms of "action at a distance." They imagined a charge (or mass) situated at one point in space mysteriously influencing a charge (or mass) at another point, with no linkage or connection of any kind between the charges (or masses). Faraday proposed to explain electricity as a mechanical system. He asserted that the instrumentality of electric and magnetic action was lines of force running through space—not merely imaginary lines but actual, physical entities, with properties of tension, attraction, repulsion, motion and so on.

Maxwell admirably summarized the cleavage between the two views: "Faraday, in his mind's eye, saw lines of force traversing all space, where the mathematicians saw centres of force attracting at a distance; Faraday saw a medium where they saw nothing but distance; Faraday sought the seat of the phenomena in real actions going on in the medium, they were satisfied that they had found it in a power of action at a distance impressed on the electric fluids."

Maxwell believed in Faraday's concept, and he set out to develop it. In his first paper, "On Faraday's Lines of Force," he tried to imagine a physical model, embodying Faraday's lines, whose behavior could be reduced to formulas and numbers. He did not suggest that the model represented the actual state of things, but he felt that it was important "to lay hold of a clear physical conception, without being committed to any theory founded on the physical science from which that conception is borrowed." Such a method would protect the investigator against being led into a blind alley of abstractions or being "carried beyond the truth by a favorite hypothesis."

Maxwell proposed a hydrodynamic model, in which he incorporated Faraday's lines of force in the form of "tubes of flow" carrying an incompressible fluid such as water. The fluid moving through the tubes represented electricity in motion; the form and diameter of the tubes gave information as to the strength and direction of the flow. The velocity of the fluid was the equivalent of electrical force; differences of fluid pressure were analogous to differences of electrical pressure or potential; pressure transmitted from tube to tube by way of the elastic tube surfaces

167

furnished an analogue to electric induction. By applying the
established equations of hydrodynamics to such a system, Maxwell was able to account for many of the observed facts concerning electricity.

It was a wonderful paper, and Faraday expressed his appreciation. "I was at first almost frightened," he wrote Maxwell, "when
I saw such mathematical force made to bear upon the subject,
and then wondered to see that the subject stood it so well." Other
students, however, thought the subject stood it not at all well.
Electricity was mysterious enough without adding tubes and
incompressible fluids. But Maxwell, who had had good training
in being considered queer, went on with the task of extending
Faraday's ideas.

Maxwell's second great memoir, "On Physical Lines of Force,"
was published after he returned to the subject of electricity in
London. He now constructed a more elaborate model to account
not only for electrostatic effects but also for magnetic attraction
and electromagnetic induction. In the new model "molecular
vortices" rotating in space were the agents that produced magnetic fields. A molecular vortex may be thought of as a slender
cylinder which rotates around the lines of magnetic force. The
velocity of rotation depends on the intensity of the magnetic
force. Two mechanical effects are associated with the cylinders:
tension in the direction of the lines of force, and lateral pressure
arising from the centrifugal force produced by the rotating
cylinders. Combined, these effects mechanically reproduce magnetic phenomena: magnetism is a force exerted both along the
axis and outward from the axis.

Maxwell proceeded to show how this curious arrangement
might explain the production of a magnetic field by an electric
current and of a current by a changing field. He supposed first
that a uniform magnetic field consists of a portion of space filled
with cylinders rotating at the same velocity and in the same

direction "about axes nearly parallel." But immediately a puzzle confronted him. Since the cylinders are in contact, how can they possibly rotate in the same direction? As everyone knows, a rotating wheel or cylinder causes its neighbor to rotate in the opposite direction. Maxwell hit upon a pretty idea. He supposed that rows of small spheres, like layers of ball bearings, lay between the cylinders and acted as gears (in Maxwell's words, "idle wheels"). Thus the cylinders all rotated in the same direction.

And now, as just reward for his ingenuity, Maxwell found that the spheres could be made to serve another even more valuable purpose. Think of them as particles of electricity. Then by purely mechanical reasoning it can be shown that their motions in the machine of which they are a part serve to explain many electrical phenomena.

Consider these examples. In an unchanging magnetic field the cylinders all rotate at the same constant rate. The little rotating spheres keep their position; there is no flow of particles, hence no electric current. Now suppose a change in the magnetic force. This means a change in the velocity of rotation of the cylinders. As each cylinder is speeded up, it transmits the change in velocity to its neighbors. But since a cylinder now rotates at a slightly different speed from its neighbor, the spheres between them are torn from their positions by a kind of shearing action. This motion of translation of the particles is an electric current.

Observe now how the model begins to live a life of its own. Though designed primarily to demonstrate how magnetic changes produce electric currents, it also suggested to Maxwell a mechanism whereby a change in electric force might produce magnetism. Assume the spheres and cylinders are at rest. If a force is applied to the spheres of electricity, causing them to move, the cylinders of magnetism with which they are in contact will begin to rotate, thereby producing a magnetic force. Moreover, the model holds up even as to details. Take a single illustration. An examination of Maxwell's model shows that the cylinders will rotate in the direction perpendicular to the motion of the spheres, thus bearing out the observation that a magnetic field acts at right angles to the flow of a current!

"I do not bring it forward," Maxwell wrote of his system, "as a mode of connection existing in Nature. . . . It is, however, a mode of connection which is mechanically conceivable and easily investigated, and it serves to bring out the actual mechanical connections between the known electromagnetic phenomena." Among the other "mechanical connections" Maxwell was able to demonstrate were electrical repulsion between two parallel wires carrying currents in opposite directions (ascribed to the centrifugal pressures of the revolving cylinders on the electrical particles in the model) and the induction of currents (the result of communication of rotary velocity from one cylinder to another).

Maxwell was not done with the model. It had yet to pass the supreme test: that is, to supply a mechanical explanation of the origin of electromagnetic waves. To orient ourselves in this matter we must examine briefly the question of condensers and insulators.

Faraday in his experiments had come upon a curious fact. The type of insulating material used in a condenser made a considerable difference in the condenser's capacity to take or to hold a charge. This was difficult to understand if all insulators were equally impermeable to an electric current. With the help of his model, Maxwell advanced a bold hypothesis. In an insulating material the little electrical particles somehow are unable to move freely from cylinder to cylinder; hence no current can flow. However, it was known that "localized electric phenomena" did occur in insulators. Maxwell suggested that these phenomena were currents of a special kind. When an electric force acts on an insulator, the particles of electricity are "displaced" but not torn loose; that is, they behave like a ship riding at anchor in

170

a storm. They move only a limited distance, to the point where the force pushing them is balanced by the resistance of the elastic cylinders. As soon as the impelling force ceases to act, the particles snap back to their original positions. When a particle snaps back, it overshoots and oscillates about its fixed position. The oscillation is transmitted through the insulator as a wave. Thus for a brief instant a displacement current flows, for the wave is the current. If the electric force applied to the insulator is varied continually, it will produce a continually varying displacement wave: in other words, a continuing current.

Maxwell next arrived at an epoch-making conclusion. It had to do with the relation of the velocity of the displacement wave, or current, to that of light. For the point of departure we must go back to earlier work by the German physicists Wilhelm Weber and Friedrich Kohlrausch on the relationship between electrostatic and electrodynamic forces. The electrostatic unit of charge was defined as the repulsion between two like unit charges at unit distance apart. The electrodynamic unit was defined as the repulsion between two measured lengths of wire carrying currents "which may be specified by the amount of charge which travels past any point in unit time." In order to compare the repulsion between static charges with that between moving charges, a factor of proportionality must be introduced, since the units are different. This factor turns out to be a velocity, for since the length of the wires is fixed, and the number of units of electricity passing a given point in a given time can be measured, what the investigator must consider is length divided by time, or velocity. Weber and Kohlrausch had found that the velocity of propagation of an electric disturbance along a perfectly conducting wire was close to 3×10^{10} centimeters per second. This was an astonishing coincidence, for the figure was about the same as the velocity of light, determined a few years earlier.

Maxwell pursued the coincidence. He himself confirmed the Weber-Kohlrausch results, using an ingenious torsion balance to compare the repulsion between two static charges and two wires carrying currents, and at about the same time he calculated the velocity of displacement currents in a dielectric (nonconductor). The resulting values tallied closely. In other words, currents in a perfect conductor, displacement currents in a dielectric, and light in empty space (which of course is a dielectric) all traveled with the same velocity. With this evidence at hand Maxwell did not hesitate to assert the identity of the two phenomena—electrical disturbances and light. "We can scarcely avoid the inference," he said "that light consists in the transverse undulations of the same medium which is the cause of electric and magnetic phenomena."

Maxwell now had to outgrow his model. In "A Dynamical Theory of the Electromagnetic Field," published in 1864, he displayed the architecture of his system, as Sir Edmund Whittaker has said, "stripped of the scaffolding by aid of which it had first been erected." The particles and cylinders were gone; in their place were the field and the ether, a special kind of "matter in motion by which the observed electromagnetic phenomena are produced." The matter composing the ether had marvelous properties. It was very fine and capable of permeating bodies; it filled space with an elastic medium. It was the vehicle of "the undulations of light and heat."

For all its refinements and subtleties the ether was no less a mechanical rig than the cylinders and balls. It could move, transmit motions, undergo elastic deformations, store potential (mechanical) energy and release it when the deforming pressures were removed. As a mechanism, Maxwell said, it "must be subject to the general laws of dynamics, and we ought to be able to work out all the consequences of its motion, provided we know the form of the relation between the motions of the parts." Applying himself to this task, he devised the famous Maxwellian equations of the electromagnetic field. In their most finished form they appear in his *Treatise on Electricity and Magnetism*, which presents the results of 20 years of thought and experiment.

Maxwell based the equations on four principles: (1) that an electric force acting on a conductor produces a current proportional to the force; (2) that an electric force acting on a dielectric produces displacement proportional to the force; (3) that a current produces a magnetic field at right angles to the current's lines of flow and proportional to its intensity; (4) that a changing magnetic field produces an electric force proportional to the intensity of the field. The third and fourth principles exhibit a striking symmetry. The third is Faraday's law of electromagnetic induction, according to which "the rate of alteration in the number of lines of magnetic induction passing through a circuit is equal to the work done in taking unit electric charge round the circuit." Maxwell's complementary law, the fourth principle, is that "the rate of alteration in the number of lines of electric force passing through a circuit is equal to the work done in taking a unit magnetic pole round it."

On this foundation two sets of symmetrical equations can be erected. One set expresses the continuous nature of electric and magnetic fields; the second set tells how changes in one field produce changes in the other.

How does the concept of the field enter the theory? We have followed Maxwell as he stripped his model of its particles and cylinders and reduced it to an ethereal medium. Now he robs the medium of almost all its attributes other than form. Its properties are all purely geometric. The grin is left but the cat is gone. It is a perfect example of mathematical abstraction.

The ether is a thing that quivers when it is prodded, but does nothing on its own. An electromagnetic field consists of two kinds of energy: electrostatic or potential energy, and electrodynamic, or kinetic, energy. The ether, like a universal condenser, may be conceived as storing energy—in which case, being elastic, it is deformed. Since the ether fills all space and therefore penetrates conductors as well as dielectrics, it no longer makes any difference whether we deal with a conduction current or a displacement current; in either case the ether is set in motion. This motion is communicated mechanically from one part of the medium to the next and is apprehended by us as heat, light, mechanical force (as in the repulsion between wires) or other phenomena of magnetism and electricity. The ruling principle of all such phenomena, it should be observed, is that of least action. This is the grand overriding law of the parsimony of nature: every action within a system is executed with the least possible expenditure of energy. It was of the first importance to Maxwell that electrical phenomena should satisfy the principle, for otherwise his mechanical explanation of the phenomena would not have been possible.

With these points in mind, we may examine a set of Maxwell's equations in a form which describes the behavior of an electromagnetic field in empty space. No conductors or free charges are present; the source of the field is some other region of space.

The first equation then reads:

$$\text{div } E = 0$$

E represents the electric field strength, which varies in time and from place to place. Div is an abbreviation for divergence. It signifies a mathematical operation which gives a rate of change. The equation says that the number of electric lines of force (representing the field strength) which enter any tiny volume of space must equal the number leaving it. That is, the rate of change in the number of lines is zero, and they can neither be created nor destroyed.

The second equation reads:

$$\text{div } H = 0$$

It makes the same assertion for the magnetic field H as the first equation makes for the electric field.

The third equation is:

$$\text{curl } E = -\frac{1}{c}\frac{\partial H}{\partial t}$$

This is Maxwell's statement of Faraday's law of induction: it describes what happens in a changing magnetic field. The expression $\partial H/\partial t$ simply states the rate of change of the magnetic field. The changing magnetic field creates an electric field, and this fact is expressed on the left side of the equation, where the term "curl" signifies a mathematical operation dealing with rotation. The equation is more than analytic; it actually gives a picture of the event. Suppose the existence of a magnetic field uniform over a region of space. A bundle of parallel lines represents the intensity and direction of this field. If the field is changed (by motion or by increase or reduction of strength), it produces an electric field which acts in a circle around the lines of magnetic force. By summing the work done in moving unit electric charge around the circle we obtain what is called the net electromotive force around the circle. If the circle were made of wire, the changing magnetic lines would of course induce the flow of a current; but even without a wire a force would be induced. Dividing this force by the area enclosed by the circle gives the net electromotive force (per unit area) which "curls" around the circle. Now imagine the circle growing smaller and smaller and shrinking finally to the point P. By this limiting process we obtain a limiting value of the net electromotive force per unit area: this is curl E at P. Thus the equation says that the limiting value of electromotive force per unit area equals the rate of change of H at the point P, multiplied by the tiny negative fraction, $-1/c$. The symbol c here stands for the ratio of the electrostatic to the electromagnetic units of electricity. It is required to translate E (an electrostatic phenomenon) and H (an electrodynamic phenomenon) into the same system of units. The equation explains how Maxwell was able to connect electrical and magnetic phenomena with the velocity of light, for c is in fact that velocity.

The last equation is:

175

$$\text{curl } H = \frac{1}{c}\frac{\partial E}{\partial t}$$

It says that except for the change of algebraic sign (which has to do with the directions of the fields), the roles of E and H in the preceding equation may be reversed. At any given point and instant the magnetic force per unit of area created by a changing electric field is equal to the time rate of change of the electric field multiplied by the tiny positive fraction $1/c$. Now this rate of change is none other than Maxwell's displacement current. For since the changes are taking place in the dielectric known as empty space, the only currents that can flow are displacement currents. Prior to Maxwell it was thought that a magnetic field could be produced only by currents which flowed in wires. It was Maxwell's great discovery, deduced mechanically from his model and expressed mathematically in this equation, that a time-varying electric field produced a magnetic force even in an insulator or empty space.

According to Maxwell's theory the introduction of a time-varying electric force in a dielectric produces displacement waves with the velocity of light. These periodic waves of electric displacement are accompanied by a periodic magnetic force. The wave front itself comprises electric vibrations at right angles to the direction of propagation, and a magnetic force at right angles to the electric displacement. The compound disturbance is therefore called an electromagnetic wave. A light wave (a displacement wave), as Henri Poincaré later elaborated, is "a series of alternating currents, flowing in a dielectric, in the air, or in interplanetary space, changing their direction 1,000,000,000,000,-000 times a second. The enormous inductive effect of these rapid alternations produces other currents in the neighboring portions of the dielectric, and thus the light waves are propagated from place to place."

The electromagnetic theory of light was testable experimentally, and stood up remarkably well in laboratory trials. There were also other ways of testing Maxwell's theory. If his reasoning was correct, different sources of disturbance should produce other electrical waves at frequencies different from those of light. They would not be visible; yet it should be possible to detect them with appropriate instruments. Maxwell did not live to see their discovery, but 10 years after his death Heinrich Hertz won the race to demonstrate their existence. In a series of brilliant experiments he succeeded in generating electric radio waves. He concluded that the connection "between light and electricity . . . of which there were hints and suspicions and even predictions in the theory, is now established. . . . Optics is no longer restricted to minute aether waves, a small fraction of a millimetre in length; its domain is extended to waves that are measured in decimetres, metres and kilometres. And in spite of this extension, it appears merely . . . as a small appendage of the great domain of electricity. We see that this latter has become a mighty kingdom."

Maxwell completed his great work on electromagnetic theory while "in retirement" at Glenlair. It drew only part of his energy. As a "by-work" during the same period he wrote a textbook on heat and a number of papers on mathematics, color vision and topics of physics. He maintained a heavy scientific and social correspondence, enlarged his house, studied theology, composed stanzas of execrable verse, rode his horse, went on long walks with his dogs, visited his neighbors and played with their children, and made frequent trips to Cambridge to serve as moderator and examiner in the mathematical tripos.

In 1871 a chair in experimental physics was founded at Cambridge. It is hard to realize that at the time no courses in heat, electricity and magnetism were being taught there, and no laboratory was available for the pursuit of these arcane matters. The University, as a contemporary scholar delicately observed, "had lost touch with the great scientific movements going on outside her walls." A committee of the faculty began to bestir itself, a report was issued, and the lamentable facts fell under the gaze of the Duke of Devonshire, chancellor of the University. He offered the money for the building and furnishing of the famous Cavendish Laboratory. Maxwell, though at first reluctant to leave Glenlair, yielded to the urging of his friends to offer himself as a candidate for the chair. He was promptly elected.

He now devoted himself to the task of designing and superintending the erection of the laboratory. His aim was to make it the best institution of its kind, with the latest apparatus and the most effective arrangements for research. He presented to the laboratory all the apparatus in his own possession and supplemented the Duke's gift by generous money contributions. With so many details to be taken care of, the structure and its appointments were not completed until 1874. The delay, while inevitable, was inconvenient. "I have no place," wrote Maxwell, "to erect my chair, but move about like the cuckoo, depositing my notions in the Chemical Lecture Room in the first term, in the Botanical in Lent and in the Comparative Anatomy in Easter." His "notions" were the courses he gave on heat, electricity and electromagnetism.

Maxwell's classic *Matter and Motion*, "a small book on a great subject," was published in 1876. About this time he contributed articles on various subjects—"Atom," "Aether," "Attraction," "Faraday," among others—to the famous ninth edition of the Encyclopaedia Britannica. His public lectures include a charming discourse "On the Telephone," which, though delivered when he was already very ill, is not only as clear as his best expositions but filled with gay, amusing asides. Speaking of "Professor Bell's invention," he commented on "the perfect symmetry of the whole apparatus—the wire in the middle, the two telephones at the ends of the wire, and the two gossips at the ends of the telephones." Maxwell spent five years editing 20 packets of unpublished scientific papers of Henry Cavendish. This splendid two-volume work, published in 1879, did much to fix the reputation of the immensely gifted eighteenth-century investigator, whose important work on electricity was unknown to his contemporaries because the results were confided only to his manuscripts. Maxwell repeated Cavendish's experiments and showed that he had anticipated major discoveries in electricity, including Ohm's law.

As Maxwell grew older, friends remarked on his "ever-increasing soberness" of spirit. He continued to see his many friends, to write light verse and parodies, to promenade with his dog Toby, to play small practical jokes. But he became somewhat more reticent, and more and more concealed his feelings and reflections beneath an ironical shell. The tough, rational, Scottish common-sense cord of his nature had always been intertwined with threads of mysticism. He had faith in science; yet he was at bottom skeptical as to how much could be learned from science alone about nature and meaning. His contemporaries described him as both modest and intellectually scornful, tentative in his scientific opinions and dogmatic when others seemed to him to be immoderately self-assured.

The most striking of Maxwell's traits was his gentleness. An extraordinary selflessness characterized his relationship to those close to him. When his brother-in-law came to London to undergo an operation, Maxwell gave up the ground floor of his house to the patient and nurse and lived in a room so small that he frequently breakfasted on his knees because there was no room for a chair at the table. Mrs. Maxwell had a serious and prolonged illness in the last years of Maxwell's life, and he insisted on nursing her. It is reported that on one occasion he did not sleep in a bed for three weeks. But his work went on as usual and he was as cheerful as if he enjoyed the ordeal—which may indeed have been the case. Nor did he give the slightest sign of being downcast or show self-pity when his own fatal illness seized him.

In the spring of 1877 he began to be troubled with pain and a choking sensation on swallowing. For some strange reason he consulted no one about his symptoms for almost two years, though his condition grew steadily worse. His friends at Cambridge observed that he was failing, that the spring had gone out of his step. When he went home to Glenlair for the summer of 1879, he was so obviously weakening that he called for medical help. He was in terrible pain, "hardly able to lie still for a minute together, sleepless, and with no appetite for the food which he so required." He understood thoroughly that his case was hopeless, yet his main concern seemed to be about the health of his wife. On November 5 he died. "No man," wrote his physician, Dr. Paget, "ever met death more consciously or more calmly." When Maxwell was buried in Parton Churchyard at Glenlair, the world had not yet caught up with his ideas. Even today it has not fully explored the kingdom created by his imagination.

PART 5 THE STUDY OF LIFE

I. WILLIAM HARVEY *by Frederick G. Kilgour*

Librarian of the Yale Medical Library since 1948, Frederick G. Kilgour was born in Springfield, Mass., in 1914. Upon receiving his A.B. from Harvard College in 1935, he joined the staff of its library, serving there until 1942 when he went off to war as an intelligence officer in the Office of Strategic Services. He was demobilized in 1945 with a Legion of Merit award and went to the State Department as deputy director of the office of collection and dissemination of intelligence. In 1948 he returned to academic life at Yale where, in addition to his work as librarian, he lectures in the history of science and conducts the editorial affairs of the *Yale Journal of Biology and Medicine*.

II. CHARLES DARWIN *by Loren C. Eiseley*

Chairman of the Department of Anthropology at the University of Pennsylvania and the curator of the division covering early man in the University Museum, Loren C. Eiseley was born in Lincoln, Nebraska, in 1907. He attended the University of Nebraska and took his doctorate at the University of Pennsylvania. In anthropology he has specialized in archaeological studies of man in the New World and has done extensive field research in the western United States and Mexico. Eiseley also is a prolific writer, both in and outside his professional field. He was one of the editors of a recent Wenner-Gren Foundation publication entitled *An Appraisal of Anthropology Today*. His short stories and verse have appeared in popular magazines. At present he is at work, under commission of the American Philosophical Society, on a bibliography of Darwin to be published for the Society in celebration of the centenary of the *Origin of Species* in 1959. A central feature of this project is the assembling of material on evolution to shed light on the correspondence between Darwin and Sir Charles Lyell, which the Philosophical Society has purchased. Eiseley is also writing

a history of evolutionary thought for the Doubleday Anchor
Book series.

III. PAVLOV *by Jerzy Konorski*

In 1927, while Jerzy Konorski was still an undergraduate at the
University of Warsaw, Pavlov published his great work on the
conditioned reflex. Reading the book out of course, Konorski
was inspired to devote his talents to the new field which it
opened up. He soon realized that the Pavlov work did not take
into account the so-called voluntary movements and that these
could not be accounted for by the classical conditioned reflex.
With his colleague S. Miller, Konorski developed a program of
research which led to the concept of "Type II" or "instru-
mental" conditioning. Their work attracted Pavlov's attention,
and they spent several years working with him at his laboratory
in Leningrad. Returning to Warsaw in 1933, Konorski organized the Nencki Institute of Experimental Biology. He
carried on his work there until the devastation of the city by
the German invasion in 1939. Konorski and his colleagues re-
activated their institute on the heels of the German retreat,
first at a temporary seat in Lodz and now again in Warsaw.
His *Conditioned Reflexes and Neuron Organization,* published
in 1948, provoked harsh attack from orthodox Pavlovians. This
book outlines Konorski's approach to the task of establishing the
functional significance of the various parts of the cerebral cortex
by means of conditioned reflex methods. His work continues
actively along these lines today.

WILLIAM HARVEY

by Frederick G. Kilgour

And I remember that when I asked our famous Harvey, *in the only Discourse I had with him, (which was but a while be fore he dyed). What were the things that induc'd him to think of a* Circulation of the Blood? *He answer'd me, that when he took notice that the Valves in the Veins of so many several Parts of the Body, were so Plac'd that they gave free passage to the Blood Towards the Heart, but oppos'd the passage of the Venal Blood the Contrary way: He was invited to imagine, that so Provident a Cause as Nature had not so Plac'd so many Valves without design: and no Design seem'd more probable than that, since the Blood could not well, because of the interposing Valves, be sent by the Veins to the Limbs; it should be sent through the Arteries and Return through the Veins, whose Valves did not oppose its course that way.*

THE IRISH CHEMIST Robert Boyle reported this interview with William Harvey in his *Disquisition about Final Causes of Natural Things,* published 31 years after Harvey's death. It is the only recorded statement from Harvey of the clue that led him to his great discovery—an Alpine peak in the history of biology. This man who laid the basis of modern medicine is hardly known today except as a name. His classic work, written in Latin and titled *Exercitatio Anatomica de Motu Cordis et Sanguinis in Animalibus* (Anatomical Studies on the Motion of the Heart and Blood in Animals), is widely celebrated but little read. Both the man and the work are actually much more interesting than their conspicuous obscurity might suggest.

"Our famous *Harvey*" was born of yeoman stock at Folkestone in 1578; his father later became mayor of the city. Harvey was a schoolboy of 10 when the Spanish Armada sailed against England; he set up practice as a physician in London in the last year of Elizabeth's reign; he gave his first lecture on the circulation of the blood in 1616, the year that Shakespeare died. Like Shakespeare, Harvey left us his works but not very much about himself. Most of our knowledge about his person and character derives from the librarian and biographer John Aubrey, who wrote a "Brief Life" on him. Harvey, says Aubrey, was a very short man with a "little eie, round, very black, full of spirit." He was temperamental and had his eccentricities. As a young blood he wore a dagger in the fashion of the day and was wont to draw it on slight provocation. It is a matter of record that he married at the age of 26, but nothing is known about his wife or family life, except that he had no children. In his later years (he lived to the age of 79) Harvey liked to be in the dark, because he could think better, and he had underground caves constructed at his house in Surrey for meditation.

Harvey is known to have been a copious scribbler. He wrote hastily, and all but illegibly, in a mixture of Latin and English, and was a careless speller: in one place in his notes appears the word "piggg"—an unusually liberal number of "g's" even for seventeenth-century English. Aside from his classic *De Motu Cordis*, few of his writings survive. One reason is that he lost many of his papers during the Civil War of 1642, when rioters looted his house in London and destroyed his manuscripts while he was away in Nottingham with Charles I, to whom Harvey was Physician-in-Ordinary. Harvey later said this loss was the most crucifying he had ever experienced.

A dynamic little man, he spent his life in the ardent pursuit of learning, and he wrote at least a dozen treatises on various sub-

BERNARDA
BRYSON

jects, but these, like the manuscripts destroyed by the looters, were never published and none is now known to exist. Of his few published works perhaps the most important, next to *De Motu Cordis,* was *De Generatione* (On Reproduction), which made several valuable contributions to embryology.

His work on the circulation of the blood remains, however, his one great monument. It was remarkable not only as a history-making discovery but as a pioneering expression of the scientific method in biology. Harvey was a contemporary of Galileo, Kepler, Bacon and Descartes. The scientific revolution of the Renaissance, which swept away the system of classical philosophy and established the methods upon which modern science is based, found in him one of its earliest prodigies. Harvey was the first biologist to use quantitative methods to demonstrate an important discovery. To weigh, to measure, to count and thus to arrive at truth was such a new idea in the seventeenth century that even a man of Harvey's genius could do it only badly. But his application of quantitative procedures to biology ushered in the modern age for that science.

Harvey graduated from Cambridge University in 1597 and went to study medicine at the University of Padua, the greatest scientific school of the day. The anatomy and physiology of the heart, arteries, veins and blood then being taught was still mainly the system that had been constructed 14 centuries earlier by the Greek physician Galen. According to Galen, chyle (a kind of lymph) passed from the intestines to the liver, which converted it to venous blood and at the same time added a "natural spirit." The liver then distributed this blood through the venous system, including the right ventricle of the heart. Galen knew from experiment that when he severed a large vein or artery in an animal, blood would drain off from both the veins and the arteries. He realized, therefore, that there must be some connection between the veins and the arteries, and he believed he had found such a connection in the form of pores in the wall dividing the left side of the heart from the right. He argued that the venous blood oozed through these supposed pores to the left heart, was there charged with *vital spirit* coming from the lungs and thus took on the bright crimson color of arterial blood. According to the Galenic scheme, blood flowed to various parts of the body through both the veins and the arteries to supply the body members with nourishment and spirit. There was no real circulation or motive power; the blood in the vessels simply ebbed back occasionally to the heart and lungs for the removal of impurities.

To Galen's scheme two important modifications had been made by Harvey's time. Andreas Vesalius of Padua, the founder of modern anatomy, had announced in 1555 that Galen's "pores" did not exist, and Vesalius' successor Realdo Colombo had discovered the system whereby the blood flows from the right side of the heart through the pulmonary arteries to the lungs and thence via the pulmonary veins to the left side of the heart. He showed by animal experiments that the pulmonary veins contain arterial blood, not "vital spirit." The second important discovery, made by Fabricius ab Aquapendente at Padua, had been that the veins possess valves—"little doors," he called them. Fabricius did not realize their function; he suggested, following Galen's ideas, that they were designed to slow the flow of blood into the extremities.

Harvey, with his doctor's degree from Padua, returned to England in 1602. Whether or not he had begun to form his notion of the circulation of the blood when he left Padua we do not know. In any event, he proceeded to practice medicine in London and rose rapidly in his profession. In 1615 the Royal College of Physicians, of which he was a fellow, honored him with the lifetime post of Lumleian Lecturer. In his first series of Lumleian lectures, given in 1616, he began to describe the circulation of the blood. We have his 98-page set of notes outlining these lectures. In them he describes some of his experiments, including the one which satisfied him "that so Provident a Cause as Nature had not Plac'd so many Valves without design" and which gave him the idea of the circulation, as he later told Robert Boyle.

The notes make clear that Harvey was already convinced that the blood circulates through the body and that the heart is its pumping engine. He concluded his 1616 series of lectures with this statement:

"It is proved by the structure of the heart that the blood is continuously transferred through the lungs into the aorta, as by two clacks of a water bellows to raise water. It is proved by the ligature that there is a passage of blood from the arteries to the veins. It is therefore demonstrated that the continuous movement of the blood in a circle is brought about by the beat of the heart. Is this for the sake of nutrition, or the better preservation of the blood and members by the infusion of heat, the blood in turn being cooled by heating the members and heated by the heart?"

Twelve years later Harvey, having carried out further experiments to prove his circulation theory, published *De Motu Cordis*. It is a book of only 72 pages. The volume contains two dedications (to King Charles and to Doctor Argent, President of the Royal College), an introduction and 17 brief chapters presenting his arguments.

After giving in Chapter I his reasons for writing the book (among them the desire to protect himself from ridicule), Harvey devoted the next four chapters to a remarkable analysis of the movements of the heart, arteries and auricles and an equally remarkable analysis of the function of the heart. He had despaired at first of ever understanding the movement of the heart in warm-blooded animals, because its pulsation was so rapid, but he had found that he could analyze heart motions in cold-blooded animals and in dying warm-blooded ones. So far as direct inspection is concerned, such observations are still our principal sources for knowledge of heart motion.

Harvey gave the first clear statement of the apex beat, of the muscular character of the heart, and of the origin of the heart-beat in the right auricle and its conduction to the other auricle and the ventricles. He also demonstrated that the pulse in the arteries is due to the impact of blood ejected by the heart, as when "one blows into a glove," an image he used first in his 1616 lectures. Harvey correctly concluded that "the principal function of the heart is the transmission and pumping of the blood through the arteries to the extremities of the body."

He went on to review the movement of the blood from the right side of the heart through the lungs to the left side of the heart, as Colombo had described it, and to demonstrate how the blood passes from the left heart through the arteries to the extremities and thence via the veins back to the right heart. This section of the book contains the core of Harvey's discovery. He employed three "propositions" to prove that the blood must circulate: (1) the amount of blood transmitted from the veins to the arteries is so great that all the blood in the body must pass through the heart in a short time; this quantity could not be produced by the food consumed, as Galen held; (2) the amount of blood going to the extremities is much greater than needed for the nutrition of the body; (3) the blood continuously returns to the heart from the extremities through the veins.

It was to prove the first proposition that Harvey engaged in his famous quantitative work—the determination of the volume of blood pumped by the heart. To make this calculation, he had to measure the amount of blood that the heart ejects with each beat and to establish the pulse rate. The measurement of cardiac output is a tough problem, and even today there are wide variations in the measurements obtained by the various methods. But Harvey got a figure that is only one eighteenth of the lowest estimate used today. How could he have arrived at such a ridiculously incorrect figure and at the same time have used it successfully to demonstrate such an important discovery?

Harvey based his reckoning on the fact that in a cadaver he once examined the left ventricle of the heart held more than two ounces of blood. (It must have been a dilated heart.) He assumed that between contractions the ventricle might hold as little as an ounce and a half. Assuming further that the ventricle with each contraction ejects, "a fourth, a fifth, sixth or only an eighth" of its contents (we now think it ejects nearly all), he finally calculated that the cardiac output must be at least 3.9 grams per beat. According to a present-day estimate, it is actually in the neighborhood of 89 grams. Harvey can certainly be excused for not obtaining any close estimate of the output of the human heart, but he got virtually as poor results when he tried to measure the output of a sheep's heart. If he had severed a sheep's aorta and weighed the amount of blood ejected in one minute while counting the heartbeats for that minute, he could have obtained a reasonably accurate figure for cardiac output in sheep. But he never performed that obvious experiment.

Harvey also missed the mark widely in his other important measurement—the pulse rate. Somehow he counted it to be 33 per minute, about half the actual average rate, and although he obtained other values, he generally used this figure. We cannot explain this error on the ground that it is a difficult measurement to make; why he went so wrong will always be a mystery. With his two estimates—3.9 grams for cardiac output and 33 pulse beats per minute—he obtained a figure for the rate of blood flow which is one 36th of the lowest value accepted today. One of his calculations reads: "In half an hour the heart will make 1,000 beats, in some as many as two, three, and even four thousand. Multiplying the number of drams ejected by the number of beats there will be in half an hour either 3,000 drams, 2,000 drams, 500 ounces of some proportionate quantity of blood transferred into the arteries by the heart, but always a larger quantity than is contained in the whole body." In this summation, the lowest weight, 2,000 drams, equals 17.1 pounds, which is well in excess of the total of 15 pounds of blood contained by an average human body weighing 150 pounds.

Even with his faulty calculations, Harvey proved his main point: that each half hour the blood pumped by the heart far exceeds the total weight of blood in the body. This was a blow to the Galenic concept, for it was obvious that the food a man eats could not produce blood continuously in any such volume.

Less impressive was Harvey's demonstration of the second proposition: that the amount of blood going to the extremities is much greater than is needed for the nutrition of the body. He used no specific measurements and argued largely by inference. However, in this discussion he made the important point that the blood must pass from the arteries to the veins in the extremities. And he described here the experiment that had first suggested the circulation idea. By employing a bandage in such a way as to stop the flow in the veins while leaving the arteries open, he showed that the veins would swell but not the arteries. When he increased pressure enough to cut off the arteries as well, the veins did not swell. From these observations, Harvey reasoned correctly that the blood entered the extremities through the arteries and passed somehow to the veins. He later looked for the channels of connection but could not find them.

By another historic experiment Harvey proved his third proposition: that the blood flows in the veins toward the heart and not away from it, as the Galenic concept held. He showed that if one pressed a finger on a vein and moved the finger along the vein from below one valve to above the next, the blood thus pushed up the vein did not return to the emptied section. In short, the valves were one-way; the blood did not flow back and forth in the venous system.

What are the principal features of Harvey's discovery? The essential factors of the cardiovascular system which effect the circulation of the blood are the pumping heart, the passage of the blood from one side of the heart through the lungs to the other side and its subsequent passage through the arteries to every part of the body and back through the veins to the heart again. Harvey already knew of the passage through the lungs when he began his work; his great contribution was to demonstrate the circulation through the arteries and veins and to integrate it with the pulmonary passage, thus establishing one comprehensive system for the movement of blood through the body. There remained, of course, one final uncharted link: How did the blood pass from the arteries to the veins in the extremities in order to return to the heart? Thirty-three years after the appearance of *De Motu Cordis* the Italian anatomist Marcello Malpighi filled in that link by discovering the capillaries and so completed Harvey's scheme.

The direct contributions of Harvey's discovery to medicine and surgery are obviously beyond measuring: it is the basis for all work in the repair of damaged or diseased blood vessels, the surgical treatment of high blood pressure and coronary disease, the well-known "blue baby" operation, and so on. It is general physiology, however, that is most in his debt. For the notion of the circulating blood is what underlies our present understanding of the self-stabilizing internal environment of the body. In the dynamics of the human system the most important role is played by the fluid whose circulation Harvey discovered by a feat of great insight.

CHARLES DARWIN

by Loren C. Eiseley

In the autumn of 1831 the past and the future met and dined in London—in the guise of two young men who little realized where the years ahead would take them. One, Robert Fitzroy, was a sea captain who at 26 had already charted the remote, sea-beaten edges of the world and now proposed another long voyage. A religious man with a strong animosity toward the new-fangled geology, Captain Fitzroy wanted a naturalist who would share his experience of wild lands and refute those who used rocks to promote heretical whisperings. The young man who faced him across the table hesitated. Charles Darwin, four years Fitzroy's junior, was a gentleman idler after hounds who had failed at medicine and whose family, in desperation, hoped he might still succeed as a country parson. His mind shifted uncertainly from fox hunting in Shropshire to the thought of shooting llamas in South America. Did he really want to go? While he fumbled for a decision and the future hung irresolute, Captain Fitzroy took command.

"Fitzroy," wrote Darwin later to his sister Susan, "says the stormy sea is exaggerated; that if I do not choose to remain with them, I can at any time get home to England; and that if I like, I shall be left in some healthy, safe and nice country; that I shall always have assistance; that he has many books, all instruments, guns, at my service. . . . There is indeed a tide in the affairs of men, and I have experienced it. Dearest Susan, Goodbye."

They sailed from Devonport December 27, 1831, in H.M.S. *Beagle*, a 10-gun brig. Their plan was to survey the South American coastline and to carry a string of chronometrical measurements around the world. The voyage almost ended before it began, for they at once encountered a violent storm. "The sea ran very high," young Darwin recorded in his diary, "and the vessel pitched bows under and suffered most dreadfully; such a night I never passed, on every side nothing but misery; such a whistling of the wind and roar of the sea, the hoarse screams of the officers and shouts of the men, made a concert that I shall not soon forget." Captain Fitzroy and his officers held the ship on the sea by the grace of God and the cat-o'nine-tails. With an almost irrational stubbornness Darwin decided, in spite of his uncomfortable discovery of his susceptibility to seasickness, that "I did right to accept the offer." When the *Beagle* was buffeted back into Plymouth Harbor, Darwin did not resign. His mind was made up. "If it is desirable to see the world," he wrote in his journal, "what a rare and excellent opportunity this is. Perhaps I may have the same opportunity of drilling my mind that I threw away at Cambridge."

So began the journey in which a great mind untouched by an old-fashioned classical education was to feed its hunger upon rocks and broken bits of bone at the world's end, and eventually was to shape from such diverse things as bird beaks and the fused wing-cases of island beetles a theory that would shake the foundations of scientific thought in all the countries of the earth.

The intellectual climate from which Darwin set forth on his historic voyage was predominantly conservative. Insular England had been horrified by the excesses of the French Revolution and was extremely wary of emerging new ideas which it attributed to "French atheists." Religious dogma still held its powerful influence over natural science. True, the seventeenth-century notion that the world had been created in 4004 B.C. was beginning to weaken in the face of naturalists' studies of the rocks and their succession of life forms. But the conception of a truly ancient and evolving planet was still unformed. No one could dream that

196

the age of the earth was as vast as we now know it to be. And the notion of a continuity of events—of one animal changing by degrees into another—seemed to fly in the face not only of religious beliefs but also of common sense. Many of the greatest biologists of the time—men like Louis Agassiz and Richard Owen —tended to the belief that the successive forms of life in the geological record were all separate creations, some of which had simply been extinguished by historic accidents.

Yet Darwin did not compose the theory of evolution out of thin air. Like so many great scientific generalizations, the theory with which his name is associated had already had premonitory beginnings. All of the elements which were to enter into the theory were in men's minds and were being widely discussed during Darwin's college years. His own grandfather, Erasmus Darwin, who died seven years before Charles was born, had boldly proposed a theory of the "transmutation" of living forms. Jean Baptiste Lamarck had glimpsed a vision of evolutionary continuity. And Sir Charles Lyell—later to be Darwin's lifelong confidant— had opened the way for the evolutionary point of view by demonstrating that the planet must be very old—old enough to allow extremely slow organic change. Lyell dismissed the notion of catastrophic extinction of animal forms on a world-wide scale as impossible, and he made plain that natural forces—the work of wind and frost and water—were sufficient to explain most of the phenomena found in the rocks, provided these forces were seen as operating over enormous periods. Without Lyell's gift of time in immense quantities, Darwin would not have been able to devise the theory of natural selection.

If all the essential elements of the Darwinian scheme of nature were known prior to Darwin, why is he accorded so important a place in biological history? The answer is simple: Almost every great scientific generalization is a supreme act of creative synthesis. There comes a time when an accumulation of smaller discoveries and observations can be combined in some great and comprehensive view of nature. At this point the need is not so much for increased numbers of facts as for a mind of great insight capable of taking the assembled information and rendering it intelligible. Such a synthesis represents the scientific mind at its highest point of achievement. The stature of the discoverer is not diminished by the fact that he has slid into place the last piece of a tremendous puzzle on which many others have worked. To finish the task he must see correctly over a vast and diverse array of data.

Still it must be recognized that Darwin came at a fortunate time. The fact that another man, Alfred Russel Wallace, conceived the Darwinian theory independently before Darwin published it shows clearly that the principle which came to be called natural selection was in the air—was in a sense demanding to be born. Darwin himself pointed out in his autobiography that "innumerable well-observed facts were stored in the minds of naturalists ready to take their proper places as soon as any theory which would receive them was sufficiently explained."

Darwin, then, set out on his voyage with a mind both inquisitive to see and receptive to what he saw. No detail was too small to be fascinating and provocative. Sailing down the South American coast, he notes the octopus changing its color angrily in the waters of a cove. In the dry arroyos of the pampas he observes great bones and shrewdly seeks to relate them to animals of the present. The local inhabitants insist that the fossil bones grew after death, and also that certain rivers have the power of "changing small bones into large." Everywhere men wonder, but they are deceived through their thirst for easy explanations. Darwin, by contrast, is a working dreamer. He rides, climbs, spends long days on the Indian-haunted pampas in constant peril of his life. Asking at a house whether robbers are numerous, he receives the cryptic reply: "The thistles are not up yet." The huge thistles, high as a horse's back at their full growth, provide ecological cover for bandits. Darwin notes the fact and rides on. The thistles are over-running the pampas; the whole aspect of the vegetation is altering under the impact of man. Wild dogs howl in the brakes; the common cat, run wild, has grown large and fierce. All is struggle, mutability, change. Staring into the face of an evil relative of the rattlesnake, he observes a fact "which appears to me very curious and instructive, as showing how every character, even though it may be in some degree independent of structure . . . has a tendency to vary by slow degrees."

He pays great attention to strange animals existing in difficult environments. A queer little toad with a scarlet belly he whimsically nicknames *diabolicus* because it is "a fit toad to preach in the ear of Eve." He notes it lives among sand dunes under the burning sun, and unlike its brethren, cannot swim. From toads to grasshoppers, from pebbles to mountain ranges, nothing escapes his attention. The wearing away of stone, the downstream travel of rock fragments and boulders, the great crevices and upthrusts of the Andes, an earthquake—all confirm the dynamic character of the earth and its great age.

Captain Fitzroy by now is anxious to voyage on. The sails are set. With the towering Andes on their right flank they run north for the Galápagos Islands, lying directly on the equator 600 miles off the west coast of South America. A one-time refuge of buccaneers, these islands are essentially chimneys of burned-out volcanoes. Darwin remarks that they remind him of huge iron foundries surrounded by piles of waste. "A little world in itself," he marvels, "with inhabitants such as are found nowhere else." Giant armored tortoises clank through the undergrowth like prehistoric monsters, feeding upon the cacti. Birds in this tiny Eden do not fear men: "One day a mocking bird alighted on the edge of a pitcher which I held in my hand. It began very quietly to sip the water, and allowed me to lift it with the vessel from the ground." Big sea lizards three feet long drowse on the beaches, and feed, fantastically, upon the seaweed. Surveying these "imps of darkness, black as the porous rocks over which they crawl,"

Darwin is led to comment that "there is no other quarter of the world, where this order replaces the herbivorous mammalia in so extraordinary a manner."

Yet only by degrees did Darwin awake to the fact that he had stumbled by chance into one of the most marvelous evolutionary laboratories on the planet. Here in the Galápagos was a wealth of variations from island to island—among the big tortoises, among plants and especially among the famous finches with remarkably diverse beaks. Dwellers on the islands, notably Vice Governor Lawson, called Darwin's attention to these strange variations, but as he confessed later, with typical Darwinian lack of pretense, "I did not for some time pay sufficient attention to this statement." Whether his visit to the Galápagos was the single event that mainly led Darwin to the central conceptions of his evolutionary mechanism—hereditary change within the organism coupled with external selective factors which might cause plants and animals a few miles apart in the same climate to diverge—is a moot point upon which Darwin himself in later years shed no clear light. Perhaps, like many great men, nagged long after the event for a precise account of the dawn of a great discovery, Darwin no longer clearly remembered the beginning of the intellectual journey which had paralleled so dramatically his passage on the seven seas. Perhaps there had never been a clear beginning at all—only a slowly widening comprehension until what had been seen at first mistily and through a veil grew magnified and clear.

The paths to greatness are tricky and diverse. Sometimes a man's weaknesses have as much to do with his rise as his virtues. In Darwin's case it proved to be a unique combination of both. He had gathered his material by a courageous and indefatigable pursuit of knowledge that took him through the long vicissitudes of a voyage around the world. But his great work was written in sickness and seclusion. When Darwin reached home after the voyage of the *Beagle,* he was an ailing man, and he remained so to the end of his life. Today we know that this illness was in some degree psychosomatic, that he was anxiety-ridden, subject to mysterious headaches and nausea. Shortly after his voyage Darwin married his cousin Emma Wedgwood, granddaughter of the founder of the great pottery works, and isolated himself and his family in a little village in Kent. He avoided travel like the plague, save for brief trips to watering places for his health. His seclusion became his strength and protected him; his very fears and doubts of himself resulted in the organization of that enormous battery of facts which documented the theory of evolution as it had never been documented before.

Let us examine the way in which Darwin developed his great theory. The nature of his observations has already been indicated —the bird beaks, the recognition of variation and so on. But it is an easier thing to perceive that evolution has come about than to identify the mechanism involved in it. For a long time this problem frustrated Darwin. He was not satisfied with vague references to climatic influence or the inheritance of acquired characters. Finally he reached the conclusion that since variation in individual characteristics existed among the members of any species, selection of some individuals and elimination of others must be the key to organic change.

This idea he got from the common recognition of the importance of selective breeding in the improvement of domestic plants and livestock. He still did not understand, however, what selective force could be at work in wild nature. Then in 1838 he chanced to read Thomas Malthus, and the solution came to him. Malthus had written in 1798 a widely read population study in which he pointed out that the human population tended to increase faster than its food supply, precipitating in consequence a struggle for existence.

Darwin applied this principle to the whole world of organic life and argued that the struggle for existence under changing environmental conditions was what induced alterations in the physical structure of organisms. To put it in other words, fortuitous and random variations occurred in living things. The struggle for life perpetuated advantageous variations by means of heredity. The weak and unfit were eliminated and those with the best heredity for any given environment were "selected" to be the parents of the next generation. Since neither life nor climate nor geology ever ceased changing, evolution was perpetual. No organ and no animal was ever in complete equilibrium with its surroundings.

This, briefly stated, is the crux of the Darwinian argument. Facts which had been known before Darwin but had not been recognized as parts of a single scheme—variation, inheritance of variation, selective breeding of domestic plants and animals, the struggle for existence—all suddenly fell into place as "natural selection," as "Darwinism."

While he developed his theory and marshaled his data Darwin remained in seclusion and retreat, hoarding the secret of his discovery. For 22 years after the *Beagle*'s return he published not one word beyond the bare journal of his trip (later titled *A Naturalist's Voyage around the World*) and technical monographs on his observations.

Let us not be misled, however, by Darwin's seclusiveness and illness. No more lovable or sweet-tempered invalid ever lived. Visitors, however beloved, always aggravated his illness, but instead of the surly misanthropy which afflicts most people under similar circumstances, the result in Darwin's case was merely nights of sleeplessness. Throughout the long night hours his restless mind went on working with deep concentration; more than once, walking alone in the dark hours of winter, he met the foxes trotting home at dawn.

Darwin's gardener is said to have responded once to a visitor who inquired about his master's health: "Poor man, he just stands and stares at a yellow flower for minutes at a time. He would be better off with something to do." Darwin's work was of an intangible nature which eluded people around him. Much of it consisted in just such standing and staring as his gardener reported. It was a kind of magic at which he excelled. On a visit to the Isle of Wight he watched thistle seed wafted about on offshore winds and formulated theories of plant dispersal. Sometimes he engaged in activities which his good wife must surely have struggled to keep from reaching the neighbors. When a friend sent him a half ounce of locust dung from Africa, Darwin triumphantly grew seven plants from the specimen. "There is no error," he assured Lyell, "for I dissected the seeds out of the middle of the pellets." To discover how plant seeds traveled, Darwin would go all the way down a grasshopper's gullet, or worse, without embarrassment. His eldest son, Francis, spoke amusedly of his father's botanical experiments: "I think he personified each seed as a small demon trying to elude him by getting into the wrong heap, or jumping away all together; and this gave to the work the excitement of a game."

The point of his game Darwin kept largely to himself, waiting until it should be completely finished. He piled up vast stores of data and dreamed of presenting his evolution theory in a definitive, monumental book, so large that it would certainly have fallen dead and unreadable from the press. In the meantime, Robert Chambers, a bookseller and journalist, wrote and brought out anonymously a modified version of Lamarckian evolution, under the title *Vestiges of the Natural History of Creation*. Amateurish in some degree, the book drew savage onslaughts from the critics, including Thomas Huxley, but it caught the public fancy and was widely read. It passed through numerous editions both in England and America—evidence that *sub rosa* there was a good deal more interest on the part of the public in the "development hypothesis," as evolution was then called, than the fulminations of critics would have suggested.

Throughout this period Darwin remained stonily silent. Many explanations of his silence have been ventured by his biographers: that he was busy accumulating materials; that he did not wish to affront Fitzroy; that the attack on the *Vestiges* had intimidated him; that he thought it wise not to write upon so controversial a subject until he had first acquired a reputation as a professional naturalist of the first rank. Primarily, however, the basic reason lay in his personality—a nature reluctant to face the storm that publication would bring about his ears. It was pleasanter to procrastinate, to talk of the secret to a few chosen companions such as Lyell and the great botanist Joseph Hooker.

The Darwin family had been well-to-do since the time of grandfather Erasmus. Charles was independent, in a position to devote all his energies to research and under no academic pressure to publish in haste.

"You will be anticipated," Lyell warned him. "You had better publish." That was in the spring of 1856. Darwin promised, but again delayed. We know that he left instructions for his wife to see to the publication of his notes in the event of his death. It was almost as if present fame or notoriety were more than he could bear. At all events he continued to delay, and this situation might very well have continued to the end of his life, had not Lyell's warning suddenly come true and broken his pleasant dream.

Alfred Russel Wallace, a comparatively unknown, youthful naturalist, had divined Darwin's great secret in a moment of fever-ridden insight while on a collecting trip in Indonesia. He, too, had put together the pieces and gained a clear conception of the scheme of evolution. Ironically enough, it was to Darwin, in all innocence, that he sent his manuscript for criticism in June of 1858. He sensed in Darwin a sympathetic and traveled listener.

Darwin was understandably shaken. The work which had been so close to his heart, the dream to which he had devoted 20 years, was a private secret no longer. A newcomer threatened his priority. Yet Darwin, wanting to do what was decent and ethical, had been placed in an awkward position by the communication. His first impulse was to withdraw totally in favor of Wallace. "I would far rather burn my whole book," he insisted, "than that he or any other man should think that I had behaved in a paltry spirit." It is fortunate for science that before pursuing his quixotic course Darwin turned to his friends Lyell and Hooker, who knew the many years he had been laboring upon his *magnum opus.* The two distinguished scientists arranged for the delivery of a short summary by Darwin to accompany Wallace's paper before the Linnaean Society. Thus the theory of the two men was announced simultaneously.

The papers drew little comment at the meeting but set in motion a mild undercurrent of excitement. Darwin, though upset by the death of his son Charles, went to work to explain his views more fully in a book. Ironically he called it *An Abstract of an Essay on the Origin of Species* and insisted it would be only a kind of preview of a much larger work. Anxiety and devotion to his great hoard of data still possessed him. He did not like to put all his hopes in this volume, which must now be written at top speed. He bolstered himself by references to the "real" book—that Utopian volume in which all that could not be made clear in his abstract would be clarified.

His timidity and his fears were totally groundless. When the *Origin of Species* (the title distilled by his astute publisher from Darwin's cumbersome and halfhearted one) was published in the fall of 1859, the first edition was sold in a single day. The book which Darwin had so apologetically bowed into existence was, of course, soon to be recognized as one of the great books of all time. It would not be long before its author would sigh happily and think no more of that huge, ideal volume which he had imagined would be necessary to convince the public. The public and his brother scientists would find the *Origin* quite heavy going enough. His book to end all books would never be written. It did not need to be. The world of science in the end could only agree with the sharp-minded Huxley, whose immediate reaction upon reading the *Origin* was: "How extremely stupid not to have thought of that!" And so it frequently seems in science, once the great synthesizer has done his work. The ideas were not new, but the synthesis was. Men would never again look upon the world in the same manner as before.

No great philosophic conception ever entered the world more fortunately. Though it is customary to emphasize the religious and scientific storm the book aroused—epitomized by the famous debate at Oxford between Bishop Wilberforce and Thomas Huxley—the truth is that Darwinism found relatively easy acceptance among scientists and most of the public. The way had been prepared by the long labors of Lyell and the wide popularity of Chambers' book, the *Vestiges*. Moreover, Darwin had won the support of the great Hooker and of Huxley, the most formidable scientific debater of all time. Lyell, though more cautious, helped to publicize Darwin and at no time attacked him. Asa Gray, one of America's leading botanists, came to his defense. His codiscoverer, Wallace, as generous-hearted as Darwin, himself advanced the word "Darwinism" for Darwin's theory, and minimized his own part in the elaboration of the theory as "one week to 20 years."

This sturdy band of converts assumed the defense of Darwin before the public, while Charles remained aloof. Sequestered in his estate at Down, he calmly answered letters and listened, but not too much, to the tumult over the horizon. "It is something unintelligible to me how anyone can argue in public like orators do," he confessed to Hooker, though he was deeply grateful for the verbal swordplay of his cohorts. Hewett Watson, another botanist of note, wrote to him shortly after the publication of the *Origin*: "Your leading idea will assuredly become recognized as an established truth in science, i.e., 'Natural Selection.' It has the characteristics of all great natural truths, clarifying what was obscure, simplifying what was intricate, adding greatly to previous knowledge. You are the greatest revolutionist in natural history of this century, if not of all centuries."

Watson's statement was clairvoyant. Not a line of his appraisal would need to be altered today. Within 10 years the *Origin* and its author were known all over the globe, and evolution had become the guiding motif in all biological studies.

Summing up the achievement of this book, we may say today, first, that Darwin had proved the reality of evolutionary change beyond any reasonable doubt, and secondly, that he had demonstrated, in natural selection, a principle capable of wide, if not universal, application. Natural selection dispelled the confusions that had been introduced into biology by the notion of individual creation of species. The lad who in 1832 had noted with excited interest "that there are three sorts of birds which use their wings for more purposes than flying; the Steamer [duck] as paddles, the Penguin as fins, and the Ostrich (*Rhea*) spreads its plumes like sails" now had his answer—"descent with modification." "If you go any considerable lengths in the admission of modification," warned Darwin, "I can see no possible means of drawing the line, and saying here you must stop." Rung by rung, was his plain implication, one was forced to descend down the full length of life's mysterious ladder until one stood in the brewing vats where the thing was made. And similarly, rung by rung, from mudfish to reptile and mammal, the process ascended to man.

Darwin had cautiously avoided direct references to man in the *Origin of Species*. But 12 years later, after its triumph was assured, he published a study of human evolution entitled *The Descent of Man*. He had been preceded in this field by Huxley's *Evidences as to Man's Place in Nature* (1863). Huxley's brief work was written with wonderful clarity and directness. By contrast, the *Descent of Man* has some of the labored and inchoate quality of Darwin's overfull folios of data. It is contradictory in spots, as though the author simply poured his notes together and never fully read the completed manuscript to make sure it was an organic whole.

209

One of its defects is Darwin's failure to distinguish consistently between biological inheritance and cultural influences upon the behavior and evolution of human beings. In this, of course, Darwin was making a mistake common to biologists of the time. Anthropology was then in its infancy. In the biological realm, the *Descent of Man* did make plain in a general way that man was related to the rest of the primate order, though the precise relationship was left ambiguous. After all, we must remember that no one had yet unearthed any clear fossils of early man. A student of evolution had to content himself largely with tracing morphological similarities between living man and the great apes. This left considerable room for speculation as to the precise nature of the human ancestors. It is not surprising that they were occasionally visualized as gorilloid beasts with huge canine teeth, nor that Darwin wavered between this and gentler interpretations.

An honest biographer must record the fact that man was not Darwin's best subject. In the words of a nineteenth-century critic, his "was a world of insects and pigeons, apes and curious plants, but man as he exists, had no place in it." Allowing for the hyperbole of this religious opponent, it is nonetheless probable that Darwin did derive more sheer delight from writing his book on earthworms than from any amount of contemplation of a creature who could talk back and who was apt stubbornly to hold ill-founded opinions. In any case, no man afflicted with a weak stomach and insomnia has any business investigating his own kind. At least it is best to wait until they have undergone the petrification incident to becoming part of a geological stratum.

Darwin knew this. He had fled London to work in peace. When he dealt with the timid gropings of climbing plants, the intricacies of orchids or the calculated malice of the carnivorous sundew, he was not bedeviled by metaphysicians, by talk of ethics, morals or the nature of religion. Darwin did not wish to leave man an exception to his system, but he was content to consider man simply as a part of that vast, sprawling, endlessly ramifying ferment called "life." The rest of him could be left to the philosophers. "I have often," he once complained to a friend, "been made wroth (even by Lyell) at the confidence with which people speak of the introduction of man, as if they had seen him walk on the stage and as if in a geological sense it was more important than the entry of any other mammifer."

Darwin's fame as the author of the theory of evolution has tended to obscure the fact that he was, without doubt, one of the great field naturalists of all time. His capacity to see deep problems in simple objects is nowhere better illustrated than in his study of movement in plants, published some two years before his death. He subjected twining plants, previously little studied, to a series of ingenious investigations of pioneer importance in experimental botany. Perhaps Darwin's intuitive comparison of plants to animals accounted for much of his success in this field. There is an entertaining story that illustrates how much more perceptive than his contemporaries he was here. To Huxley and another visitor, Darwin was trying to explain the remarkable behavior of *Drosera*, the sundew plant, which catches insects with grasping, sticky hairs. The two visitors listened to Darwin as one might listen politely to a friend who is slightly "touched." But as they watched the plant, their tolerant poise suddenly vanished and Huxley cried out in amazement: "Look, it *is* moving!"

As one surveys the long and tangled course that led to Darwin's great discovery, one cannot but be struck by the part played in it by oceanic islands. It is a part little considered by the general public today. The word "evolution" is commonly supposed to stand for something that occurred in the past, something involving fossil apes and dinosaurs, something pecked out of the rocks of eroding mountains—a history of the world largely demonstrated and proved by the bone hunter. Yet, paradoxically, in Darwin's time it was this very history that most cogently challenged the evolutionary point of view. Paleontology was not nearly so extensively developed as today, and the record was notable mainly for its gaps. "Where are the links?" the critics used to rail at Darwin. "Where are the links between man and ape—between your lost land animal and the whale? Show us the fossils; prove your case." Darwin could only repeat: "This is the most obvious and gravest objection which can be urged against my theory. The explanation lies, as I believe, in the extreme imperfection of the geological record." The evidence for the continuity of life must be found elsewhere. And it was the oceanic islands that finally supplied the clue.

Until Darwin turned his attention to them, it appears to have been generally assumed that island plants and animals were simply marooned evidences of a past connection with the nearest continent. Darwin, however, noted that whole classes of continental life were absent from the islands; that certain plants which were herbaceous (nonwoody) on the mainland had developed into trees on the islands; that island animals often differed from their counterparts on the mainland.

Above all, the fantastically varied finches of the Galápagos particularly amazed and puzzled him. The finches diverged mainly in their beaks. There were parrot-beaks, curved beaks for probing flowers, straight beaks, small beaks—beaks for every conceivable purpose. These beak variations existed nowhere but on the islands; they must have evolved there. Darwin had early observed: "One might really fancy that, from an original paucity of birds in this archipelago, one species had been taken and modified for different ends." The birds had become transformed, through the struggle for existence on their little islet, into a series of types suited to particular environmental niches where, properly adapted, they could obtain food and survive. As the ornithologist David Lack had remarked: "Darwin's finches form a little world of their own, but one which intimately reflects the world as a whole."

Darwin's recognition of the significance of this miniature world, where the forces operating to create new beings could be plainly seen, was indispensable to his discovery of the origin of species. The island worlds reduced the confusion of continental life to more simple proportions; one could separate the factors involved with greater success. Over and over Darwin emphasized the importance of islands in his thinking. Nothing would aid natural history more, he contended to Lyell, "than careful collecting and investigating of *all the productions* of the most isolated islands. . . . Every sea shell and insect and plant is of value from such spots."

Darwin was born in precisely the right age even in terms of the great scientific voyages. A little earlier the story the islands had to tell could not have been read; a little later much of it began to be erased. Today all over the globe the populations of these little worlds are vanishing, many without ever having been seriously investigated. Man, breaking into their isolation, has brought with him cats, rats, pigs, goats, weeds and insects from the continents. In the face of these hardier, tougher, more aggressive competitors, the island faunas—the rare, the antique, the strange, the beautiful—are vanishing without a trace. The giant Galápagos tortoises are almost extinct, as is the land lizard with which Darwin played. Some of the odd little finches and rare plants have gone or will go. On the island of Madagascar our own remote relatives, the lemurs, which have radiated into many curious forms, are now being exterminated through the destruction of the forests. Even that continental island Australia is suffering from the decimation wrought by man. The Robinson Crusoe worlds where small castaways could create existences idyllically remote from the ravening slaughter of man and his associates are about to pass away forever. Every such spot is now a potential air base where the cries of birds are drowned in the roar of jets, and the crevices once frequented by bird life are flattened into the long runways of the bombers. All this would not have surprised Darwin, one would guess.

Of Darwin's final thoughts in the last hours of his life in 1882, when he struggled with a weakening heart, no record remains. One cannot but wonder whether this man who had no faith in paradise may not have seen rising on his dying sight the pounding surf and black slag heaps of the Galápagos, those islands called by Fitzroy "a fit shore for Pandemonium." None would ever see them again as Darwin had seen them—smoldering sullenly under the equatorial sun and crawling with uncertain black reptiles lost from some earlier creation. Once he had cried out suddenly in anguish: "What a book a devil's chaplain might write on the clumsy, wasteful, blundering, low and horribly cruel works of nature!" He never spoke or wrote in quite that way again. It was more characteristic of his mind to dwell on such memories as that Edenlike bird drinking softly from the pitcher held in his hand. When the end came, he remarked with simple dignity, "I am not in the least afraid of death."

It was in that spirit he had ventured upon a great voyage in his youth. It would suffice him for one more journey.

PAVLOV

by Jerzy Konorski

IVAN PETROVICH PAVLOV, the great Russian physiologist, was one of those rare personages in science whose work is known in every country during his own time. Indeed, the character of his fame reminds one a little of the Pavlov dog whose mouth always watered at the sound of a bell: the mention of Pavlov's name instantly evokes in every literate person's mind the great contribution with which he is inseparably associated—"the conditioned reflex."

Pavlov's work left imperishable marks on physiology, neurology and psychology. Despite his wide fame, however, he was not intimately known outside his own country. Obviously one cannot attempt to give a comprehensive review of his work in a single article; there will be set down here simply some personal recollections of Pavlov, and an estimate of some of his most important researches.

Pavlov was a man with obvious natural gifts—a brilliant mind, an incomparable memory, boundless energy and immeasurable enthusiasm—but with all that he remained to the end of his life a transparently simple human being. His laboratory in Leningrad when I worked under him was a tumultuous beehive. Pavlov was then over 80 years old; nonetheless he still possessed a vast enthusiasm for scientific investigation which he communicated to all those around him. He was the moving spirit in most of the laboratory's projects, and he would greet the successful completion of an experiment with a dance of joy. His laboratory was operated like a town meeting; on Wednesdays his several dozen scientific associates gathered to discuss and argue their problems.

Pavlov, who had a gift for dramatic narrative, fascinated his colleagues. He fought tooth and nail for his ideas against all arguments; but after he had cooled down he was quick to admit his error if his opponent turned out to be right.

There is a story about Pavlov that illustrates amusingly his general attitude toward his work. During his early studies of the digestive system, he found that hydrochloric acid, when supplied to an animal's duodenum, caused the pancreas to secrete juice. Pavlov believed that the acid acted through some mechanism in the nervous system to produce this result. Some time later, however, the British physiologists Sir William Bayliss and Ernest H. Starling showed that the pancreatic secretion was initiated by a hormone mechanism: when the mucous membrane of the duodenum was stimulated by hydrochloric acid, it produced a hormone, secretin, which then acted on the pancreas. Pavlov at first pronounced this result incredible. When, having repeated the Bayliss-Starling experiments himself, he found that their conclusion was indeed correct, he exclaimed wrathfully, not in envy but in astonishment and self-reproach: "So we're not the only ones to make discoveries!"

Pavlov was born in 1849 in the provincial town of Ryazan, in central Russia. He was the son of an Orthodox village priest, and inevitably was educated in a religious seminary. But he soon found that his interests lay elsewhere, and he transferred to the Faculty of Natural Sciences in St. Petersburg University. He went on to study medicine in the Military Medical Academy, graduating in 1879. While still a student, he began his first researches in the physiology of blood circulation. He was appointed to the staff of the Clinic for Internal Diseases. The head of the clinic entrusted Pavlov with the responsibility for organizing a physiological laboratory to combine medical theory with practice in the clinic. Except for a two-year period, 1884–86, during which Pavlov went to study with the German physiologist Carl F. W.

BERNARDA
BRYSON

Ludwig at Leipzig, he did most of his early work in this meager laboratory at the St. Petersburg clinic.

His facilities were of the most primitive kind. The laboratory was a small wooden building, hardly more than a shed. He had to finance his research largely out of his own very small salary. He had no regular assistants. Nevertheless, by his own uncommon energy, assiduity and self-sacrifice he made rapid and fruitful headway, and his work won him a recognition out of all proportion to the modesty of his laboratory. In 1890 he was appointed to the chair of pharmacology in the Military Medical Academy, and in 1891 he was placed in charge of the physiological laboratory at the Institute of Experimental Medicine which was then being established in St. Petersburg.

By the end of the nineteenth century Pavlov was generally recognized as one of the world's outstanding physiologists. In 1904 he was awarded the Nobel prize for his work on the physiology of digestion. In 1907 he was elected to the Russian Academy of Sciences, and later he became the director of the Academy's Physiological Institute, which post he retained to the end of his life. In the 1930s a biological station was built for him in Koltuszi, now called Pavlovo, near Leningrad. He died of pneumonia in February, 1936, at the ripe age of 87.

Omitting Pavlov's interesting but not pre-eminent early studies of the regulation of blood pressure, his lifework divided into two periods. From the 1880s to 1902, he devoted himself to detailed investigation of the functions of the alimentary tract. From 1902 until his death, he went on to explore a new branch of knowledge which he himself created—the physiology of higher nervous activity.

As is well known, Pavlov's research work on the secretory function of the alimentary tract became the lasting foundation of our present-day knowledge in this field. In these studies, as well as in his later investigations of the nervous system, he was guided by certain ideas which, while not entirely original with him, he perhaps developed most consistently.

The first of these principles was that the organism functions as an integrated whole, and that the investigation of separate organs in the artificial conditions of isolated experiments cannot provide an adequate idea of how those organs act in their normal situation. Hence Pavlov tried to carry out his physiological experiments in conditions approximating the normal as closely as possible. In his work on the alimentary tract he resorted to a number of ingenious operations to maintain the normal functioning of an animal's organs while exposing them to observation. For example, he developed a method of exposing the ducts of the salivary and pancreatic glands without removing the organs from the body. He learned how to isolate a part of an organ without detaching it from the nervous system. One of his typical operations was the so-called "Pavlov pouch." In this operation, performed on a dog, one part of the stomach is isolated and formed into a blind pouch, with an opening to the abdominal wall. The nervous network of the pouch is uninjured, so that its secretory function is an exact replica of the functioning of the rest of the stomach, to which food passes, and it can be examined with great precision.

Obviously to make such operations come off successfully and keep the animals healthy Pavlov had to develop aseptic operating conditions and facilities for proper care of the animals after the operation. Today the existence of such adjuncts is taken for granted, but in those days the idea was quite novel.

Pavlov's second guiding principle was what he called "nervism," meaning the hypothesis that all functions of the body were controlled by the nervous system. It must be remembered that in those days the study of endocrinology was only in its beginnings. Pavlov believed that the nervous system was the only mechanism regulating and integrating the organism's activity, and so in all his researches he concentrated on elucidating the role of the nerves. One of his most beautiful experiments was a set of operations on a dog's gastric system to investigate the mechanism of secretion by the stomach. He severed the dog's gullet from its stomach so that the food it ate would not pass into the stomach but fall outside the body. He also made a tubular opening into the stomach to examine its behavior. He found that even though no food actually entered the stomach, it still secreted gastric juice, being powerfully stimulated by the animal's chewing and other acts of eating. And Pavlov proved that this reaction was mediated by the vagus nerves, for if these nerves were cut, the gastric secretion elicited by the act of eating stopped immediately. Pavlov's devotion to the theory of the central role of the nervous system helps to explain his incredulity and astonishment at the later discovery by Bayliss and Starling that hormones also play a part in the process of digestion.

The third principle that strongly motivated Pavlov's work was his conviction that physiological experimentation was of great significance for practical medicine. This idea, accepted without question today, was not so universally recognized then; at any rate not, so far as I know, in Russia.

Pavlov's switch to the nervous system and the investigation of conditioned reflexes, which marked the second phase of his career, was a natural sequel to his work on the digestive system. During that work he had been impressed by the discovery that a dog secretes saliva and gastric juice not only as the result of direct action of the food on the mucous membranes of the mouth and stomach, but even in response to the mere sight of food, or to other signals heralding feeding. This indicated that gastric secretions, which Pavlov had considered a purely physiological phenomenon, might also have a psychological basis and be related to the dog's experiences.

To a physiologist this was then a shocking idea. Up to that time physiology and psychology had been regarded as two entirely separate fields. Physiology was concerned solely with the innate responses of the body, mainly those controlled by the lower parts of the nervous system, while acquired or learned responses were the exclusive domain of psychology. Pavlov was confronted with a vexing problem. Must he now give up physiological methods and turn to psychology to investigate the dog's gastric behavior? This he could not bring himself to do, for he could see no way to verify theories in the realm of psychology by means of experiment.

After long hesitation and tormenting indecision, Pavlov found a characteristically imaginative and resolute answer to his dilemma: He would attack the psychological problem with purely physiological methods. After all, the secretion of saliva or gastric juice was exactly the same phenomenon whether it had a directly physiological origin or a psychic one. By applying physiological experiments to the investigation of acquired behavior, he might open up an enormous new field of study.

For several well-considered reasons, Pavlov chose the salivary glands as the focus of his experiments He knew from previous research that the salivary gland is a very sensitive and selective reacting mechanism. Moreover, its activity is much more restricted and specific than that of the motor organs, the chief effectors of acquired behavior. Above all, Pavlov judged that investigation of the salivary glands would involve much less danger of anthropomorphic and psychological interpretation of the results, an error he wished to avoid at all costs.

So Pavlov and his collaborators began their studies of acquired, or, as he himself called them, conditioned (in Russian "conditional") reflexes. The first experiments were made on "natural" conditioned reflexes, those established spontaneously in an animal in response to the sight and the smell of food, and so on. Only later, as the method was perfected, did the Pavlov group begin to develop conditioned reflexes to special signals, such as the beat of a metronome, the ringing of a bell, or the lighting of a lamp.

An important early finding in these experiments was that conditioning works two ways: it can inhibit as well as produce a response. When a conditioned stimulus ceases to be "reinforced," i.e., to be accompanied by the presentation of food, the conditioned reflex is extinguished. Pavlov showed that this extinction is effected by a special mechanism which he called internal inhibition.

During the first period of research the Pavlov group occupied themselves chiefly with the properties and interrelations of the excitatory and inhibitory conditioned reflexes. Later they extended the investigation to two new and important spheres. First, they showed by repetition of identical experiments on a great many dogs that animals vary greatly in the speed with which conditioned reflexes are formed, their permanence, the influence of inhibitory on excitatory reflexes, and so on. This provided a basis for the development of a classification of types of nervous system, a subject which has been worked at extensively in recent years. Attempts have even been made at the Biological Station in Pavlovo to show that an individual's type of nervous system may be inherited. Secondly, at the end of the second decade of research into conditioned reflexes the Pavlov investigators came quite accidentally upon the discovery of a neurotic state in dogs, caused by a conflict between excitatory and inhibitory reflexes.

The latter finding led to extensive investigation of so-called experimental neuroses, their pathogenesis, symptomatology and therapy. In these experiments the salivary conditioned reflexes proved to be a very sensitive and precise indicator both of normal and of pathological nervous conditions. Toward the end of Pavlov's life a psychiatric and a psychoneurological clinic were attached to his laboratories, and in these the attempt was made to analyze various cases of human neuroses by resort to the laws discovered in experiments on animals. Thus even in this long, difficult and fundamental inquiry Pavlov realized his lifelong hope of applying his experimental research on animals directly to human pathology.

I have summarized in general outline the main scientific achievements that Pavlov and the physiological school he created have given us. So far as his researches into the physiology of digestion are concerned, there is no need to stress their value. But it is more difficult to estimate the value and scope of the science of conditioned reflexes.

It is generally accepted that conditioned reflexes have played a very considerable part in the development of modern psychology, and today there are whole trends of psychological investigation based to a large extent on the achievements of the Pavlov school. But, since the psychological applications of conditioned reflexes have been developed mainly in the United States, I do not think that I, a European far removed from the centers of these trends, am competent to discuss them. As for the practical applications of the Pavlov achievements to the fields of psychoneurology, psychic hygiene and teaching, it is still too early to estimate their ultimate importance. And so I shall confine myself to surveying the significance of conditioned reflexes to neurophysiology itself.

Pavlov often called his teaching on conditioned reflexes "the true physiology of the brain." For him the study of conditioned reflexes was not an end in itself, but rather a means for understanding the central mechanism controlling them, namely, the cerebral cortex. Pavlov conceded that other methods of investigation of the activity of the cerebral cortex, such as electrical stimulation of the cortex in an anesthetized animal, could be very valuable, but he held that the true picture of this activity could be obtained only by studying the normal functioning of the organ, as in conditioned-reflex experiments. He was strengthened in this conviction by the fact that his view had been thoroughly and brilliantly justified in his work on the alimentary tract.

224

It is an interesting fact that Pavlov's attitude and methods were closely related to those of a great British contemporary, Sir Charles Sherrington. Both Sherrington and Pavlov based their physiological studies on work with quantitatively and qualitatively defined stimuli and their combinations. Both investigated the central mechanism of reflexes by examining the reactions of animals. But in Sherrington's case the preparation studied was a spinal animal; i.e., one with its higher brain centers surgically disengaged; whereas in Pavlov's it was an animal with the cerebral cortex intact. Sherrington studied the innate activity of the nervous system, while Pavlov was concerned with its acquired activity.

Within the last few decades, owing to the tremendous development of modern electrophysiological methods, the chief ideas put forward by the genius of these two men have gained increasingly secure experimental confirmation. At the time Pavlov and Sherrington were doing their work, the notion of the "nerve center," either in the spinal cord or in the cerebral cortex, was not much more than a useful abstraction created to establish a bridge between the stimulus and the response. Today, however, the nerve center is growing ever more concrete and tangible. Perhaps we are not far from that time when the beautiful fancy of Pavlov about *"seeing"* through the skull what is going on in the watching brain will become a reality.

PART 6 THREE MATHEMATICIANS

I. CHARLES BABBAGE
by Philip and Emily Morrison

Philip Morrison is associate professor of physics at Cornell University. He graduated from the Carnegie Institute of Technology in 1936, then studied theoretical physics under J. Robert Oppenheimer at the University of California, where he received his doctorate in 1940. When World War II broke out, Morrison left a lectureship at the University of Illinois to join the Metallurgical Laboratory of the University of Chicago, and later became a group leader at the Los Alamos Laboratory of the Manhattan District. He was a member of the group of physicists that managed the last phase of the fateful enterprise in the Marianas Islands and was one of the first to survey its consequences in Japan. In 1946 he demobilized to accept his present appointment at Cornell. There his activities have diversified to include "studies on the origin of cosmic rays, nuclear structure theory and, with no very hopeful progress, experiments on the nature of information transfer in cells." Emily Morrison, also a graduate of Carnegie Tech, is her husband's collaborator in the popularization of science, an interest they warmly share.

II. LEWIS CARROLL by Warren Weaver

Warren Weaver is vice president for the natural and medical sciences of The Rockefeller Foundation and director of its division of natural sciences and agriculture. This is his second career; he was first a mathematician at the University of Wisconsin, where he was chairman of the mathematics department until 1932. When he joined The Rockefeller Foundation Weaver declared that his objective in allocating its funds would be to greatly increase "the emphasis on biology and psychology, and on those special developments in mathematics, physics and chemistry which are themselves fundamental to biology." The flourishing state of American science in these fields today is in no small part the reflection of this policy. A vital and tirelessly enterprising man, Weaver has made the public affairs of science a major concern of his life. He has stirred such venerable and immovable institutions as the American Association for the Advancement of Science and the National Academy of Sciences into surprisingly active involvement in the promotion of public understanding of science and the defense of the freedom of science. At home in New Milford, Connecticut, he has what is perhaps the largest private collection of Lewis Carroll's works; it includes mathematical manuscripts as well as editions in many languages of *Alice's Adventures in Wonderland* and *Through the Looking-Glass*.

III. SRINIVASA RAMANUJAN
by James R. Newman

Better known as a writer on mathematics, through such works as *Mathematics and the Imagination* (page 1) and *The World of Mathematics* (page 109), James R. Newman is also author of *The Atomic Energy Industry, an Emperiment in Hybridization* and coauthor of *The Control of Atomic Energy*. These two works bespeak his experience as counsel to the Senate Committee on Atomic Energy in 1945–46 and as a contributor to the drafting of the original United States atomic energy legislation.

CHARLES BABBAGE

by Philip and Emily Morrison

Dᴜʀɪɴɢ the Festival of Britain in 1951 the center of the stage in a section of the Exhibition of Science at the South Kensington Science Museum was held by a glowing, streamlined computer called Nimrod. A visitor who wandered away from the main attractions might have found, tucked away in a remote gallery, a dust-covered ancestor of Nimrod. It is a complicated collection of wheels and rods labeled "Babbage's Difference Engine." Made in 1833, it was the work of a designer who consumed his years and his fortune in the attempt to build mathematical machines for which his age was not ready but which have now been realized.

Charles Babbage is a name known to some mathematicians today. Few of his own contemporaries recognized the value of his work, and he was held a crackpot by his London neighbors, who knew him chiefly as a crotchety crusader against street organ-grinders; indeed, when he died the London *Times* identified him in the first paragraph of its obituary as a man who had lived to almost 80 "in spite of organ-grinding persecutions." Today mathematicians recognize him as a man far ahead of his time. To an article on one of the modern United States calculating machines the British magazine *Nature* gave the title "Babbage's Dream Comes True."

Babbage was a versatile fellow. He wrote a book, *On the Economy of Manufactures and Machinery,* which foreshadowed what is now known as operations research; he made a determined campaign for government subsidy of scientific research at a time when research was still to a large extent a gentleman's hobby;

he published a widely used table of logarithms from 1 to 108,000; he plotted mortality tables and made a pioneering attempt to popularize life insurance; he designed machine tools; he proposed a number of inventions, from schemes for preventing railroad wrecks to a system of lighthouse-signaling; he wrote papers on physics, geology, astronomy and archaeology. But mathematical machines were his great lifelong passion.

Babbage was born in Devonshire in 1792, the son of a banker, from whom he eventually inherited a considerable fortune. Because of poor health he was educated by private teachers until he entered Trinity College at Cambridge in 1810. Already passionately fond of mathematics, he was discouraged to find that he knew more than his tutor. His most intimate friends at the University were John Herschel, son of the eminent astronomer William Herschel, and George Peacock. The three undergraduates entered into a compact to "do their best to leave the world wiser than they found it." In 1812, as their first step in this direction, they founded the Analytical Society, primarily to encourage English mathematicians to replace the Newtonian mathematical notation with the Leibnitz scheme used on the Continent. Newton denoted a rate of change by placing a dot over the symbol in question; Leibnitz, by placing a d in front of it. Babbage founded the Society, he once remarked, to advocate the "principles of pure 'd-ism' as opposed to the '*dot*-age' of the University." In spite of considerable opposition, the Society had a profound effect on the future development of mathematics in England.

Babbage, believing that he was certain to be beaten in the tripos by both Herschel and Peacock, transferred from Trinity College to Peterhouse in his third year, preferring to be first at Peterhouse rather than third at Trinity. He did, indeed, graduate first from Peterhouse, and went on to take his M.A. in 1817. Babbage, Herschel and Peacock continued to be friends after they left school. Each in his own way lived up to their joint

BERNARDA
BRYSON

compact, though their careers were very different. Peacock joined the ministry and soon became Dean of Ely. Herschel, after a brief apprenticeship at law, decided to follow his father into astronomy. Not only did he distinguish himself in astronomy, but he was knighted by the Crown, served as Master of the Mint, avoided all scientific feuds, and his biographers report that his life was full of serenity and innocence.

Babbage, in contrast, was to spend a life of bitter frustration on his mathematical machines. Toward the end of his life he remarked once to friends that he had never had a happy day in his life, and spoke "as though he hated mankind in general, Englishmen in particular, and the English government and organ-grinders most of all. Actually it was not as bad as that: for much of his life he was a most social and gregarious man with a sense of humor. Once, on a visit to France with Herschel, Babbage ordered two eggs for each of them for breakfast by telling the waiter *"pour chacun deux."* The waiter called out to the kitchen, *"Il faut faire bouillir cinquante-deux oeufs pour Messieurs les Anglais."* They succeeded in stopping the cook in time, but the story preceded them to Paris and quickly ran through several editions. Asked by a guest at a dinner party soon afterward whether he thought the tale of two young Englishmen who had eaten 52 eggs and a pie for breakfast was probable, Babbage replied soberly that "there was no absurdity a young Englishman would not occasionally commit." An Edinburgh professor who was once asked to dinner by Babbage reported that "it was with the greatest difficulty that I escaped from him at two in the morning after a most delightful evening." On his frequent trips to the Continent Babbage constantly sought the company of all sorts of people: members of the aristocracy, mathematicians, skilled mechanics.

Nonetheless, Babbage's obsession with his machines transformed him from a cheerful young man into a bitter old one. He was first seized with this obsession, according to the most credible of his own differing versions, as the result of a chance conversation with his friend Herschel. The latter had brought in some calculations made for the Astronomical Society. In their tedious checking of the figures Herschel and Babbage found a number of errors, and at one point Babbage said, "I wish to God these calculations had been executed by steam." "It is quite possible," remarked Herschel. The more Babbage thought about it, the more convinced he became that it was possible to make machinery to compute and print mathematical tables. He set down a rough outline of his first idea, and made a small model consisting of 96 wheels and 24 axes, which he later reduced to 18 wheels and 3 axes. In 1822 he wrote a letter about his idea to Sir Humphrey Davy, the president of the Royal Society, pointing out the advantages of his "difference engine" and proposing to construct one for the government's use. The Royal Society reported favorably on his project, and the Chancellor of the Exchequer made a vague verbal agreement to underwrite the enterprise with government funds.

Babbage had expected the project to take three years, but he was constantly having new ideas about the machine and scrapping all that had been done, and at the end of four years he was not yet in sight of his goal. The government built him a fireproof building and workshops next to his home. After a visit by the Duke of Wellington himself to inspect the shops, it made a further liberal grant to continue the work. After a time Babbage and his very excellent engineer Joseph Clement had a "misunderstanding" about salary payments. Clement abruptly dissolved the workshop, dismissed his men and departed with all the tools, of which he was legally the owner, and all the drawings.

At this critical juncture Babbage had a brand-new idea: an analytical engine, which would be simpler to build, would operate more rapidly and would have far more extensive powers than the difference engine. He put the scheme enthusiastically to the government, asking whether he should continue with the difference engine or work on the new idea. For eight years he pressed for an official decision; at last he was advised that the government must regretfully abandon the project. The government had already spent £17,000 on it; Babbage had also spent a comparable amount from his own pocket. Now the unfinished difference engine, in which he had lost interest, was deposited in the Museum of King's College, London; eventually the bones of his dream went to the South Kensington Museum, where they are now.

For several years Babbage worked on his analytical engine, using his own funds. Then he dropped it and decided to design a second difference engine, which would include all the improvements and simplifications suggested by his work on the analytical engine. He again asked for government support, but the Chancellor of the Exchequer declined. Babbage bitterly denounced him as "the Herostratus of Science, [who] if he escapes oblivion, will be linked with the destroyer of the Ephesian Temple."

In the end Babbage never completed a working engine. His vision was greater than the means then available for achieving it. Babbage aimed at something higher than a mere desk calculator; he planned to make a machine that could compute lengthy mathematical tables and set them up directly in type. He remarked: "Machinery which will perform . . . common arithmetic . . . will never be of that utility which must arise from an engine which calculates tables."

His difference engine was to be based on the principle of constant differences. To illustrate the principle let us take a problem the engine was designed to solve, namely, to compute the squares of the successive numbers: 1^2, 2^2, 3^2, 4^2, and so on. The squares of all whole numbers, as far as we have the patience to go, can be obtained by the simple process of addition, with the use of the number 2 as the constant difference. We set up three columns. In the first we always set down the constant 2 (representing the second power). The second column starts with 1 and adds the constant 2 at each successive step. This sum is fed into the third column, which starts with 1, and then gives the answer. For example, 1 plus 2 plus the square of 1 gives 4, the square of 2; 3 plus 2 plus 4 gives 9, the square of 3; 5 plus 2 plus 9 gives 16, the square of 4; and so on. The table looks like this:

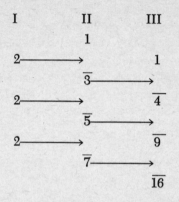

Now these simple operations can easily be performed by a machine, in much the same manner as the mileage indicator on an automobile, which adds by turning wheels with numbers on them. Babbage's first preliminary model for the difference engine, made with toothed wheels on shafts that were turned by a crank, could produce a table of squares up to five places. But the engine he proposed to build was to be on a much grander scale. Babbage's plans called for no less than 20-place capacity, up to differences of the sixth order, instead of only the second. Furthermore, each number as it appeared in the answer column was to be transmitted through a set of levers and cams to a collection of steel punches, which would stamp the number on a copper engraver's plate.

Mechanically all this was an enormous order. Imagine the variety and number of bolts and nuts, claws, ratchets, cams, links, shafts and wheels that would be needed, and remember that standardized machine parts, not requiring hand-fitting, were practically nonexistent! Babbage attacked the problem with great skill. He and his assistants designed each part with great care, providing supplementary mechanisms to minimize wear. He became an expert technician, developing tools which were superior for the time, and methods which foreshadowed some of the modern practices of instrument design. But perhaps the very care and thoroughness of the design were its greatest weakness. If the machine had ever been finished, it would have comprised some two tons of novel brass, steel and pewter clock-work, made as nothing before it to gauged standards.

What Babbage saw when he went on from the difference to the analytical engine idea was a really grand vision. He had early conceived a notion which he picturesquely described as "the Engine eating its own tail." By this he meant that the results appearing in the answer column might be made to affect the earlier columns, and thus change the instructions set into the machine. The analytical engine was to be capable of carrying out *any* mathematical operation. The instructions set into it would tell it what operations to carry out, and in what order. It would be able to add, subtract, multiply and divide; it would have a memory with a capacity of 1,000 50-digit numbers; it would draw on auxiliary functions such as logarithm tables, of which it would possess its own library. It would compare numbers, and act upon its judgments, thus proceeding on lines not uniquely specified in advance by the machine's instructions.

All or much of this, of course, has come to pass in modern computers. But Babbage was limited to trying to carry it out mechanically; his design did not envision any help from electrical circuits, to say nothing of electronic tubes. He proposed to do it all with punched cards—not the fast-shuffled Hollerith cards moving over handy electrical-switch feelers that we have today, but cards modeled on those used in the Jacquard loom. The instructions and numerical constants would be punched in the cards, as coded columns of holes. When the cards were fed into the machine, feeler wires would brush over them. Whenever the holes were in the appropriate pattern, the wires would pass through them and link together the motion of "chains" of columns and whole subassemblies. In this manner the machine would carry out all its operations. The great complexity of the system did not discourage Babbage, for he owned a colored portrait of Joseph Jacquard, woven in silk, in the weaving of which some 20,000 punched cards had been employed!

This is the barest sketch of the machine. Charles Babbage would be proud to see how completely the logical structure of his analytical engine has been adopted in today's big electronic computers.

Besides the concept itself, Babbage originated many mechanical devices of immediate practical use. Just as a team designing mathematical machines today soon becomes involved in a welter of problems about the properties of vacuum tubes and electronic circuits, so Babbage became deeply involved in the problems of the machine shop and the drafting room. He and his group invented a number of new tools to use with a lathe. Among the highly skilled workmen who worked in his shop was one J. Whitworth, later Sir Joseph Whitworth, Bart., who became the foremost manufacturer of precision tools in England. Babbage's drawings for his various machines, covering altogether more than 400 square feet of paper, were described by contemporary experts as perhaps the best specimens of mechanical drawing ever executed.

Babbage's operations-research book, *On the Economy of Manufactures and Machinery,* ran through several editions, was reprinted in the United States and was translated into German, French, Italian and Spanish. In it he took to pieces the manufacture of pins—the operations involved, the kinds of skill required, the expense of each process—and suggested improvements in the current practices. He proposed some general methods for analyzing factories and processes and finding the proper size and location of factories. Babbage treasured as one of the best compliments he ever received a remark by an English workman who told him: "That book made me think."

When he was past 70, Babbage wrote an autobiography which he titled *Passages from the Life of a Philosopher*. A peevish but not humorless book, it bears on the title page a staggering list of learned societies (chiefly foreign) after his name. His autobiography is as much a record of his disappointments as of his achievements. He wrote it, he said, "to render . . . less unpalatable" the history of his calculating machines.

But there was no need for apology. The conception of the engines was ingenious. His whole story bears witness to the strong interaction between purely scientific innovation, on the one hand, and the social fabric of current technology, public understanding, and support on the other. His great engines never cranked out answers, for ingenuity can transcend but not ignore its context. His monument is not the dusty controversy of books, nor priority in a mushrooming branch of science, nor the few wheels in a museum. His monument, by no means wholly beautiful but very grand, is the kind of research that is epitomized today by the big digital computers.

LEWIS CARROLL

by Warren Weaver

"Lewis carroll—wasn't he a first-class mathematician too?" This is a typical remark when the name of the author of *Alice in Wonderland* comes up. That Carroll's real name was Charles Lutwidge Dodgson and that his main lifelong interest was mathematics is fairly common knowledge. In fact, among his literary admirers there has long been current a completely false but unstoppable story that Queen Victoria read *Alice*, liked it, asked for another book by the same author and was sent Dodgson's very special and dry little book on algebraic determinants.

Lewis Carroll was so great a literary genius that we are naturally curious to know the caliber of his work in mathematics. There is a common tendency to consider mathematics so strange, subtle, rigorous, difficult and deep a subject that if a person is a mathematician he is of course a "great mathematician"—there being, so to speak, no small giants. This is very complimentary, but unfortunately not necessarily true. Carroll produced a considerable volume of writing on many mathematical subjects, from which we may judge the quality of his contributions. What sort of mathematician, in fact, was he?

The story of his academic career is quickly told. C. L. Dodgson was born in 1832 near Daresbury in Cheshire. His father was a clergyman, as had been his grandfather, great-grandfather and great-great-grandfather. He went up to Oxford in 1850 after six unhappy years in English "public" schools. At the end of 1852 he was given first class honors in mathematics and was appointed to a "studentship" (what we would call a fellowship) on condition that he remain celibate and proceed to holy orders. He took his B.A. with first class honors in the final mathematical school in 1854 and his M.A. in 1857. In 1855, at the age of 23, he was given a scholarship that paid the princely sum of 20 pounds a year, and was appointed senior student, or don, at Christ Church, and mathematical lecturer in the University. He lived, a bachelor, in college quarters in Tom Quad from 1868 until he died, 66 years old, in 1898. His academic life was enlivened, if you will pardon the expression, by the very Victorian activities of being made a sublibrarian in 1855; being ordained a deacon in 1861, and as a climax, when he was 50, being made curator of the Common Room—a sort of club steward.

The even tenor of this secluded life gave him ample time for writing, both as Charles Lutwidge Dodgson and as Lewis Carroll. There must be few authors who wrote so much and are remembered for so little. The standard bibliography of his work lists 256 items printed during his lifetime, and nearly 900 items in all. Of these 16 are books—about six for children and about 10 devoted to mathematics and logic. One has to say "about" because it is hard to tell whether some were intended for children or adults, whether others are mathematical or fantasy. In addition Carroll wrote nearly 200 pamphlets. About 50 related to minor academic quarrels at Christ Church, about 30 to word games, ciphers and the like, and more than 50 to wildly miscellaneous subjects: how to memorize dates, how to bowdlerize Shakespeare for young girls, how to score tennis tournaments, common errors in spelling, rules for reckoning postage, and so on.

Of the 256 items printed during his lifetime, 58 were devoted to mathematics and logic. If we consult these works for an estimate of Carroll's—or perhaps we should now say Dodgson's—stature as a mathematician, we discover that he was first of all a teacher, earnestly concerned with methods of instruction in elementary subjects. He wrote nearly two dozen texts for students in arithmetic, algebra, plane geometry, trigonometry and analytical geometry.

BERNARDA
BRYSON

Dodgson's largest and most serious work on geometry, *Euclid and His Modern Rivals,* gives us an insight into his approach to mathematics. It shows him as a militant conservative, dedicated to defending Euclid against any modern move to improve or change him in any way. Dodgson sought to prove in this book that Euclid's axioms, definitions, proofs and style simply could not be changed for the better. He even insisted that the order and numbering of Euclid's theorems be preserved. Dodgson skillfully ridiculed contemporary geometers who tried to restate Euclid's parallel axiom, and threw out all their attempts as "simply monstrous." (It is, however, worth noting that in a later book entitled *A New Theory of Parallels* Dodgson himself sought to replace the classical axiom by one of his own devising.)

Euclid and His Modern Rivals must be classed as amusing, ridiculously opinionated and scientifically unimportant. It reflects nothing of the growing realization among contemporary mathematicians that the axiom of parallels was not a self-evident fact of nature but an arbitrarily adopted and unprovable postulate. Non-Euclidean geometry, with its revolutionary consequences for mathematics and science, was not dreamt of in Dodgson's philosophy.

The bleak impression of the Reverend Dodgson created by his pedagogical works is pleasantly relieved when we turn to his other mathematical writings. He comes closer to the man we know as Lewis Carroll in, for example, a strange little book called *Pillow Problems*. Here Dodgson presents 72 problems—chiefly in algebra, plane geometry and trigonometry—all of which he had worked out in bed at night without pencil or paper. Dodgson suffered from insomnia, and while he was careful to point out that mathematics would put no one to sleep, he argued that it would occupy the mind pleasantly and prevent worry. It is characteristic of his severely pious attitude that he offered mathematical thinking, during wakeful hours, as a remedy for "skeptical thoughts, which seem for the moment to uproot the firmest faith . . . blasphemous thoughts, which dart unbidden into the most reverent souls . . . unholy thoughts which torture with their hateful presence the fancy that would fain be pure."

The problems in this book, while elementary, are nevertheless complicated enough to require real skill in concentration and visualization, if one is to solve them in his head. Here is an example:

"On July 1, at 8 a.m. by my watch it was 8 h. 4 m. by my clock. I took the watch to Greenwich, and when it said *noon*, the true time was 12 h. 5 m. That evening, when the watch said 6 h. the clock said 5 h. 59 m. On July 30, at 9 a.m. by my watch, it was 8 h. 57 m. by my clock. At Greenwich, when the watch said 12 h. 10 m. the true time was 12 h. 5 m. That evening, when the watch said 7 h., the clock said 6 h. 58 m. My watch is only wound up for each journey, and goes uniformly during any one day: the clock is always going, and goes uniformly. How am I to know when it is true noon on July 31?"

Triangle paradox leads to the impossible conclusion that 64 equals 65. The square at top, composed of 8 × 8 square units, is cut into the four parts shown. These may then be fitted together to form the rectangle of apparent area 5 × 13 square units, shown at bottom. Close inspection of the rectangle, however, shows that the angle of inclination of the hypotenuse of each triangle is not quite the same as that of the slanting side of the tetragon next to its shortest side. The extra "square" unit is actually spread out in the resulting open space between the upper and lower parts of the rectangle. Carroll generalized this paradox in an algebraic equation that yields the dimensions of all the possible squares that can be cut in the same paradoxical fashion; for example, squares with sides 21 and 55.

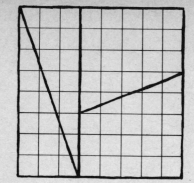

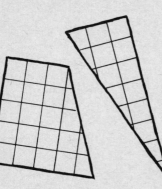

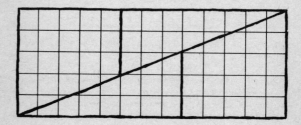

Dodgson's solutions of the problems in this collection are generally clever and accurate, but one of them ludicrously exposes the limitations in his mathematical thinking. The problem is: "A bag contains 2 counters, as to which nothing is known except that each is either black (B) or white (W). Ascertain their colors without taking them out of the bag." In his attack on this problem (which as stated cannot actually be solved) he makes two dreadful mistakes. First he assumes, incorrectly, that the statement implies that the probabilities of BB, BW and WW (the three possible constitutions of the bag) are ¼, ½, and ¼ respectively. Then he adds a black ball to the bag, calculates that the probability of now drawing a black ball is ⅔ and makes his second fatal error in concluding that the bag now must contain BBW. His line of reasoning thus leads him to the conclusion that the two original balls were one B and one W! This is good Wonderland, but very amateurish mathematics. It has been pointed out that if one applies Dodgson's argument to a bag containing three unknown balls (black or white), he can come out with the conclusion that it was impossible for there to have been three balls at all.

Dodgson's zest for mathematical puzzles produced a second little book which he called *A Tangled Tale*. The problems are named "Knots," and Knot I, for example presents this tangle: Two travelers spend from 3 o'clock until 9 o'clock in walking along a level road, up a hill, back down the hill, along the same road, and home. Their pace on the level is 4 miles per hour, uphill it is 3, and downhill 6 miles per hour. Find the distance walked, within a half hour, when they were on the summit.

My collection of Dodgson's manuscripts includes his two favorite puzzles, which he did not publish. One, called "Where Does the Day Begin?", considers the paradox that a man who travels westward around the earth at the same speed as the sun will find that though he started on a Tuesday, when he returns to his starting point the day is now called Wednesday. Where and when did the date change? Dodgson troubled many officials in government offices and telegraph companies with correspondence on this question, which he first posed in 1860. No one could answer it, of course, until the arbitrary International Date Line was established in 1884.

Dodgson's other favorite puzzle, named "The Monkey and Weight," was equally baffling to his contemporaries. A weightless, perfectly flexible rope is hung over a weightless, frictionless pulley. At one end is a monkey, at the other a weight which exactly counterbalances the monkey. The monkey starts to climb. What does the weight do?

In a restricted sense one cannot in detail say just what the weight will do unless he knows just what the monkey does— whether he pulls gently on the rope, jerks it hard, or whatever. But in a general sense, one can at once give a complete and simple solution. For under the assumed conditions of the problem, the rope exerts on the weight exactly the same force, at any moment, that it exerts on the monkey. However the monkey moves, the weight moves in exactly the same way.

In all of Dodgson's mathematical writing it is evident that he was not an important mathematician. As we have seen, in geometry his ideas were old-fashioned even for his time; in the probability problem cited he failed to grasp the principle of insufficient reason; in algebra he once wrote in his notes: "that $2(x^2 + y^2)$ is always the sum of two squares seems true but unprovable." It took him some time to recall the fact, familiar to any high-school student of elementary algebra that $2(x^2 + y^2) = (x + y)^2 + (x - y)^2$. In calculus his concept of infinitesimals was the wholly confused one that these were queer shadowy quantities which were noninfinite, nonfinite and also nonzero! His notes record such logical monstrosities as "infinitesimal unit," "infinity unit," "minimum finite fraction." He did not understand the basic concept of the limiting process in the calculus, as is indicated by the remark in his notes: "The notion that because a variable magnitude can be proved *as nearly equal* to a fixed one as we please, it is therefore equal, is to my mind unsatisfactory, as we only *reduce* the difference, and never annihilate it."

But before we write Dodgson off as a mathematician we must consider his contributions to formal logic. Nearly half of his mathematical writings were in this field.

The most important were *The Game of Logic,* published in 1886, and an expansion of it 10 years later into a longer and somewhat more serious book called *Symbolic Logic: Part I, Elementary.* In these works Carroll developed the use of a scheme which had first been introduced by the Swiss mathematician Leonhard Euler in 1761. It involves the representation of sets of similar propositions by spatial diagrams, together with a symbolic language for translating the diagrams back into verbal statements. The examples he invented for the use of the method were characteristically clever and amusing.

For instance, from the premises:

> All dragons are uncanny,
> All Scotchmen are canny;

he derived the comforting conclusions:

> All dragons are not-Scotchmen,
> All Scotchmen are not-dragons.

Another example of the fun he had with simple logic is the following (deduce a conclusion from the given premises):

> "It is most absurd of you to offer it! You might have known, if you had any sense, that no old sailors ever like gruel!"
> "But I thought, as he was an uncle of yours . . ."

"An uncle of mine indeed! Stuff!"

"You may call it stuff if you like. All I know is, *my* uncles are all old men: and they like gruel like anything"

"Well then, *your* uncles are—" [not sailors].

Amusing as Carroll's games of logic were, they were neither technically original nor profound. In his formal works on logic, as in geometry, he remained a resolute conservative. The British logician R. B. Braithwaite has pointed out that Carroll "did not accept the doctrine that has done so much to simplify traditional formal logic—the interpretation of a universal proposition as not involving the existence of its subject-term." Thus to Carroll the statement "All frogs that jump more than 20 feet croak loudly" necessarily implied a world of discourse within which there exist frogs that jump more than 20 feet.

Near the end of his life, however, Carroll did make one formal contribution to logic that has intrigued serious mathematicians. It was a problem containing a paradox which no one has conclusively resolved. A barbershop has three barbers, A, B, and C. (1) A is infirm, so if he leaves the shop B has to go with him. (2) All three cannot leave together, since then their shop would be empty. Now with these two premises, let us make an assumption and test its consequences. Let us assume that C goes out. Then it follows that if A goes out, B stays in (by premise 2). But (by premise 1) if A goes out, B goes out too. Thus our assumption that C goes out has led to a conclusion we know to be false. Hence the assumption is false, and hence C can't go out. But this is nonsense, for C obviously can go out without disobeying either of these restrictions. C can in fact go out whenever A stays in. Thus strict reasoning from apparently consistent premises leads to two mutually contradictory conclusions.

Some readers will wish, at this point, to say, "This barbershop and its three proprietors present a perfectly simple and clear situation, and I can make several obviously correct, and noncontradictory remarks about who goes out and who doesn't." This is all well and good. But it fails to meet the real point. The question is not "Can you say something noncontradictory?" The question is "What is specifically wrong with Carroll's argument?"

Bertrand Russell tried to get around the difficulty by saying that the statement "If A goes out then B must go out" is not contradictory to the statement that "If A goes out then B must stay in." He argues that they can both be jointly true on the condition that "A stays in." But this is the same as arguing that there is no disagreement between the statement by one politician that "If the Republicans win, things will improve," and the statement by another politician that "If the Republicans win, things won't improve." Neither politician would be satisfied by a logician's assurance that a Socialist victory would make both their statements true.

Other readers will wish to say, "Having assumed C out, one is then not free to go on and say, 'Then if A goes out, B stays in.'"

In the *Principia Mathematica* of Whitehead and Russell, one of the basic rules of procedure is the so-called Principle of Exportation. This may be stated in words: if p and q jointly imply r, then p implies that q implies r. As applied to our situation this Principle of Exportation permits one to proceed from the statement: "If C and A are both out, then B must be in" to the statement: "If C is out, then if A is out B is in."

Thus under the formal rules of what has now become classical logic, the second of these statements can, in fact, be "exported" from the former. Having reached this point, one either has to concede the Russell position (that "if A goes out then B must go out" is not contradictory to "if A goes out, then B must stay in"), or he has the paradoxical conclusions that C can't go out. Thus if one does not like the Russell escape, then he must find some way around the standard application of the Principle of Exportation.

The paradox has recently been answered in a more complicated and interesting way by two logicians in a paper published in the British Journal *Mind*. Still another approach has been proposed in the pages of the journal *Philosophy of Science* by Dr. Arthur W. Burks of the University of Michigan. Under the title "Dispositional Statements," he proposes a new (as I understand it) distinction between what he calls *causal implication* and *material implication*, the former of these not being "exportable" in the way that the latter is. This distinction thus furnishes an escape from the Barbershop Paradox, but only by what many would consider a pretty close shave.

As Braithwaite observes, "Carroll was ploughing deeper than he knew. His mind was permeated by an admirable logic which he was unable to bring to full consciousness and explicit criticism. It is this that makes his Symbolic Logic so superficial . . . and his casual puzzles so profound."

It would be hard to state better than Braithwaite does in these words the conclusion of the matter. The Reverend Dodgson was a dull, conscientious and capable teacher of elementary mathematics. Lewis Carroll was, in a tantalizingly elusive way, an excellent and unconsciously deep logician. But when he tried to approach logic head on, in a proper professional way, he was only moderately successful. It was when he let logic run loose that he demonstrated his true subtlety and depth. In fact, for a full measure of his stature as a logician we must look into Wonderland.

Alice and her companions have often been quoted in books on logic and philosophy. P. E. B. Jourdain, in his delightful book, *The Philosophy of Mr. B*rtr*nd R*ss*ll*, relies heavily on Carroll to demonstrate the key notions of logic. The sampling of Carroll's virtuosity which follows is taken from that book.

Logicians have for ages struggled with "theories of identity." Just when is one justified in saying "X is identical with Y," or "X is the same as Y," or "X is Y"? This matter was entirely clear to Carroll's little friends:

"The day is the same length as anything that is the same length as *it*." (*Sylvie and Bruno*)

"Bruno observed that when the Other Professor lost himself, he should shout. 'He'd be sure to hear hisself, 'cause he couldn't be far off.'" (*Sylvie and Bruno*)

Most logicians—and most of the rest of us for that matter—have to be very careful about precision in definitions and about the confusing overlap between what words denote and what they connote. But this was not a matter of confusion on the other side of the looking glass:

"Tweedledum and Tweedledee were, in many respects, indistinguishable, and Alice, walking along the road, noticed that 'wherever the road divided there was sure to be two finger-posts pointing the same way, one marked "TO TWEEDLEDUM'S HOUSE" and the other "TO THE HOUSE OF TWEEDLEDEE."'

"'I do believe,' said Alice at last, 'that they live in the *same* house! . . .'"

"'When *I* use a word,' Humpty Dumpty said, in rather a scornful tone, 'it means just what I choose it to mean—neither more nor less.'

"'The question is,' said Alice, 'whether you *can* make words mean different things.'

"'The question is,' said Humpty Dumpty, 'which is to be master—that's all.'"

Extremely subtle and intricate problems in modern mathematical logic hinge on the question whether there exists any such thing as a universal class of all possible things. But even the

Gnat had that one figured out. The Gnat had told Alice that the Bread-and-butter-fly lives on weak tea with cream in it:

> " 'Supposing it couldn't find any?' she suggested.
> " 'Then it would die, of course.'
> " 'But that must happen very often,' Alice remarked thoughtfully.
> " 'It always happens,' said the Gnat." (*Through the Looking-Glass*)

If existence is difficult to analyze, then nonexistence is perhaps even more elusive, but not to Alice:

> " 'I see nobody on the road,' said Alice.
> " 'I only wish *I* had such eyes,' the [White] King remarked in a fretful tone. 'To be able to see Nobody! And at that distance too! Why, it's as much as *I* can do to see real people, by this light!' " (*Through the Looking-Glass*)

> ". . . The Dormouse went on, . . . : 'and they drew all manner of things—everything that begins with an M——'
> " 'Why with an M?' said Alice.
> " 'Why not?' said the March Hare.
> "Alice was silent.
> ". . . [The Dormouse] went on: '—that begins with an M, such as mouse-traps, and the moon, and memory, and muchness—you know you say things are "much of a muchness"—did you ever see such a thing as a drawing of a muchness?'
> " 'Really, now you ask me,' said Alice, very much confused, 'I don't think——'
> " 'Then you shouldn't talk,' said the Hatter." (*Alice's Adventures in Wonderland*)

Those interested in the logic of modern science are by no means agreed as to the significance and validity of imaginary experiments, particularly if they involve unrealizable conditions. This is a matter which did not worry the White Queen:

"Alice laughed. 'There's no use trying,' she said; 'one *can't* believe impossible things.'

"'I daresay you haven't had much practice,' said the White Queen. 'When I was your age, I always did it for half-an-hour a day. Why, sometimes I've believed as many as six impossible things before breakfast.'" (*Through the Looking-Glass*)

So rare and so great were Carroll's true talents that we need not be condescending about the shortcomings of his formal mathematical writings. Carroll himself had no pretensions about them, and pronounced his own modest verdict in his diary. The very first entry in this two-volume record, which he wrote down on January 1, 1855, at the age of 23, says: "tried a little mathematics unsuccessfully."

SRINIVASA RAMANUJAN

by James R. Newman

THIS IS a brief account, from the scanty materials available, of
the poor Indian boy who became, as one eminent authority has
written, "quite the most extraordinary mathematician of our
time." Srinivasa Ramanujan died in India of tuberculosis on
April 26, 1920, at the age of 33. Except among mathematicians,
his name is almost unknown. He was a mathematician's mathematician, and as such, did not attract wide attention outside his
field. But his work has left a memorable imprint on mathematical
thought.

The late G. H. Hardy of Cambridge, a leading mathematician
of his time, was professionally and personally closest to Ramanujan during his fruitful five years in England. His obituary of Ramanujan and his notable course of Ramanujan lectures at Harvard
provide the bulk of the material to be found here; the rest comes
from a brief biographical sketch by P. V. Seshu Aiyar and R.
Ramachandra Rao to be found in Ramanujan's *Collected Works*.
There is enough here, however, to suggest the quality of Ramanujan's personality and genius.

Srinivasa Ramanujan Aiyangar, according to his biographer
Seshu Aiyar, was a member of a Brahman family in somewhat poor
circumstances in the Tanjore district of the Madras presidency.
His father was an accountant to a cloth merchant at Kumbakonam, while his mother, a woman of "strong common sense," was
the daughter of a Brahman petty official in the Munsiff's (or legal
judge's) Court at Erode. For some time after her marriage she
had no children, "but her father prayed to the famous goddess
Namagiri, in the neighboring town of Namakkal, to bless his

daughter with offspring. Shortly afterwards, her eldest child, the mathematician Ramanujan, was born on 22nd December 1887."

He first went to school at five and was transferred before he was seven to the Town High School at Kumbakonam, where he held a scholarship. His extraordinary powers appear to have been recognized almost immediately. He was quiet and meditative and had an extraordinary memory. He delighted in entertaining his friends with theorems and formulae, with the recitation of complete lists of Sanskrit roots and with repeating the values of *pi* and the square root of two to any number of decimal places.

When he was 15 and in the sixth form at school, a friend of his secured for him the loan of Carr's *Synopsis of Pure Mathematics* from the library of the local Government College. Through the new world thus opened to him Ramanujan ranged with delight. It was this book that awakened his genius. He set himself at once to establishing its formulae. As he was without the aid of other books, each solution was for him a piece of original research. He first devised methods for constructing magic squares. Then he branched off to geometry, where he took up the squaring of the circle and went so far as to get a result for the length of the equatorial circumference of the earth which differed from the true length by only a few feet. Finding the scope of geometry limited, he turned his attention to algebra. Ramanujan used to say that the goddess of Namakkal inspired him with the formulae in dreams. It is a remarkable fact that, on rising from bed, he would frequently note down results and verify them, though he was not always able to supply a rigorous proof. This pattern repeated itself throughout his life.

He passed his matriculation examination to the Government College at Kumbakonam at 16, and secured the "Junior Subrahmanyam Scholarship." Owing to weakness in English—for he gave no thought to anything but mathematics—he failed in his next examination and lost his scholarship. He then left Kumbakonam, first for Vizagapatam and then for Madras. Here he

presented himself for the "First Examination in Arts" in December 1906, but failed and never tried again. For the next few years he continued his independent work in mathematics. In 1909 he was married and it became necessary for him to find some permanent employment. In the course of his search for work he was given a letter of recommendation to a true lover of mathematics, Diwan Bahadur R. Ramachandra Rao, who was then Collector at Nelore, a small town 80 miles north of Madras. Ramachandra Rao had already seen one of the two fat notebooks kept by Ramanujan into which he crammed his wonderful ideas. His first interview with Ramanujan is best described in his own words.

"Several years ago, a nephew of mine perfectly innocent of mathematical knowledge said to me, 'Uncle, I have a visitor who talks of mathematics; I do not understand him; can you see if there is anything in his talk?' And in the plenitude of my mathematical wisdom, I condescended to permit Ramanujan to walk into my presence. A short uncouth figure, stout, unshaved, not overclean, with one conspicuous feature—shining eyes—walked in with a frayed notebook under his arm. He was miserably poor. He had run away from Kumbakonam to get leisure in Madras to pursue his studies. He never craved for any distinction. He wanted leisure; in other words, that simple food should be provided for him without exertion on his part and that he should be allowed to dream on.

"He opened his book and began to explain some of his discoveries. I saw quite at once that there was something out of the way; but my knowledge did not permit me to judge whether he talked sense or nonsense. Suspending judgment, I asked him to come over again, and he did. And then he had gauged my ignorance and showed me some of his simpler results. These transcended existing books and I had no doubt that he was a remarkable man. Then, step by step, he led me to elliptic integrals and hypergeometric series and at last his theory of divergent series not yet announced to the world converted me. I asked him what he wanted. He said he wanted a pittance to live on so that he might pursue his researches."

Ramachandra Rao undertook to pay Ramanujan's expenses for a time. After a while, other attempts to obtain a scholarship having failed and Ramanujan being unwilling to be supported by anyone for any length of time, he accepted a small appointment in the office of the Madras Port Trust.

But he never slackened his work in mathematics. His earliest contribution was published in the *Journal of the Indian Mathematical Society* in 1911, when Ramanujan was 23. His first long article was on "Some Properties of Bernoulli's Numbers" and was published in the same year. In 1912 he contributed two more notes to the same journal and also several questions for solution.

By this time Ramachandra Rao had induced a Mr. Griffith of the Madras Engineering College to take an interest in Ramanujan, and Griffith spoke to Sir Francis Spring, the chairman of the Madras Port Trust, where Ramanujan was employed. From that time on it became easy to secure recognition of his work. Upon the suggestion of Seshu Aiyar and others, Ramanujan began a correspondence with G. H. Hardy, then Fellow of Trinity College, Cambridge. His first letter to Hardy, dated January 16, 1913, which his friends helped him put in English, follows:

"Dear Sir,

"I beg to introduce myself to you as a clerk in the Accounts Department of the Port Trust Office at Madras on a salary of only £20 per annum. I am now about 23 years of age. [*He was actually 25—Ed.*] I have had no University education but I have undergone the ordinary school course. After leaving school I have been employing the spare time at my disposal to work at Mathematics. I have not trodden through the conventional regular course which is followed in a University course, but I am striking out a new path for myself. I have made a special investigation of divergent series in general and the results I get are termed by the local mathematicians as 'startling'. . . .

"I would request you to go through the enclosed papers. Being poor, if you are convinced that there is anything of value I would like to have my theorems published. I have not given the actual investigations nor the expressions that I get but I have indicated the lines on which I proceed. Being inexperienced I would very highly value any advice you give me. Requesting to be excused for the trouble I give you.

I remain, Dear Sir, Yours truly,

S. Ramanujan."

To the letter were attached about 120 theorems. Hardy commented on these:

"I should like you to begin by trying to reconstruct the immediate reactions of an ordinary professional mathematician who receives a letter like this from an unknown Hindu clerk.

"The first question was whether I could recognise anything. I had proved things rather like (1.7) myself, and seemed vaguely familiar with (1.8). Actually (1.8) is classical; it is a formula of Laplace first proved properly by Jacobi; and (1.9) occurs in a paper published by Rogers in 1907. I thought that, as an expert in definite integrals, I could probably prove (1.5) and (1.6), and did so, though with a good deal more trouble than I had expected. . . .

"The series formulae (1.1)-(1.4) I found much more intriguing, and it soon became obvious that Ramanujan must possess much more general theorems and was keeping a great deal up his sleeve. The second is a formula of Bauer well known in the theory of Legendre series, but the others are much harder than they look. . . .

"The formulae (1.10)-(1.13) are on a different level and obviously both difficult and deep. An expert in elliptic functions can see at once that (1.13) is derived somehow from the theory of 'complex multiplication,' but (1.10)-(1.12) defeated me completely; I had never seen anything in the least like them before. A single look at them is enough to show that they could only be written down by a mathematician of the highest class. They must be true because, if they were not true, no one would have the imagination to invent them. Finally . . . the writer must be completely honest, because great mathematicians are commoner than thieves or humbugs of such incredible skill. . . .

"While Ramanujan had numerous brilliant successes, his work on prime numbers and on all the allied problems of the theory was definitely wrong. This may be said to have been his one great failure. And yet I am not sure that, in some ways, his failure was not more wonderful than any of his triumphs. . . ."

Ramanujan's notation of one mathematical term in this area, wrote Hardy, "was first obtained by Landau in 1908. Ramanujan had none of Landau's weapons at his command; he had never seen a French or German book; his knowledge even of English was insufficient to qualify for a degree. It is sufficiently marvellous that he should have even dreamt of problems such as these, problems which it has taken the finest mathematicians in Europe a hundred years to solve, and of which the solution is incomplete to the present day."

At last, in May of 1913, as the result of the help of many friends, Ramanujan was relieved of his clerical post in the Madras Port

Trust and given a special scholarship. Hardy had made efforts from the first to bring Ramanujan to Cambridge. The way seemed to be open, but Ramanujan refused at first to go because of caste prejudice and lack of his mother's consent.

"This consent," wrote Hardy, "was at last got very easily in an unexpected manner. For one morning his mother announced that she had had a dream on the previous night, in which she saw her son seated in a big hall amidst a group of Europeans, and that the goddess Namagiri had commanded her not to stand in the way of her son fulfilling his life's purpose."

When Ramanujan finally came, he had a scholarship from Madras of £250, of which £50 was allotted to the support of his family in India, and an allowance of £60 from Trinity.

"There was one great puzzle [Hardy observes of Ramanujan]. What was to be done in the way of teaching him modern mathematics? The limitations of his knowledge were as startling as its profundity. Here was a man who could work out modular equations, and theorems of complex multiplication, to orders unheard of, whose mastery of continued fractions was, on the formal side at any rate, beyond that of any mathematician in the world, who had found for himself the functional equation of the Zeta-function and the dominant terms of many of the most famous problems in the analytic theory of numbers; and he had never heard of a doubly periodic function or of Cauchy's theorem, and had indeed but the vaguest idea of what a function of a complex variable was. His ideas as to what constituted a mathematical proof were of the most shadowy description. All his results, new or old, right or wrong, had been arrived at by a process of mingled argument, intuition, and induction, of which he was entirely unable to give any coherent account.

"It was impossible to ask such a man to submit to systematic instruction, to try to learn mathematics from the beginning once more. I was afraid too that, if I insisted unduly on matters which Ramanujan found irksome, I might destroy his confidence or break the spell of his inspiration. On the other hand there were things of which it was impossible that he should remain in ignorance. Some of his results were wrong, and in particular those which concerned the distribution of primes, to which he attached the greatest importance. It was impossible to allow him to go through life supposing that all the zeros of the Zeta-function were real. So I had to try to teach him, and in a measure I succeeded, though obviously I learnt from him much more than he learnt from me. . . .

"I should add a word here about Ramanujan's interests outside mathematics. Like his mathematics, they shewed the strangest contrasts. He had very little interest, I should say, in literature as such, or in art, though he could tell good literature from bad. On the other hand, he was a keen philosopher, of what appeared, to followers of the modern Cambridge school, a rather nebulous kind, and an ardent politician, of a pacifist and ultraradical type. He adhered, with a severity most unusual in Indians resident in England, to the religious observances of his caste; but his religion was a matter of observance and not of intellectual conviction, and I remember well his telling me (much to my surprise) that all religions seemed to him more or less equally true. Alike in literature, philosophy, and mathematics, he had a passion for what was unexpected, strange, and odd; he had quite a small library of books by circle-squarers and other cranks . . . He was a vegetarian in the strictest sense—this proved a terrible difficulty later when he fell ill—and all the time he was in Cambridge he cooked all his food himself, and never cooked it without first changing into pyjamas. . . .

"It was in the spring of 1917 that Ramanujan first appeared to be unwell. He went to a Nursing Home at Cambridge in the early summer, and was never out of bed for any length of time again. He was in sanatoria at Wells, at Matlock, and in London, and it was not until the autumn of 1918 that he shewed any decided symptom of improvement. He had then resumed active work, stimulated perhaps by his election to the Royal Society, and some of his most beautiful theorems were discovered about this time. His election to a Trinity Fellowship was a further encouragement; and each of those famous societies may well congratulate themselves that they recognized his claims before it was too late."

Early in 1919 Ramanujan went home to India, where he died in the following year.

For an evaluation of Ramanujan's method and work in mathematics we must again quote from Hardy:

"I have often been asked whether Ramanujan had any special secret; whether his methods differed in kind from those of other mathematicians; whether there was anything really abnormal in his mode of thought. I cannot answer these questions with any confidence or conviction; but I do not believe it. My belief is that all mathematicians think, at bottom, in the same kind of way, and that Ramanujan was no exception. He had, of course, an extraordinary memory. He could remember the idiosyncrasies of numbers in an almost uncanny way. It was Mr. Littlewood (I believe) who remarked that 'every positive integer was one of his personal friends.' I remember once going to see him when he was lying ill at Putney. I had ridden in taxi-cab No. 1729, and remarked that the number seemed to me rather a dull one, and that I hoped it was not an unfavorable omen. 'No,' he replied, 'it is a very interesting number; it is the smallest number expressible as a sum of two cubes in two different ways.' I asked him, naturally, whether he knew the answer to the corresponding problem for fourth powers; and he replied, after a moment's thought, that he could see no obvious example, and thought that the first such number must be very large. His memory, and his powers of calculation, were very unusual, but they could not reasonably be called 'abnormal.' If he had to multiply two large numbers, he multiplied them in the ordinary way; he could do it with unusual rapidity and accuracy, but not more rapidly or more accurately than any mathematician who is naturally quick and has the habit of computation.

"It was his insight into algebraical formulae, transformations of infinite series, and so forth, that was most amazing. On this side most certainly I have never met his equal, and I can compare him only with Euler or Jacobi. He worked, far more than the majority of modern mathematicians, by induction from numerical examples; all of his congruence properties of partitions, for example, were discovered in this way. But with his memory, his patience, and his power of calculation, he combined a power of generalisation a feeling of form and a capacity for rapid modification of his hypotheses, that were often really startling, and made him, in his own field, without a rival in his day.

"It is often said that it is much more difficult now for a mathematician to be original than it was in the great days when the foundations of modern analysis were laid; and no doubt in a measure it is true. Opinions may differ as to the importance of Ramanujan's work, the kind of standard by which it should be judged, and the influence which it is likely to have on the mathematics of the future. It has not the simplicity and the inevitableness of the very greatest work; it would be greater if it were less strange. One gift it has which no one can deny— profound and invincible originality. He would probably have been a greater mathematician if he had been caught and tamed a little in his youth; he would have discovered more that was new, and that, no doubt, of greater importance. On the other hand he would have been less of a Ramanujan, and more of a European professor and the loss might have been greater than the gain."

BIBLIOGRAPHY

READERS interested in further reading on the topics covered in this book may find the list below helpful. It is *not* a bibliography of source material. The books chosen are for the most part addressed to the general reader; they include also some of the more accessible textbooks and survey volumes. The list is by no means exhaustive. Nor does it embrace the full range of interest of this book, since much of the work reported here is not yet represented in the pages of any other book. (The date given in italics under each chapter title is the date of its original publication in SCIENTIFIC AMERICAN.)

GALILEO
August 1949

Galileo: His Life and Work. John Joseph Fahie. John Murray, 1903.
Galileo and the Freedom of Thought. F. Sherwood Taylor. Watts & Co., 1938.
The Crime of Galileo. Giorgio de Santillana. University of Chicago Press, 1955.

ISAAC NEWTON
December 1955

Isaac Newton. E. N. da C. Andrade. The Macmillan Company, 1954.
Opticks, or a Treatise on the Reflections, Refractions, Inflections & Colours of Light. Isaac Newton. Dover Publications, Inc., 1952.
The Royal Society of London Newton Tercentenary Celebrations. Cambridge University Press, 1947.
Sir Isaac Newton's Mathematical Principles of Natural Philosophy and His System of the World. Translated by Andrew Motte and edited by Florian Cajori. University of California Press, 1954.

ROBERT HOOKE
December 1954

"Robert Hooke." E. N. da C. Andrade in *Proceedings of the Royal Society,* Series A, Vol. 201, No. 1067, pages 439–473; May 23, 1950.

The Diary of Robert Hooke, 1672–1680. Edited by Henry W. Robinson and Walter Adams. London: Taylor & Francis, 1935.

LAPLACE
June 1954

Men of Mathematics. Eric Temple Bell. Simon and Schuster, 1936.
L'Oeuvre scientifique de Laplace. H. Andoyer. Payot & Cie., 1922.
Pioneers of Science. Sir Oliver Lodge. The Macmillan Company, 1930.

WILLIAM ROWAN HAMILTON
May 1954

Life of Sir William Rowan Hamilton. R. P. Graves. Hodges, Figgis and Company, Ltd., 1882–89.

G. F. FITZGERALD
November 1953

The Scientific Writings of the Late George Francis FitzGerald. Dublin University Press Series, 1902.

PRIESTLEY
October 1954

Joseph Priestley. T. E. Thorpe. E. P. Dutton & Co., Inc., 1906.
Joseph Priestley, 1733–1804. R. M. Caven. Institute of Chemistry of Great Britain and Ireland, 1933.
The Discovery of Oxygen. Part I. Joseph Priestley. Alembic Club Reprint No. 7. Oliver and Boyd, Edinburgh, 1923.
Priestley in America, 1794–1804. Edgar F. Smith. P. Blakiston's Son & Co., 1920.

LAVOISIER
May 1956

Antoine Lavoisier: Scientist, Economist, Social Reformer. Douglas McKie. Henry Schuman, Inc., 1952.
A Bibliography of the Works of Antoine Laurent Lavoisier, 1743–1794. Denis I. Duveen and Herbert S. Klickstein. Wm. Dawson & Sons, Ltd., 1954.
Torch and Crucible: The Life and Death of Antoine Lavoisier. S. J. French. Princeton University Press, 1941.

BENJAMIN FRANKLIN
August 1948

Benjamin Franklin's Experiments. A New Edition of Franklin's Experiments and Observations on Electricity. Edited by I. Bernard Cohen. Harvard University Press, 1941.
Benjamin Franklin. Carl Van Doren. Viking, 1938.
Benjamin Franklin's Autobiographical Writings. Selected and edited by Carl Van Doren. Viking, 1945.

MICHAEL FARADAY
October 1953

Faraday's Diary. Seven volumes. Edited by Thomas Martin. G. Bell and Sons, Ltd., 1932–36.
Experimental Researches in Electricity. Michael Faraday. Three volumes. Richard and John Edward Taylor, 1839–1855.
Faraday's Discovery of Electromagnetic Induction. Thomas Martin. Edward Arnold & Co., 1949.

JOSEPH HENRY
July 1954

The Discovery of Induced Electric Currents. Edited by Joseph S. Ames. American Book Company, 1900.
Famous American Men of Science. James G. Crowther. W. W. Norton and Co., Inc., 1937.
Joseph Henry, His Life and Work. Thomas Coulson. Princeton University Press, 1950.
Scientific Writings of Joseph Henry. Smithsonian Institution, 1886.

JAMES CLERK MAXWELL
June 1955

The Life of James Clerk Maxwell. Lewis Campbell and William Garnett. Macmillan and Co., 1882.
The Scientific Papers of James Clerk Maxwell. Edited by W. D. Niven. Dover Publications, Inc., 1953.
A Treatise on Electricity and Magnetism. James Clerk Maxwell. Dover Publications, Inc., 1954.

273

WILLIAM HARVEY
June 1952

Exercitatio Anatomica de Motu Cordis et Sanguinis in Animalibus. William Harvey. With an English translation and annotations by C. D. Leake. Charles C Thomas, ·1928.

CHARLES DARWIN
February 1956

The Foundations of the Origin of Species. Charles Darwin. Cambridge University Press, 1909.
The Life and Letters of Charles Darwin. Edited by Francis Darwin. D. Appleton and Company, 1888.

PAVLOV
September 1949

Conditioned Reflexes and Neuron Organization. Jerry Konorski. The Macmillan Company, 1948.
Lectures on Conditioned Reflexes: Twenty-Five Years of Objective Study of the Higher Nervous Activity (Behavior) of Animals. Ivan Petrovich Pavlov. International Publishers, 1928–1941.

CHARLES BABBAGE
April 1952

Babbage's Calculating Engines. Edited by Henry P. Babbage. E. and F. N. Spon, London, 1889.

LEWIS CARROLL
April 1956

"Lewis Carroll as Logician." R. B. Braithwaite in the *Mathematical Gazette,* Vol. 16, No. 219, pages 175–178; July, 1932.
"Lewis Carroll—Mathematician." D. B. Eperson in the *Mathematical Gazette,* Vol. 17, No. 223, pages 92–100; May, 1933.

SRINIVASA RAMANUJAN
June 1948

Ramanujan. G. H. Hardy. Cambridge University Press, 1940.
Collected Papers of Srinivasa Ramanujan. Edited by G. H. Hardy, P. V. Seshu Aiyar and B. M. Wilson. Cambridge University Press, 1947.